ON MOON SQUARE

"A Boy And His Dogma"

E REKSTEIN

ISBN: 1479245984
ISBN 13: 9781479245987
Cover artwork: Josef Lada 1953
"Josifek v mesicni navsi" "Little Josef on moon square."
rekstein@gmail.com

Prague

womb

At the beginning of my freshman year, some upperclassmen told me that their fraternity was the best and I believed them. They looked the coolest and the most colorful, yet were said to hold dark mysterious secrets.

But Colin, my new best friend, did not attempt, like I, to join them.

I

I first met Colin in the dorm laundry room, and I didn't know what the rest of our freshman herd thought about him but I was curious what he might have to say—he was bright-eyed and quietly confident. I left with the group, but later I wandered up to his room.

Colin Vonn's parents were divorced, and Mrs. Vonn's second husband had sent Colin to a Texas preparatory school. He starched his shirts, dated debutantes, and read etiquette magazines—he shared with me that proper dining meant to chew your bite, wipe your mouth, and only then sip from your glass. I stared, confused. He took me down to Columbia to meet Patrick Pearsall, a handsome black Texan from Colin's starchy school. Colin said, "And you think *I'm* a bad influence?"

They told me about Patrick's latest conquest, with a black Columbia model. "Standing up," said Colin, "in her bedroom while the rest of the group was waiting to go out." I stared, listening. The three of us walked a Manhattan sidewalk and I heard Colin's curt laugh—he had winked at a passing girl even though she was holding her boyfriend's hand. Colin whispered to me, "You can do that, you know." I hadn't known. "I will fuck your ass up mother fucker," said the boyfriend, seeing it differently. He was looking back at us on the sidewalk. But he was smaller than we were and we were walking onward, the other way.

Coming to New York also meant meeting his mother's first husband, Mr. Mike Vonn, youngest partner at Goldman Sachs. We stayed at his deluxe apartment above the avenues. He was successful and imposing. We looked up to him, literally. On his walls were photos of the children from his own second marriage. Colin whispered, "And he's free and single like we are."

Back in Boston though, and without Colin, I was soon pledging the fraternity, pursuing the camaraderie and deep mystique that I had glimpsed among the members.

During Hell Week our breakfast was a raw egg and a shot of gin, whereupon a senior Brother led our jog around campus. He wore fresh white running shoes and we followed in heavy work boots and hypnosis. Lunch was a raw hotdog which we promptly puked. We fixed up the House during the days and at night we were made to drink and to perform their required random mayhem such as stealing pizzas from a delivery car. If we passed out on the floor or pool table, we could sleep a few hours before again following the new-shoed Brother around the dawn campus.

The week ended but the hell was skillfully stretched all year, finally to end at Initiation, during which a whole night passed with me standing blindfolded in a dark corner of the House. The next night was the same. At times I heard distant clatter. I was moved elsewhere, to stand in more endless quiet. Deep into the hours, I was dragged into a dark room and pushed down into a chair.

A bright light was shone into my face, and voices shot at me. It was the seniors. Had I broken a rule during Hell Week by eating a cafeteria meal? Yes, I confessed it. They seemed to know all. Did I own a shot glass with House letters on it, hidden in my dorm drawer? Yes. "You are not a Brother of this House yet." No, I confessed I was not.

"Reks," a voice asked in the dark, "do you know who I am?" I scoured my mind. They yelled, "He's a senior who lives in the House—what does that say about your commitment? The rest of the pledges were initiated tonight. They are Brothers. You, we are de-pledging. Get out."

I was escorted down the dark staircase. I was blindfolded again and placed in a coffin. Hammers nailed it shut. The coffin was lifted up and I smelled smoke and heard voices chanting, "Ashes to ashes, dust to dust."

When the coffin was opened, I was in a lit room filled with smiling faces. I was a Brother. It was four-thirty in the morning. There was a keg. We freshmen nodded with satisfaction. The seniors explained, "It's so you appreciate it more."

For our sophomore year, Colin promptly professed our new mission. "To have a devoted girlfriend you take a cut in looks." He had me write it down. He put it right into effect, with his charm, clarity, and new Camaro. The instant conquest was freshman Tammy, who listened to the Grateful Dead and laughed at Colin's jokes and slept with him twice a day. "Rekstein," he said, "it's so great."

Extra-starch Colin now grew his hair long and wore tie-dye and pushed me to read *Be Here Now* by some smiley Ram Dass. "So wise," said Colin. "And dude, get the girlfriend. You won't believe how great it is." So he was absent for days.

As a full-fledged Brother now, I could freely explore the halls of the House. Late one evening, I meandered to the top rooms and climbed out the window and up the rooftop, where "Blaze" and "Fish" were shrooming—they were staring down at the moonlit campus. Blaze said, "There's more on the table." I shook my head. Blaze said, "You aren't committed to the Brotherhood. Eat the shrooms."

I said, "I have a Russian test." Fish socked me hard in the arm. Blaze said, "Clueless, you are so random. You're chasing after windmills, thinking they're something else. You do it with girls too, you chase these fairy-tale beauties who aren't really real."

"Clueless" had been my pledge name but hadn't really stuck—Blaze liked to call me it with an understood irony between us. He asked me, "So you going to the Soviet Union, is that why you take those random courses?" I shrugged. I ate the mushrooms on Saturday, during the campus carnival, to which the school invited local children and allowed us to provide clowns, not knowing that random mayhem was the sole objective.

We were fully committed—we donned clown hair to clown shoes. My shift included "Sven" and "Satan". Sven was as black as night but for his white smile and purple paint. Satan had wavy hair and a fiendish snicker. I flopped out the front door after them.

In moments we turned orderly children into screaming chasers of clowns. We led figure eights around the grassy quad while the white-shirted guides chased their flocks. When we walked among the carnival rides, crowds parted. Bright faces looked up and we frowned. Little arms clung to the guides. Purple-wigged Sven looked like a wild tribal leader. The mushrooms made the sunny day buzz with that heavy ponderousness. Should I pursue it?

These kids thought we were clowns—I was getting this now. Yes, I was dressed like a clown but I'd figured they knew I was a college kid thinking about his homework. Instead they were hurrying over to us with their hopes, and these we crushed. I felt sorry for them all. Maybe I could be a good clown. Why not? My clown partners were ahead of me, off to join the Brothers at lunch. "I'm a good clown," I told a little boy. He smiled wide. Yes, I would tell my partners this shroom epiphany—perhaps they felt it too.

I was racing to catch them. "They think we're clowns, they think we're clowns!" I was hurrying down Professors Lane, and mothers shielded their children, and fellow students stared with shock. I was so happy. But everyone was aghast. Indeed, I was flop-sprinting down the middle of the street yelling, "Satan, Satan, Satan!"

I froze. I stood there thinking. I returned to my room and sat at my desk and stared at my Russian homework while still in my baggy clown garb.

One night, Colin came in with Tammy and sat down and put a hand through his thick brown hair and looked at me and sighed. They'd been at a House party and two seniors had looked calmly in Colin's eyes and said the word "Luther" to one another. Then they'd walked off. "It was code," explained Colin. Tammy stood beside him in support.

Colin said, "There's a dark side, an inner circle. Think, Reks, you know it's there, you know who's in."

Tammy said, "They make you say things like, 'Worship the House, worship the House.'"

"They don't make us."

"But they go around accusing you, 'You don't worship the House, you blow off the House.'"

I asked, "A fraternity within the fraternity?"

Colin answered, "I know it's hard to accept."

Actually, it sounded cool and exciting. I was eager to room there next year—I would be a junior, allowed to live in the House, the place. First, Colin and I drove off to California for the summer. That Texas man had moved Colin's mother there, and then divorced her.

Her goal now was just to hold on to the house though it stretched her financially. The backyard had a big swimming pool. Colin and I lounged there. He had sold Electrolux here last summer. He told me, "It's truly a great machine, otherwise I wouldn't even suggest we do this. Right?" I stared, and nodded.

The vacuum office was abuzz that next morning—Colin's return energized the staff, as did Manager Bill Sidhu springing up to speak. He seemed to dance in the air, this happy skinny little man from India. He started us clapping. The other salesmen were locals from Bakersfield, which had few trees and some gravel lawns painted green.

I knocked on my first door. Colin was there in support. We could hear a television. I knocked again. I felt ready. The door opened. A tree of a man, shirtless and blindly drunk, stared down toward us and belched. It didn't seem like he was going to buy a vacuum cleaner. But Colin said the pitch. Then he said to me as we walked back to the sidewalk, "Your worst possible door is behind you. You're even readier now for sales."

He had me walk my own suburb alone. No one was home. Bill Sidhu had instructed us to just get in the door, do a thorough vacuuming with her machine, then mention that we might have our own in the car. Then we were to do her carpet all over again, dump out the new dirt from our vacuum and ask, "Was there something wrong with yours?"

When a door finally opened, a woman in an apron said, "Honey, I'm not interested, but I really hope you find many who are." She was speaking through bars on her door. I found a woman in a business suit. She said, "No, thank you." When I re-opened my mouth she repeated strongly, "No, thank you." She was too seasoned, I too weak. She closed her door on me. Bill Sidhu said at Morning Meeting, "Keep knocking. We have the happiest lightest vacuum ever, just push it along with one finger." He danced it across the carpet. "The hardest door is your car door. Don't drip."

This was what they called inaction. Colin also hadn't sold any this year, but at every meeting Bill found someone to tell a success story. That evening, a door opened and an old lady in a bathrobe said, "I am so happy to see you. I love you. God sent you to me today."

So I got inside. But she wasn't paying attention to my dirt piles. Her sun-weathered husband came in from the backyard and the wife said, "He was in the hospital and was nearly dead. Now look. God has blessed us and let him live."

"You need a new vacuum."

Her smile flattened. She said, "All of our money goes to medical expenses. He's still very, very sick. We are blessed he's alive." She wanted me to kneel and say some prayer with her—it would cause something to happen.

I asked, "If God loves you so much then why is your husband so sick?" She frowned again, darker than when I had told her she needed a vacuum. When I made it back on the street, I breathed out relief. When I got home, Colin's mother consoled me about my latest fruitless day. Her being lonely added to the air of struggle. That blue pool sat cool and empty every day. Colin flew off to visit Tammy in Chicago.

I dripped. I sat in the Camaro and stared at the doors. I knew that getting in them was important. I sat in a park. There were people here who didn't knock on doors and work for no pay. A skinny blonde walked across the grass. She had a big chest. She disappeared into a house. I knocked on its door. I told her the vacuum thing. She wasn't smiling, but I talked on for several more minutes. She didn't get a thing I was trying to say. She was shielding most of her body with the door. She said, "I just walked home across the oil field. They blaspheme there. I could not believe it. They blasphemed." I left. I knocked her whole suburb.

Bill Sidhu said at Morning Meeting, "Just smile at them, that's all." He brought his wide grin right toward my face. I smiled. He said, "See? That's all you have to do." He called up someone to relate another late-night success. I drove to my next suburb and sat in the hot Camaro here in this town where the blaspheming oil fields had laid off staff and everyone knew our dirt-dumping gag.

I knocked fifty hot doors and I sulked home. Colin was back, sitting by the pool. He said, "Let's quit and camp across the country." Oh I wanted to cry with joy. The next day we smoked up and went in to Morning Meeting. The clapping was extra loud—there were two new guys and Bill Sidhu was on fire. He got us all singing. When Colin and I stepped outside, I said, "Being stoned made that weird."

Colin smiled, his handsome blue eyes bloodshot. "You've been brainwashed this summer," he said, "I thought you realized." We walked into a sports store and there stood a dome tent on sale for $29.99. We bought it and headed east. I didn't have to knock on doors. It was no longer the only thing.

Colin had us ask strangers whether we could pitch the tent on their property. I stood silently beside him. In Western Colorado, a farmer pointed to a patch of trees in the distance. "You can try that crick but you'd better take this shovel to hit the ground because them rattling devils don't rattle in August." We obeyed. That night, Colin said we had become half of each other. The fire warmed the colors of his face, and I imagined it was doing the same to mine.

As we approached New York, highways grew out of the ground and spread around us. Colin wasn't returning to school. "I'm taking a year off. To search." I was to keep the Camaro for now. In the morning he left with his father to buy suits and groom his hair for a job at Goldman Sachs. Evidently, he was no longer a Be-Here-Nower. I wrote a goodbye note and sped north to the House.

Blaze, Fish, and Satan shared the attic with big-shouldered Guppy, who was facing a deadline on a paper—he spent three days typing at his table. Then, in the middle of the night, he came to the top of the staircase and screamed prolongedly and beat his chest. The paper was done, and in Guppy's mind it was appropriate for him to go to the top of the stairs and bellow it all out.

Every night, someone celebrated something. "At the very least there's always some random bass shaking the walls," said Queef, who had escaped off campus after his junior year. "Just when you settle into bed, there it is."

Someone's grandmother sent the House a Mr. Potato Head, for some reason. We stared at it. We assembled it and awarded it to Gilligan for being the week's worst Brother, because he dirtied the pots each late-night and caused our cook to quit. Mutant got it the next week for drunken urinating on the pool table. Wastoid won it for sleeping with Rockhead's girlfriend. Phoebe won it for smashing the Mr. Potato Head into little pieces in the parking lot.

Colin dumped Tammy by mail. He said, when I visited him in New York, "Sometimes I used to look at her and shudder." He said the real way to read the *Wall Street Journal* on the subway was to fold it in eighths. He told me about sleeping with some Goldman secretary. I returned to school and the Brothers asked, "Why'd you blow off the party? You don't pray to the House." I went up to my room and stared at my economics graphs for hours. I rewrote and reconstructed them, not just so I knew them but so I understood the why of each line and point. I wanted it to make total sense. Russian class meanwhile had been whittled down to students who lived in the Russian House and spoke Russian three meals a day, and me. We didn't speak much Russian at Zeta Psi. Late at night, when loud conversing came from the hall, I leaned over the banister and asked the Brothers to keep it down. "Are you a fool?" they responded. "It's a fraternity!"

Before dawn, I awoke to silhouettes climbing up my loft. I swung with no reservations. The next day during afternoon television, Fish asked how I'd slept and I wrestled him to the floor, there among the others. Blaze said, "You know what you are, Clueless, you're scrappy." I released Fish, feeling a bit sorry for him. Blaze asked again, "You going to the Soviet Union or not?" I answered, "The Iron Curtain isn't going anywhere. There's time." While I was in my last hours of sleep before my economics final, Wastoid was typing the last words of a paper. So, what would it be? How about Hendrix's *Star Spangled Banner* on the electric guitar?

Wastoid played us every note, at full volume, deep in the night. Gilligan and Conehead and others found a private house off campus, and I decided to join them for our final year.

I was out of the House. I was interning at the grad school's Institute for Foreign Policy Analysis. I stood in its little library and read Foreign Broadcast Booklets for the Soviet Union and East Europe. They were filled with dark, communist speeches. I imagined them spoken on cold, misty days. IFPA's strict consensus was that Gorbachev was just another dictator whom we couldn't let con us. But there was one co-worker who could at least laugh about it. "Why does Gorbachev have a tattoo of South America on his forehead?" Conversation with skinny grad-student Jan Surotchak wasn't quite like House banter or Colin counselings, but I soon decided to read those dark booklets in Jan's office.

At our senior house, Conehead reported that female students lived next door. "And I know the hot blonde," said Gilligan. "Friends with the hot sexy skank I used to date." We had preserved a bedroom for Colin's possible return, but he enrolled at Columbia with Patrick Pearsall. They were living in a rent-controlled Harlem apartment—they played their stereo quietly to hide its presence. Conehead and Gilligan came home with a very large television so we could watch the World Series. It went in Colin's room.

Colin called. "Patrick's a best friend, but I don't think anyone will understand me as well as you do. It's like that night we were driving and listening to Yello and it gave us this intense feeling which was impossible to explain yet *you* understood. Promise you'll move to Manhattan next year." I promised. I walked downstairs and the television was showing the Berlin Wall falling. Peaceful protests were starting in squares behind the Iron Curtain, there in the East Europe night. Someone turned to "Wheel of Fortune". I said, "Dude." We debated. We finally agreed on more baseball.

It was good background for reading Quantitative Economics. The Athletics, with huge Canseco and McGuire, dwarfed the Dodgers, with old Kirk Gibson—he limped to the plate and slugged an improbable home run—and skinny Orel Hirshchiser, who was supposed to pitch tomorrow but they brought him in to close this one. It was a huge and unusual gamble.

It paid off. The Dodgers won it all. It was October 1989. We carried the television back to the store. In the evening, I put on someone's cowboy hat and knocked on the neighboring door. Gil's sexy skanky ex-girlfriend answered. I said, "I'm walking to the store. Y'all want anything?" She turned around and yelled, "He says he lives next door, do we want anything?" She turned back with a wide smile. "That's so nice," came the other female voices. I continued on to the store. Maybe I looked good in the hat. While we played chess in our living room we could see in their living room. "But don't look," cautioned Gil. "The blonde is a heartbreaker." One night we heard footsteps on our winding staircase. It was IFPA's Jan Surotchak. I met him at the door and answered his friendly questions—I was conscious of the tall bong in the room behind me. Gil stepped up. "The girls are waiting for you to drive them to the bar."

Jan Surotchak the skinny grad-student walked off and we piled in the Camaro with Gil's ex-skank and the blonde, who started a snake through the bar crowd. I joined on. A Brother from the House was there and he mocked, "Oh, you're so cool, Reks." I said, "Packer, don't be one of those." And he seemed to sort of understand. My housemates disappeared, walking off to other bars. I sat in the Camaro with blond Stephanie, waiting for the windows to unfog.

She wrote on the windshield, "What are you thinking?" We sat there. I leaned over to kiss her. She pulled away. I felt fine about it—she was way beyond me. "Weird," she said, "that's exactly what I wanted you to do." We sat there. I leaned over and put my lips to hers. I had kissed a very beautiful girl. I felt warm and satisfied.

The next evening, I sat in their living room. I could see the chess match next door. Soon it was just me and Stephanie. We held hands. "I could just eat you up," she said to me. It was too good to be true. I looked around the room. At dawn I wrapped myself in her white comforter and scampered from her porch to mine. She yelled, "I'll come for the blanket tonight." I sat down to study Operation Barbarossa, the three million German soldiers taking their first, well-organized strides onto Russian soil.

Steph pulled me on top of her each night. I almost wanted to cry, looking into her blue eyes. They sparkled. In the morning, we lay on the bed and talked. We lay north, then east, south, west. She told me about her parents' divorce. "My mom raised us kids, but then my father had a baby with a co-worker. Right then my mom got breast cancer. How does that happen to someone?"

When she slipped off to class she left me little notes, "Can't wait to smooch you, Smoo." This was my tall pretty blonde, somehow. I played her my trippy Colin music. "And then one day you find, ten years have got behind you. No one told you when to run, you missed the starting gun."

Steph frowned. "Why do you listen to that? That's not you." I kissed her. She kissed back, with increasing aggression. Then, the winter sun heated the window while we were curled up as if in a womb, gripped together, moist, dozing in and out, unmoving.

But one morning I returned from class and Steph was frowning. "What's the matter?"

She didn't want to discuss it. Reluctantly she said, "I felt we had sex last night and then just went to sleep. I never wanted it to be like that." Speechless, I wanted her frown gone. And I wanted her back in bed.

I consulted Colin. His voice was comforting and wise. "Well, who changed? Who started acting differently?" So it really was her fault. I'd just been following what she started.

Three days later, Colin called me back—I was glad he took the issue seriously. "I spoke to Patrick. Listen, it's you. You have to respect her needs. You can't be controlled by yours." Colin's voice again had that calm authority. "But Reks, my father just bought a beach house. Move to the City."

I turned in my last papers—one professor said, with pleasant surprise, that I had indeed captured the nuances of why the Soviets needed force and a fence to preserve their flawed socio-economic system. But who cared? It was summer.

Steph dashed home to Chicago. Under my pillow I found a little note, "Visit soon, Smoo." I drove down to Harlem.

Patrick and Colin advised me which streets were safe to walk, and how to avoid saying unsafe things to anyone in the building. Patrick had joined some church. He now disapproved of clubbing and drugging. I squinted. Colin explained, "It's not the dancing, but the intent to get sexual."

Colin began visiting the church. Apparently we wouldn't be frequenting the beach house. "What the hell?" I asked. Mr. Vonn, at dinner, seemed happy to see me—he had been questioning Colin's new views. After dinner, Colin had a church thing.

"Want to come?"

"I don't even know what it is."

"It's a Bible Talk. But it's actually cool. The guy leading it's an artist. He's born again, so now he paints depictions of the scriptures." I went back to the apartment alone. In the morning, I wanted to jog. I tried the sidewalk but it was jammed with people. So I walked toward the nearest Central Park entrance—the streets were lined with trash and abandoned cars and dark stares. As I was approaching the trees, a bicyclist rode out. He was a big, mustached white guy on a junky old bike. He said, "Watch out in there bud, watch out."

Fuck, I thought, I can't even jog? I shook my head. I turned around and walked back up the littered streets. I sat inside the apartment. I browsed through the drawers. Deep in a corner lay three videos. I played one. This was incredible, two guys and a girl walked into some warehouse where there was a bed, and the girl stood between them and they took off her shirt and just kneaded her breasts. Then one guy lay down, and she lay on top, and the other on her. I leaned back on the coffee table. The glass cracked. I stared at it. I felt guilty, stupid. And now I had a table to fix.

Luckily, Pat and Colin were at another event, so I searched out a glass store. The little owner greeted. I recognized his accent. I took it as a good sign and I spoke some Russian to him and he immediately corrected me. He had a Mexican employee. "All the kid does is look out the door at the girls. That's all he thinks about." The Mexican drove me to the apartment and measured the table and came back later with the replacement. I breathed with relief. Back on the sidewalk, some guy was selling a mountain bike. He said, "Sixty bucks. Don't worry, kid, it's not from around here."

I said, "I have forty." He said, "I can get sixty." I thought about Steph and her nice white bike that she had bought and shared with me at school. When I met up with Colin, he asked, "Coming to Bible Talk?" I shook my head. He said, "I was feeling low today and just not liking New York, because the city isn't really a cool mystery, it's a nest of lost, uncaring people. So I shared my faith aloud on the subway."

He was speaking a foreign language. He looked around and then back at me and he smiled. "You should really think about getting your life in order, Rekstein." He pointed a finger into my chest. "Get rid of all that mess that Satan has taught you." He thudded his forehead. "That must sound so weird," he said. "And to think, it's actually true." I had a really bad feeling inside. "Remember this street corner, Reks." I went back to the apartment and packed up.

I would help Steph settle in for her last year of college. Then I would try to get to Russia. In Boston, we carried in her furniture and then smooched. Her housemate said, "You're still tripping over each other, it's ridiculous." Steph biked off to register for classes.

I went off to DC to submit a Master's application. The Czechoslovak president was in town and his audience asked him what help was needed for his new effort. He responded that his people needed English. A small group of Georgetown students was assembling something. I wrote them a letter. Before I returned again to Steph, Colin called me up and said, "I'm showing my summer film. It would mean a lot if you stopped in."

The film showed life in New York City, with the skyscrapers and sirens and homeless—we were watching it in a Newark hotel. The film was actually addressing their church thing, as was this whole conference. The crowd was mixed black and white. There was a tall guy who played NYU basketball. There was a short guy who designed suits. A guy named Jordan approached me and looked me over and said, "Yo." Colin took my shoulder and said, "Jordan and I took two Sisters to the movies last week. Before the show started I stood up and told the crowd that I wanted to share about Jesus. But this guy yells back, 'I'm sick and tired of people like you coming to public places and disturbing us.' So I said, 'See, New

York, I came to talk about love and this is what happens.' Then Jordan gave me a high five."

They high-fived now. We went up to their room and sat around. Jordan said, "We can order a pizza." They asked me to study the Bible with them. I was sitting on the edge of the bed. A white Columbia student wearing glasses said his goal was to spread this in Africa. The pizza came and the box sat in the middle of the floor and everyone held hands, including mine, and said thanks for the food and for me. They passed the slices around their circle, more than once, with no one accepting, and I ate mine in an instant and was starving. They were still passing theirs. Jordan said, "I was stubborn and worldly just like you. Come into the City for a week, open your heart for a week."

"I want to go to Russia."

"For who?"

"What?"

"For yourself, right?" They again urged me into the City to study with them. It sounded so unpleasant. Here in the Newark hotel I slept on the floor with about five of them sleeping around me. The beds had three in each. In the morning there was a cold, continental breakfast. I saw the guy in glasses and I asked, "You don't try to get girls?"

"When I did," he answered, "I was filled with deceit." Then a mustached guy stood at the podium and insisted, "You need to give up fornicating. Don't say you'll give it up when you get married. We all know that argument." Everyone cheered. In the lobby they surrounded me again. "Goodbye," I said. There was still a quiet Asian between me and the door. I leaned in close, to understand him. "You should join," he said. I sped up the road. I rushed back to Steph's arms.

In the mail was a letter from the girl leading that Georgetown group. She wrote that I was supposed to meet them over there. That would get me close to Russia. When the time came, I hoped Steph wouldn't get too sad.

But on that morning when she walked me outside, a giant lump dried up my throat. Steph held me. I was the one who broke into tears, it was I who cried. Finally I drove off. There was so much to look forward to. In DC I met up with high-school friends and went to a trendy dive and sat on a bar stool. I felt like I was part of some cool, post-college scene. But no, I didn't belong.

These high-school friends were arranging some group house—one guy was even engaged. How could that be, when there was all this still to do? His fiancé had found a job as a school teacher. She had brought another teacher, who had a cute brown haircut but yapped away about who knows what at this bar table. "She's practically married," said one friend.

I got on an airplane toward this Eastern Europe that had just overthrown its governments. I had been on airplanes, I had been to Europe, but now I was traveling to a mysterious sphere that had long stood separately behind its dark fence.

I dozed in and out. Another young guy had also boarded the plane and he looked European. He wore clean sandals and a trim backpack. Maybe he was ending an American adventure. He was calm and he knew the strap from which to hang his coffee mug. But he got off in Frankfurt. I was continuing on into darkness. Somewhere in the air I crossed to the other side. I felt empty and aware. I felt great distances around me. We finally descended into gray dawn over damp green fields.

Hay was stacked in unkempt, sparse piles. The airport was one small building. Figures stood on the tarmac, on balconies, behind barricades, awaiting the plane. I walked through the crowd and stepped inside the lone building—the walls were bare and old. A wall of people was waiting inside too. Their gray stares confirmed what I felt—this was an absolute beginning. These faces were awaiting passengers who had come on the day's one airplane, people who hadn't been sighted for forty years, and the rest of us were arriving somewhere we'd never been—it hadn't existed.

Evidently one of the Georgetown students had been on the flight—we had been told what bus to take, and now it dropped us at a tall, plain, concrete building, a workers' dorm. I slept the entire day. The Georgetown girl slept in the adjacent bed. That was random. My sleep was so deep that it was a pit from which I couldn't climb out. I surfaced very gradually. In fact, the dorm woman had to come knocking for us—we had another bus to catch. We hurried groggily down the hall. Horrible body odor stung at me—I sniffed at my arm pits.

"No," said the Georgetown girl, "it's her." Indeed, it was neither of the people who had spent the night on an airplane, but the lady who worked here. The Georgetown girl said, "You should walk into a bar in Africa sometime." Apparently she'd traveled in Africa, whereas I thought this dorm was the furthest place in the world. We made it to the bus and subway, and then we ascended toward the city streets. It was a stone city. The facades were all different shades of dust. Rooftops were old slate, red or black or green, slanting every way.

The group leader brought us to a poorly translated film that was flecked as if old but was oh so shockingly new. I watched with wide eyes. In fact, we might have just walked through the square where it had occurred, lanes so narrow the walls seemed to be nearly toppling. The film lasted fifteen minutes. Communism had ruled forty years. Attempts to change it had led only to jail and death—twenty years along the way a movement had tried and failed. Tanks had squashed it. This past winter another group had rallied, and out came the police, to whom these young protestors extended flowers, which the police didn't take, so showed the film. As night descended, the protestors were still there, now holding out candles to the police, who finally then bludgeoned them.

The protestors ran. They were trapped in the narrow lanes and porticos. Some were twisted into police trucks while others rushed by and away.

The next day, more came out. Something had lit the whole sphere—its squares were filling. In Prague, thousands were singing for rights, and again the red-star tanks were preparing. Still the rally dared to grow, to hundreds of thousands, filling the long square, demanding freedom in a rhythmic stamping that had just recently been unthinkable. They huddled in the cold beneath the city's black towers. Work halted. Onto a snowy balcony a leader of the Party emerged. He was burly with short, straight hair. He asked down to a mass of factory workers whether they were truly ready to follow a movement of poets and students and such, did they truly know what this might mean?

And they hissed his every word, hissed for the first time, they fearless in face, they finally and truly one voice. So the Party stepped down. The throng celebrated. A playwright, once jailed for his independent thoughts, was now hurried to the castle and told to be president—the film showed him putting on his pants as the joyful crowd came to his door.

II

Above the black towers, the castle was black too. It loomed over the rooftops and lanes and the towers themselves, below which our little group now walked—the lanes were so filled with jutting dimensions and detail and spires, it was inconsumable. And at spots along these wordless walls the new president's name had been scrawled.

Supporters were painting it amid this cheery mood—many were artists apparently. Yes, we saw them carrying black portfolios or instrument cases. "Now a writer is president," said the group leader. Benjamin, who had brought an enormous box of books, said, "I'd like to be a writer someday." Everyone borrowed from his box. We were to be shipped out to towns and villages. Some Canadians were said to be arriving too.

I so badly wanted to share this all with Steph but there was no way to phone her. The group leader had gone to the post office but no phone lines from this sphere reached that. The leader had a special number to reach a West Europe operator but the post-office women wanted no part in it. And we couldn't find a payphone. The leader said, "Postcards don't really make it out either. Yet local mail somehow arrives in a day." She shrugged. "Here's the pub."

To walk into this pub of dark-clad communist thinkers and revolution-square goers and odd artists, and for us to find a tight space within the tables and to have black beer slammed before us meant to link eyes and eventually words with people who had never met the likes of us. One communicated that he was a fisherman. We didn't understand much more. But their sad smoky eyes spoke volumes. The fisherman led us along the labyrinth of facades to a round, black door. Deep inside, a stone garden was packed with drinkers, singers, swayers. A polka band was playing. The fisherman found room for us on the benches. We kept low beneath their language and celebrating. But they found us—soldiers jumped over the table and sought out common words with us, and an old, suited man begged our girls to dance, we all then humming their polka tune down these coal-stained cobblestone lanes. This whole unknown world awaited me down the lane. I cried, "There's a payphone."

I stepped into an iron booth on a dark corner. Weepy trees hung over me. I yelled, "Is it America? Is it America?" The operator said it was, I had made it through. When Steph picked up I was still yelling. She said, "It all sounds like something I can't understand." I said, "I'll write you, write me back, I'll write you." She responded, "I'll write you back, Smoo."

Again I slept in deep drug-like sleep. At daylight I tried to wake back into this place but instead could only roll over again, and again.

A bearded man came for me in a small pale car made of plastic. It was the East German contribution to the Bloc economy. The man had a serious gaze. We puttered down the road. The countryside was green and brown and yellow. We rounded corners slowly, and there stood a thatched cottage, or an empty meadow, or a church tower peaking from a valley village. The man said, "Perhaps you'll like our nature. There is not much else here to like."

His wife opened their apartment door. They laughed at my belongings. "You knew not where you were going, yet you brought many things." They had never seen a mountain bicycle. Mine was bright black and new. I had brought a pillow. "Did you think we do not have pillows in our society?" In their dim kitchen, Jitka and Jan served me a shot of the local alcohol. They toasted me. I drank it down. Jan Mraka was the Marxist economist at the town brewery. Its workers wanted to learn English. The high-schoolers wanted it after school. Jan told me, "You will help us all." He laughed.

In the morning, he took me to his brewery office, where a woman in a lab coat stared at me with such wonder that I turned and looked behind myself. She walked us down the tight halls. Jan said, "They are curious about you. They waited a long time." In the lab, some women wore sleeveless coats, showing full underarms. The eldest mumbled about me, "Where will he shop, what will he eat, how will he live?" She asked it as if these doings required a hard old knowledge, without which I'd be lost.

Jan said, "You're the first American they've seen. Though I hear there will be one called David at the school." I walked into my brewery class and stood before the men and women who had been the mill here, laboring all these years behind the fence. I walked into my evening class at the high-school and the big eyes of the girls looked away. Surely part of their blushing was that I was opening my mouth with a once forbidden language. But there was a face among them that caused me to pause—it must have been the fair Slavic face that represented it all, the lonely pretty face that had been here all this time while life was elsewhere. She nodded politely goodbye after class.

I returned to the brewery and stared alone at the dark wooden cottage-like walls of the workers' lounge. A pebble hit the window. Three Canadian girls had been brought in to teach at the hospital and one stood in the street below. "Our students want to meet you," she yelled up. "We want to meet you." I followed her to the only housing found for them, the dark little apartment nestled in the grassy little communist zoo. I sat in an old brown chair. There was a knock at their door.

"The climbers," said Canadian Anne. They trailed in. "They climb cliffs." As they entered, the climbers bowed, so their tall packs and guitars could make it through the door. They were nearly young and they were pale but colorful, not in their gray sweaters or their sad jeans or their silence but in that I immediately felt that this was a group who thought things that I did not.

"Do you come with us tonight?"

"Where?"

"To the best pub in Eastern Europe. No, Central Europe—we used to be Eastern Europe but today we are Central Europe, because you are here. So do you come tonight to the best pub in Central Europe?"

I nodded.

"And do you come with us tomorrow?"

"Where?"

"To climb. To see our nature. To drink our special sweet young wine. Do you know about it? Come, we go now. Not to climb, but to the best pub in the Central Europe woods. Do you like our woods?" Though it was night in a small Moravian town, we swiftly caught a bus and it dropped us atop an empty road, and we trailed down toward the lights of a stone inn.

In the front room, gruff men played cards. In the back room, they played fiddles. The ceiling had old stains in shapes like strange continents. The climbers sat down at a long table and unsheathed their guitars. "Do you know how great this day is?" asked blond Andre.

I said, "I think so."

"We do not know freedom like you," said another, called Petr, married to female climber Mirka. He seemed, behind his brown eyes, to possess pent-up words. Blond Andre said, "Today is truly something else. I don't know how to explain." I myself was beginning to wonder about this trip tomorrow—I was holding their small dictionary and I asked, "Do you cook for yourselves there?" And now brown-eyed Petr spilled his thought.

"Yes I am a proud man but no not a proud citizen." I glanced down at the dictionary. Petr said onward, "So no we do not respect ourselves. We did this to ourselves. We were weak. And this is exactly what our new president now says." The group was centered around me and the Canadians. Another climber smiled at me with peaceful eyes while tuning a guitar with strong weathered hands. He said, "It is actually good that you don't climb, good that there is something we can actually teach you. Much is broken here."

"But he will fix it," blurted one from down the table. "They will fix it."

Blond Andre said, "Igor is only joking. Do not worry." Blond Karel, still tuning the guitar, continued quietly and slowly, "Climbing was good when things were bad. Climbing was where we could meet up and be true. When a climber meets an unknown climber, they already speak on familiar terms, they are already kind."

Andre added, "And now everyone can be like this." He looked around—they were all agreeing here at this table. We all slept, briefly, on the dark carpeting of the little zoo apartment. At first light they roused me for our train. And I had eaten no food and had none to take with me and none of these young men or women made mention of it. There was one auto among them—Andre took the keys and took Mirka and Canadian Anne and the extra packs. The rest of us walked from the town straight into meadows. The sun hung crisply above us. A breeze blew through the trees. There was no other sound.

Soon we plopped down on the tiny station's platform. Karel said, "We'll be patching the town buildings soon, as our new work, as now it will be wanted, and now allowed. And it's climbing work. We are climbers. That's all." He shrugged. A short, red train arrived. Two heads called out the window to our group. Karel said to me, "Soldiers." He shrugged again. "But climbers too."

We jumped up onto their train. Soon we were all walking up a quiet village lane. At the final house, more climbers awaited, and we continued through the fields, and there ahead stood the cliffs, a tall horizon before us. Suddenly I felt chilled. To get through this day I would have to get over those. At the first face, the climbers dropped their packs and paired off. Karel gave me old rubber shoes. He tied a knot through my harness. "Your life is in your hands," he said, and he shared a smile with Petr, who was preparing a rope for his wife. I watched their every move. Karel said, "But await my word."

His fingers found niches that I hadn't seen and he rose firmly up the wall. Suddenly he wasn't on our ground, but straight above us. His fingertips searched again and he moved higher. The rope between us unraveled like a snake. Karel rose into a mid-way crevice and soon I couldn't see him. The rope paused. Karel was figuring. But what and where, I couldn't know. I shook myself from all daydream. I was aware of everything, the breeze in my hair, the shadow in each niche, the warmth of the sun behind me. Finally, I heard his call.

I reached up and was soon standing above the ground, on no ground, my fingers and rubber toes clutching the rock. I rose higher and my limbs were spread awkwardly, as if grasping ground I had just fallen to. The rock was unmoved by my racing breaths. I reached for another niche and failed to hold it—that hand scrambled for a side slot, and I clutched there, and I exhaled. But I couldn't stay here long.

I scraped my toes upward, and raised myself to that higher hold. And when my pounding heart did ease and I was in fact standing flat atop the peak, I filed away in mind how fear had felt, just an instant ago.

I gazed down at the village and it didn't seem real. Its red roofs spiraled from its center like rays from a sun. Where the roofs ended, vineyards continued over the hills. The breeze bending their vines was the same breeze at my legs and lungs. Karel and I shared a smile. We watched the others rise to this spot. Then the group stood there and gazed down at the land. Their eyes told me that the day had meaning. Karel said, "Do you see the river?" It approached strongly out of the distance. "A forest once stood there. But they turned the river and drowned the forest, the Party changed the river to feed their factories, which then fed their East."

The group stood like thinking statues on these lone cliffs above the land. Karel said, "Finally the Party is gone. But so is the forest." A few stumps remained, standing in the river. Soon we were seated among the packs on the grass below, and most eyes were on Anne and me. "They've come far," whispered some. They didn't seem to know why we would have ever come here. One said shyly, "I make maps."

I pointed a pistol finger, "Soldier."

"Ne, ne, maps. Just a soldier making maps." Canadian Anne whispered to me, "Such sad clothing". We looked at the plain, pale shades. She said, "It's as if it were all made at home by mothers and wives, all from the same sad fabric." Karel sat silently on my other side. He put his hand through his thin blond strands.

"Like they are saying of you," he said, "today is now school of life for me too. School itself belonged to the Party—they admitted only their own children to university, and a few others upon many exams. I was one. But I could not stay. I could not hear it each day." Climbing sounds still clanked in the warm air. Karel said, "Nothing is worse to me than lies. Better to injure me than lie. Better to tell me the truth while injuring me than try to convince me of things untrue. I couldn't listen. I left." He shook his head. "I left and they sent me to factory work. And now we are free of it all. But now I have no schooling. So mine will be school of life. It is nice so far." He patted me on the shoulder. Petr was standing beside us with a beaming smile. He said to me excitedly, "Now I understand—you like adventure. I too." This was cause for bonding, and self-reflection.

Petr added, "Adventure in America, this has always been my dream. It sounds impossible but one day, some day, I would travel there, just to see it. This is my dream." And Petr shook his head.

"But dreams," said Karel, "they're no longer just dreams. Look what has happened—people here are good, now we know. A humanist is atop the new party, Civic Forum, a civil party, the party of a revolution, the president of a revolution. Am I dreaming? No, it's true."

Petr still couldn't sit, not with this energy. He added, "Yes, yes."

Karel's eyes were fixed afar. When he looked back at me again, he said, "When it happened, those days in the city square, those events." He shook his head, "I cannot express the feeling."

"Try," I said.

"I cannot. The feeling. In the square." He pressed his hand to his chest, and he looked at the surrounding faces. "So good," he said slowly, "no words." He again put a hand on my shoulder and shook me very softly. "It's good that you are here."

Then Karel was climbing again—just enough light remained on the nearby walls. I stood up and walked a piece away. I looked down the slope at the village and vineyards in the purple-orange sunset. I knew that this was the place, there was nowhere else, I was supposed to be right here.

It felt very good.

I decided that I would write about what was happening. The full story came to me instantly, as if it had already been in me. Or it came on this breeze that was passing through us. The story would involve a pretty girl who had been trapped here behind the fence, unhappily marrying, and only now meeting her potential savior from the other side. It was just symbolic, the characters in *Both Sides of Winter* would symbolize the nations involved in this day that was apparently something else.

I jotted notes as the sun was setting on us. I glanced up at these dusk-lit faces. I saw no hunger on them. I hoped mine didn't show. Finally, Petr donned a miner's light and we followed its small glow downward. We arrived again at the last house on the lane, and someone knocked on its door.

An old babushka opened up and pointed us down into the cellar. Other women bustled in the kitchen. We crowded around a large table. A male host plopped down a great pot and then joined us. The group looked at one another and nodded and then forks went in the pot.

Out came hot potatoes, plain and plenty. Mouths bit them off the forks. The women built up a meal of bread, cheese, peppers, and pickles. Knives split loaves and then buttered the slices. "True men carry knives," said Mirka, overwhelmed with giggling. The host plopped down two jugs. "Our sweet young wine," said Andre, "special because it lasts only a short time, you must try it." I tried it.

Everyone sipped thirstily. "So tangy," said Canadian Anne. They refilled the jugs. Their sad, hard hands strummed the guitars.

"So sweet," said Andre, "you don't feel when you've had too much." The guitars and the special young wine continued. Voices were big, and arms enwrapped the shoulders of others, and each voice tried to express this day's joy. "How it was, how it was," cried Petr, "I can't believe we're now speaking of it as past. I can't believe."

Jitka and Jan's State employment began deep in the dark morning—I woke up alone in their little flat and stepped into their sunny kitchen and stared at the pale postcards they had pinned to the wall, all showing local nature such as summer meadows and winter forests, though I did find one lone postcard from the other world, my world, not a word written on it.

"I collect them," said serious-faced Jan, suddenly in the doorway. "Yours I was handed from one who they let travel. Perhaps it could have been mailed to me, but it may not have come. Or someone else may have come, with questions." He smiled cautiously. He opened a desk drawer. "But some correspondence was allowed, if we were careful."

I looked down to see a tidy stack of road maps. "Nearly all fifty," said Jan. "I mailed a request to your each state some twenty years ago. I'm still awaiting some responses." I looked up—now he allowed a sharp, boyish laugh. "Our mail is not so reliable."

He switched on the radio. There was one station. A deep, deliberate voice began to speak. Jan sat down and listened to his new president. I stepped out with my black bicycle and rode through the town's chessboard of blocks and towers and spires and lanes. The bicycle was swift and strong. I met pale, wide stares at every corner, as if I were driving a tank. I rode through a gap in the town's surrounding wall and out into the green meadows. Deer ran alongside me, though in fact fleeing. In distant knells stood small, collective villages. Dark, forest trails branched off to unknown places. I was where for decades I would not have been allowed.

In another meadow, I gazed back down upon the town. In the grass beside me stood a smooth monument celebrating, "A Workers' Place." It was all part of a mind that was no longer. The protagonist whom I was creating for the story actually worked at the town brewery—I myself taught in its workers' lounge each evening and I wrote lessons in Jan's office but I would write it as a young American economist brought in to help the brewery find its way. The brewery, the town, the whole country was built on the communism that had just died—everyone was cheering—but soon they would need a new path.

This was symbolized in the plot. Our young heroine had married a big Commie boss named Josef and now he was gone, so she was alone. The girl of course became Lenka from that high-school class, with that rosy flush on fair cheeks. The revolution would be symbolized through Lenka walking down a leaf-strewn lane and seeing the new American on his way to the brewery and inviting him upstairs in this late-summer warmth and making love to him by candlelight. Only afterward would the mismatch be realized.

> ***Down the long lane, slowly their paths converged. His feet cracked leaves. Then the two stood upon the corner. She tucked back her hair. After a pause, she asked, 'You will come to my flat?' He felt the sunlight on him, and felt the warmth from blushing, and felt the freshness in this chance, and felt some caution too. She had a velvet couch. She lit candles. Sitting there, he knew little of her thoughts, and knew that he should know more. Then came a moment when it didn't matter what he knew, a moment when her thoughts didn't matter. Next, he saw clearly she was a stranger. He wondered what it would mean.***

Maybe launching into this was foolish. But the candles did still burn every day in that capital city, the place. They were lit on the blood-stained cobblestones where revolution-goers had been clubbed. And I did see the real Lenka in class every evening. So I jotted out more scenes up in Jan Mraka's flat. I was sleeping on the small, firm bed in their living room. One morning I walked to the dark gray school in search of the other American.

I found him sitting in the dim little library with two female students. "Oh," he said, with narrowing eyes, as if recognizing me. He was slightly shorter than I and a touch older. He took me on a walk. "It's good you're here," I said, and I meant for the sake of all that would happen. Oddly his squint seemed to say he didn't see it so. He led me down the grim square to its lone painted facade.

"The State Hotel," he said. "Rooms for Party officials and for the few West Germans they let visit. Now it's open to everyone. But we'll see only former officials and former West Germans. No one else knows how to use it." Inside the hotel, the tuxedoed waiter brought us two porcelain cups of coffee. "Look," explained David, "I was living in West Berlin. A crisp line divided them for decades. In a day the line was up and gone. Sure they're celebrating, but they also stop and gape at each other in the street—it was forty long years ago they split. The West is now a muscular machine, the East a coughing old stack. They're gonna unify? We'll see whether they speak the same language." Though the small chairs were stiff, David reclined comfortably.

He continued, "And here? They have no other half to compare themselves to, they have no idea how far down they are. Sure they've got this president and a few others who were made to sit in jails or wash windows, but what's actually changed? All their old factories are still running—they can't let them stop. Old farms and schools too. It'd be like switching which side of the street their little autos drive on, while they're all still driving. Very simple, very impossible."

He took out a local cigarette. He said, "I was working for our army in Berlin. You know what we were doing up there." Again his eyes spied over at me. He said, "So I know these languages. But you speak them too, I heard." He smiled, and sat up. "I've got to go visit a girl at the agriculture school. Very pretty. There's something about them here. I don't know what exactly. You know what I mean." We walked out into the lamp-lit dusk. It was all around me. I returned to Jan Mraka's apartment and wrote more paragraphs, about the girl's increasing worry over her new relationship. Would the new hope survive this first winter?

Her husband, Josef, burly with short dark hair, he was gone. He was seen only in photos, which Lenka had buried in the shadows of her closet, photos of a small wedding troop outside the church, photos of the couple in a summer forest. She had pushed them from memory, yet rid them she hadn't. She kept them in reach, they being of a time still inside her, a time which she wore on her silent face. By Lenka's candlelight the American saw the photos.

Jan and I departed his State Economist's office and walked to the workers' hall for lunch. We passed two chimney sweeps leaning against the facades. Beside them was the symbol of the new party, Civic Forum, its black circle smiling and winking. Beside it was the name of the little man they had just put in the castle, though he had said he just wanted to write. "I will be taking trips to other factories," Jan said as we sat with our soup. "Perhaps the answer is there somewhere."

"What's the question?"

Jan said, "What is a brewery, I suppose? What is a brewery today?" He blinked toward the food. He said, "It was just a place where three hundred came each day. The women did their tasks, and the men, we could make some details seem important." Some of these people were sitting around us. "Oh, and we made beer. We were told a certain amount to cook each month. We cooked it. Then before we began again, maybe we first raked the leaves, or cleaned the ceilings, or just sat and played chess."

Soon we scraped our fat and gravy into a bucket. This went to the hens. Back at Jan's office, the president was now on the wall. A labwoman came to the doorway and said, "I hung him there." We stared at the new photo. She asked me whether she could walk me to class. The curvy, upper passages let no more than a few strides ahead be seen.

When I returned home, a letter from Steph lay on my bed. "I miss you, Smoo. You must be having so many little adventures there. Is it actually possible that I might be there someday, snuggling you?" Hungry, the next day, I tried the unlit shops. Some wore the dust-colored State lettering, disclosing in a word what they were. The bakery had a long line out its door. The line grew backward before it moved forward. I continued down the lane. Stone faces protruded from the walls, eyes downward, as if in shame. The meat shop was locked through lunch, yet it had a line. Apparently some item not there this morning was to be briefly present this afternoon, and somehow these silent standers knew about it. Frowning Jitka stepped from the line.

We walked quietly together. "You could never understand," she said sourly. The gritty sidewalk bit at my thick soles. I looked at Jitka's thin shoes. We met Jan and the boys in the park. Jan said, "You will want to see our capital again. I too."

"Of course," I said. "And the State bus goes."

"Of course," said Jan. "But we can drive once." I raised my eyebrows—I hadn't seen his square little car since we got here. We pushed it out to where there was hill enough for the wheels to roll. Then we scrambled for our seats and Jan thrust the pedals. The motor started. "German cars," complained Jan.

"East German," I clarified.

"No difference," Jan brushed it away. He laughed his sharp, hopeful laugh. We drove along a forest road until reaching the country's little highway, a long smooth empty line through the greenery. "We were proud that we too would have such a highway," said Jan. "But here it took a very long time to build. It was not so easy to stay proud." The sun cast long shadows off the trees. Eventually the city lay in the distance. Jan said, "A man once told his tribe, 'We will settle here, between these hills.' Soon after, a princess looked out her window and imagined, 'A city of a thousand spires.'"

It looked very much like her city. We puttered through its lanes. We set tomorrow's meeting time.

Some of the Georgetown group had come in from their towns. When one of the girls saw me, she quickly spruced up her hair. How could I not notice? I was wearing my flannel shirt and black jeans. Each of these Georgetown girls was shorter and plainer than the next. With all the sharp soft Slavic faces walking around how could I think about them? I thought about brown-haired Lenka.

The group strolled across the old stone bridge. The autumn sun was setting over the castle and towers. It was all an old puppet-show stage, yet life size, and incredibly new—none of us had known about it. But I swear it was new to the Czechs too. They were smiling like we were. We were smiling because they were—it was their revolution.

The light breeze rumpled our shirts and hair. It was October 1990. History had just ended. Nothing had begun. A flutist stood in one nook of the bridge and a puppeteer in another nook and a violinist in another and black statues stared down from the ledges, and their dark river flowed calmly beneath. It surely had a name, though none of us had ever heard it.

Actually I had been trying to get to Russia, bigger and maybe even more mysterious, but now didn't seem to be the time to leave this place. On the weekend I knocked on Petr and Mirka's window. Blond Andre opened their door—he and Karel were visiting too. We all sat around their kitchen table. Andre's eye was bandaged. "It's nothing," he told me. "Some hot oil spilled from above."

I asked, "Were you attacking a castle?" He said, "Ne, ne, it's just our work, industrial climbing, it's just what we do now. But tomorrow we rock climb again. I think Karel has packed a bag for you. It's the Last Repel, last climb of the season."

We dipped into a pub, where soldiers occupied one table, gypsies another, and climbers a third. Lanterns shone from the walls. Beers were pounded to the table by the wordless barman. He was faceless too, because a patron never needed to look up. We didn't. Outside again, we huddled on the square. "It's magic," Karel was explaining to me. "The phone is magic." They pointed to the iron phonebooth atop the square. "With one coin you can dial your home. One coin, call

America. We don't know how it works, but it's real. Only we knew. We just had no one to call." I scanned their gazes and smiles.

No one had a coin. "Later," they decided, "the magic will be there." We linked shoulders and marched in song down the lanes. Beneath Igor's window they yelled up whispers. When a head finally appeared, it said, "He's sleeping."

"It's his little brother," they cried. "Wake him, wake him now. Reks is here—we're all here." The head wavered, scared. But soon the street-door opened and out came Igor in a nightcap. We marched along the cobblestone, another voice joining our chant. We marched like a castle regiment. We came to the tower in the town's surrounding wall, and up climbed Igor. He stepped on Karel's fair head, which bore the weight, cap over his eyes. And Igor tapped a second-story window, surely knocked on for the first time. But if behind the lace curtain there was any reaction, we below were quickly gone.

The next day, we put on our packs and walked through the autumn grass. And apparently all trails which this group walked led to tall rock walls, because soon the climbers were taking out their ropes and pairing off.

At dusk, we walked deeper into the forest. We arrived at a lone cottage, where a pig was sizzling above a fire, and a brewery barrel stood beneath the deck, and more climbers appeared out of the woods. They were from a neighboring town. They put down their packs and spread around the fire. One woman approached me shyly, lowering her head in apology for the interruption.

"I am a teacher," she said, "I know teachers and students in your town—the girls think you are wonderful. It is all they speak of. David, David."

I said, "They're sweet." Karel explained it to her. The woman covered her mouth. "I thought it was him." Her husband was an electrician. He strummed along with Andre and Karel. And the wife sang with a dreamy candy voice, pointed at the treetops.

The strumming grew faster—the electrician stood and spun on one foot and the others followed along, hooking arms together. It became a chant, in that deep dark other tongue. A Red Army chant, their mouths knew it. But had they ever sung it so loudly? It rose with the ashes toward the branches and sky. Then everyone collapsed, and huffing replaced the chant. "Well," rasped the electrician, "they were once our brothers." He shrugged. "No longer."

The cottage was lit by candlelight—in the attic were mats and bags for sleeping. Eventually, Canadian Anne retired there, and soon I and some others joined her. Out the little window we could hear those who remained around the fire, still talking, strumming, pausing, some of them at some point possibly to sleep, there by the fire.

In the morning, our knives found the last scraps on the pig. We walked further along the pine-needled floor and still more climbers joined our path. Another cliff wall appeared but now a drizzle forced us under its shelf. The climbers prepared the ropes but the rain strengthened, so they sat and stood and shared stories under our rock ceiling.

A group of wives emerged from the forest—they nudged the husbands hello. The husbands were bearded or shaven, shaggy or crew-cutted. There seemed to be a wife for each. They asked whether it had been done yet. It hadn't, so they stayed and shared our view to the misty trees. The rain still ruled but the season had to have a Last Repel. The climbers began braving upward. I followed.

On the wet rock, it wasn't limbs that needed to do more, but the mind. I wanted to freeze, doubt, retreat. I saw with a vividness I only knew from this spot, no floor at my feet. But again my hands safely palmed the top of the forest cliff, and soon we all stood on its edge, looking down. Andre went over first, threading backward with the rope. When it was my turn, I took that strange step, reversing fully, high in the air, edging out over nothing, blind to where I was aimed. Threading down, I tried to watch over my shoulder.

Finally I cut inward at that lower shelf, and unseen hands pulled my shoulders back. I hung upside-down and red wine was poured down my mouth, the Last Repel. They congratulated me. We marched onward through the dripping trees and came upon the State Regional Recreational Forest Lodge. Outside, it had one light-bulb against total darkness. Inside, the women had stew simmering. Someone had a violin, to join the guitars. Canadian Anne asked me, "Have you noticed? They make clothes from old curtains, keep lights off during the day, pickle for winter, fix all things. It all has meaning. And the feeling, in the air, even walking in the woods alone, even thinking lonesome thoughts maybe, it has meaning. Do you feel it too? Or am I a fool?"

I stared silently back at her. She said, "Wow, you are not nice." She shook her head at me and she checked my eyes again. I told her I felt it too, I told her I'd been walking alone a lot. At dawn, the entire assembly stood in the drizzle and nodded goodbyes. Soon Karel and I walked from the outer station toward the town.

I pointed to tidy little shacks in the grass and trees. Karel explained, "Garden space for those who live in the cube buildings." Soon we stared across a meadow at them, the cold gray statements from this last rule. "After the war they needed housing quickly. Also it was a symbol to their doctrine, of everyone having equal."

I asked, "Whom can we visit?"

"Yes, whom?"

I said, "The nurse from Anne's class?"

Karel said, "Yes, her." And we stared at each other. We shared our reasons why, and we exchanged terms.

I said, "But this is wrong."

"Terribly."

I said, "But they feel very right."

"Too right. So that it can become a need. A need that can beat a man. How to learn not to need?" We shrugged and walked on. We sat down in his grandmother's kitchen. Karel watched me as we ate. He said, "Strange, how many terrible things could happen here while in fact there were so many good people. I suppose the lie was too powerful. It made people assume that things couldn't actually be this wrong. Plus there was the fear. It prevented us from discovering how many people would have agreed if we spoke up." The daylight from the kitchen window made a tiny square in his eye. He said, "Here, a neighbor, his whole life, may have never looked you in the eye. Our neighbors have the only other door atop the stairwell, and a whole year passed when I saw nobody. It made no sense. How could they keep so quiet? How could such neighbors have no connection? One morning I was putting on my shoes and I heard footsteps and so I quickly opened the door. It was a soldier, my sister's boyfriend. He asked me where I was going with one shoe. Still the seasons were passing and I saw not a soul from that flat. So after the full year had passed, my mother baked cakes and I just took them to their door and I knocked." Karel, with shining eyes, he indeed the fair prince of this day, said, "Such a thing wasn't done. But I had to. I'm not sure why.

"And the man answered right away, as if he had been standing at the door, waiting. Now, when they go to their cottage, I water their plants. Their key hangs inside our flat. They bring me apples from their cottage tree." His old babychka handed me a bundle. "Cakes for you," explained Karel. "Take them. And come, I will show you my photos—I develop them in her flat." He showed me dim black-and-white photos of the soldiers removing the long, barbed fence, and of the crowd huddled in the winter square. "The feeling," said Karel, softly, slowly. He breathed out big toward the photos.

Anne came by at lunch the next day. "Andre says he loves me." Autumn rain had turned the town the color of wet dust. "So I asked whether he knew what love meant. He responded, 'I love you, you like me.'" We walked out of the old brewery. We walked down the square.

She said, "It's Charles Dickens land again. Who would've thought?" We walked into a shop. She scanned its open crates. "How they make meals, I don't know. What is this, a root?" It was. She said, "Couldn't you just die of thirst? Really, what do they drink?" We arrived at her hospital's grassy courts. Young nurses in skirts walked down the unlit halls. "Hairy legs," said Anne. We passed a shadowy toilet-closet. "Not a paper product in the building." We entered her cafeteria. Faces stared. Anne whispered an apology for wearing color. The smocked servers ladled us our soup and handed us our pork plates. Then they leaned back against their cabinets and muttered to each other with crowned teeth. When Anne sat she shook her head for a long slow time, as if to the thirst, the food, the wet dust. She said, "I don't need a pizza I suppose. But at least one thing green. It seems so distant. So impossible."

A student lent her a road bike and on Saturday we pedaled down the long gray road toward the town of the nearest Georgetowners. When we stood atop the hill above their town, she said, "We could easily be in some other century, on horses, with the same exact view." We arrived at their little dorm and I showered and lay back on one of their beds. It was four guys sharing a cement suite. Their floor was tangled with books and clothing and Penthouses. Tonight was the school ball. The guys lay under their covers, laugh-complaining about their existence here. "The boredom sucks."

"The food sucks."

"It all sucks."

I was skimming a book from Benjamin's giant box—he wasn't under bed covers but was a dinner guest somewhere. When he returned, I stood up toughly from his bed. "You can lie there," he said. In this new place I didn't know my exact mix of toughness and openness. I said, "Just saying hello." Maybe I was the cool unknown guy, athletic but liking books, reserved but friendly, a graduate of what Colin Vonn had taught me. Brown-haired Benjamin was similar to my town's David, without the extra years.

Lanky Craig said, "I mean the food really sucks."

Derek, who had a girlfriend still on the Georgetown sailing team, said "Sixty-seven days I'm home."

I said, "Counting days sucks."

"Look at this," he pointed at one Penthouse photo. "It's unbelievable." Anne was getting dressed in the other room. I said, "Your town has no pretty girls?"

Derek said, "They don't shave."

Craig said, "Bad enough that to wash themselves they have to squat in a tub with a hose, but they don't even do it. Have you ever stood on one of their buses and thought you were the only rider with a nose? And that's in the morning." I glanced down at that Penthouse page. The girl was slender with heavy breasts. She stood invitingly, one foot on a ladder. Craig said, "Sure it's charming when you get off the plane and there's no toilet paper in any bathroom and when you finally find a piece it's so tough you write a letter home on it. I mean I know they've suffered here. But it still sucks."

At the ball, the girls wore white lace dresses, and a flow of students sought attention from their Americans—they came to our table and pulled at the Georgetown guys, who then briefly tried the polka, and Anne and I tried a spin too. At night, the girls cooed outside our window, crying for Derek. They called and called hopingly. I said, "Derek, do something."

Craig said, "They're so young."

I said, "They mature faster here."

Derek said, "Sixty-six days."

When I arrived home, another little airmail letter lay on my bed. Steph's words were here again. She was coming over. It meant no more lying in this little bed and aching for her. It meant there'd be no Russia for me right now. It felt like a painful sacrifice. She wrote she was worried how foreign this would all be. At least I could tell the news to Jan, the climbers, and the Canadians—they'd all asked me to stay. Families wanted me at their dinner tables too. Some wanted afternoon visits for study. On Saturday, Jan took me back to the capital for the anniversary. One year ago they had totalitarian communism, today they would hear the words of a their humanist leader.

President George Bush would also speak. Jan and I rode the city subway with the students and poets and workers from those great days and nights, and then we walked those same streets. Rusted scaffolding blended into the walls. A brass band plucked and hooted with droopy instruments, droopy mustaches. Teens ran ahead with a banner bearing the Civic Forum's subtle smile. Three soldiers took nurses from an aid table and danced arm-in-arm. We flowed into that square. Bodies climbed up trees and into windowsills. Mr. Bush would speak first.

For his sake, the speaking would come from a bullet-proof black-glass booth. We heard, "Your history of freedom was written on this square, beginning a new world of revolution that linked this square with others—Gdansk, Budapest, Berlin—a revolution that joined together people fueled by the way of light, a thousand points of brave light, symbolizing your fiercely burning love of freedom.

We've seen a new world of freedom born amid shouts of joy, a beacon of hope, a light lit by humanity's essential quest for freedom, which gave birth to your new era of light." Brewery Economist Jan Mraka stood beside me as we listened. Soon his president's voice opened out, and everyone took one small step forward on the square.

"How is it that so many immediately knew what to do and none needed any advice or instruction? It is because people want something superior. Our peaceful revolution has shown the enormous human potential which was slumbering in our society." Agreement flowed toward the podium. It moved the mouths around me. I met gazes through the narrow openings. The crowd was proud. Here was that velvet voice, their gentle guide. In his thoughtful monotone he was preparing them for what they faced this winter. "For forty years you heard from my predecessors how happy we all were, and what bright perspectives were unfolding in front of us. I assume you did not propose me for this office so that I, too, would lie to you. When I flew recently I found some time to look out of the plane window. I saw the industrial complex of our State chemical factory and the giant housing right behind it. The view was enough for me to understand that for decades our leaders did not look out of the windows of their planes. The previous regime, armed with its arrogant ideology, reduced man to a force of production, and nature to a tool of production.

"But the worst thing is that we lived in a contaminated moral environment. We became used to saying something different from what we thought. Concepts such as love, friendship, and compassion lost their depth. I am talking about all of us. We had all accepted that system as unchangeable and thus helped to perpetuate it. So we cannot blame the previous rulers for everything. We are all guilty." And the crowd glared at the ground, and they nodded. They now had truth, as if it were a color long denied them and now here to paint there walls with. "We are a small country, yet at one time we were the spiritual crossroads of Europe. Is there a reason why we can't again become so?" Again approval hummed forward from the sea of hatted heads.

Under the old fluorescent lights of the bus station Jan then purchased his first *International Herald Tribune*, to his clear surprise—the vendor seemed surprised to be selling his first. Then standing on the bus, Jan said, "I am surprised to have perhaps found a very small advertisement aimed just for me." A British man wanted to learn what was happening in the world of East Europe beer and beverages. He provided a fax number. At the flat, I explained faxing. Jan shook his head, not possible. I said, "It might be his telephone too." Jitka snapped, "One call is my month's pay." She was making dough for Christmas cookies. Jan sat down to write a letter directly to the newspaper, hoping they would deliver it to the British man.

When the first snow fell, I took out my bicycle and conquered the white woods and villages. In the fading light, I pedaled slowly back along the town's long, dark school. I saw Lenka walking away. She was carrying a schoolbag over her shoulder. Her sleeves were pushed up on her pale arms. She disappeared down an old alley.

Soon I was coasting alongside her. Her hair was partly tied and partly descending in tresses. Finally she turned and saw me. Her gaze was cautious.

"I have something just for you."

"How could you have something just for me?"

I told her it was waiting at Jan Mraka's. She boarded the electric bus and rode off down her snowy streets. I returned to the flat but was stopped at the door by Jitka shaking a wooden spoon. "I am still baking. So you too will work."

Jan stepped out into the stairwell. He said, "We must search for sugar. It is night and the shops remain closed each day through all the full holiday, but we are sent for sugar." I followed him out into the evening. We turned the corner and entered another building along the town's little labyrinth.

A door clicked open. There stood the economist from the hospital and her husband. Serious Jan began to explain. But the wife just motioned us in. Jan said, "We cannot." He again began to explain. But they shook their heads, insisting. "I'm only baking cookies," said the wife. We walked past their dim living room where two tiny boys sat in pajamas. Somehow there was a plate of steaming potato pancakes waiting on the kitchen table. The husband poured red wine. The wife crouched to check the oven. She said, "We have time." We touched glasses for health. We all wore muffled grins.

We left with a tin of Christmas cookies but forgot sugar. We walked the crooked lanes until Jan stopped at a corner and looked up at a lit window. "Ivana and Yarda, they perhaps have a room for you and your Steph." The chill night compressed his voice. "Hello," said Yarda, appearing beside us on the sidewalk. He had a beer pitcher in his hand and snow in his hair.

He led us up to his family's enclave. Ivana peered around the kitchen corner and said calmly, "Jan," as if he had arrived unannounced a thousand times. Another couple was sitting there at the red kitchen table. Yarda poured them beer.

Ivana poured me hot wine. She checked her Christmas cookies in the oven. I said to the other couple, "Not baking Christmas cookies?"

The wife answered by handing me a tinful across the table. The husband answered by saying, "Yes, I too have heard of you. So, American, what do you think of our fearful streets?" His bearded grin was pointed toward Jan as he spoke.

"Do you know that Jan and I were always friends, friends who stopped and spoke in the square? We talked about work, or my hockey and his football, simple talk, and the whole time I was a bad man, a member. Or no, now I'm the bad man—in that system I was considered good and Jan was bad and now good. Can you see all this with your eyes?" His tongue played in his cheek. Jan kept a solid gaze.

"Have you seen his maps? Of course you have, probably the first day. But he showed me too, on a different day, a brave day in fact. Remember?"

"Obviously."

The others calmly sipped. Ivana brought us warm cookies. When we left, we had forgotten sugar. Snowflakes were still falling. We listened to them for a moment.

I said, "The Canadians live in the zoo." Serious-faced Jan said, "Right." We walked down the steep steps of the State outdoor theater and then into the forest and eventually to their little wooden building in the zoo.

They were drinking tea and wearing slippers and huddling under sleeping bags while writing lessons. Anne knifed open a bottle of wine. "Just like Andre showed me." We raised our glasses and gave a longer nod for it being a holiday. Jan remembered the sugar but the girls had none. When we returned to Jan's building, a lone car pulled up behind us. We stopped and stared at the black sedan in the dark night.

It was a Mercedes. I walked toward its window. The driver asked me a question in German. I shook my head. He tried another language. I almost caught it, but again shook my head. He tried English. I nodded. He said, "Oh thank goodness." He pronounced the name of the street he was seeking. He was on it. He pronounced Jan's name, as Jan walked up behind me.

So we had a very late dinner with the British beverage man. "It's incredible to actually be on this side now. I've just been through Poland." He looked at me. "You must be having a time." He was white-haired and smiley and wise. He said, "This day, you know, this joining of East and West, we shall learn things from them as well." He gave Jan a little old Toshiba laptop and tasked him to sum up the value of the town's State brewery. Stern Jan was overjoyed. He was working with the West. Jitka gave the British beverage man a tin of Christmas cookies. The next evening, Lenka visited.

We sat quietly alone on the gray couch. She was staring at me, awaiting me. The moment didn't seem real. This girl meant something, the East Europe girl, here before me, it meant something I couldn't quite grasp. Perhaps if I kissed her. Instead I showed her a *Tribune* ad for a nanny in America. Lenka said, "This is not for a girl like me, not for a girl from here." I agreed, but I suggested we send the letter anyway. I leaned over to kiss her, to touch her Slavic, pretty, real face.

She pulled backwards. "You have a girlfriend. She is coming."

"But I like you."

"You like me? For how long will you like me?"

I didn't have an answer, nor did I fully understand why she was asking. But there was time.

III

When Steph arrived and unpacked, she donned a new, peach nightgown, lighter than her skin. She had a Florida tan.

I couldn't touch her. "It's so strange," she said about our long absence. Up in our one-room flat above Ivana and Yarda we pushed together the firm little State beds. Steph and I sat at the square table by our window. "So strange," she said, "I can't express it."

I didn't think it was so strange. I really wanted to hug her and lie around with her. I said, "You'll like it here, you'll do fine. We'll do fine." The furnace clicked as it warmed our room. We were to bathe downstairs in Ivana and Yarda's flat. They said to come anytime, no need to knock.

We received a small knock on our door. Their two little daughters had come up to sit on the bed and gaze at Steph. Her face was brown, her hair a rich blond, and she wore her bright yellow fleece. The girls wore red ribbons in their pigtails. When we brought them back downstairs, Ivana motioned us to sit for dinner. I shook my head, no. Ivana nodded hers, yes. Her hair was unwashed. It swayed when she stepped to and from the stove.

"Yarda and I met at a potato planting," she told us matter-of-factly as she placed steaming soup bowls before us. "We married two weeks later." She shrugged. "It was nice."

"Sit," said Yarda, entering the flat. He pointed us to the table. "Sleep," Ivana told the little girls, who were giggling in their adjacent room. "Eat," Yarda told us. "Your people must learn that we have food here. Our food is not so good, but good, good wives. So, good dinners." The flat was cozily cramped, its shelves housing thread spools, small candles, and wooden spice jars.

Yarda said, "I too will take a trip. Through the quiet trees." His arms imitated cross-country skiing. Ivana said, "I'm sewing him a ski suit." Yarda said, "The best forests are now where the fence stood, the long, long fence to keep you out." He grinned. "No houses, no factories, no people. Now no fence. I'll take my passport, show it at the border, and make a giant circle back in. Finished, done. My trip. Alone. How exciting," he said in sweet mockery.

"Yarda is a Communist," snapped Jitka in her own kitchen on the other side of the small town. Steph and I watched her bang around her stove. Jan placed brewery bottles in front of us and quietly toasted. Jitka said, "They behaved as if all was fine, so now shouldn't they be missing it? Instead these smiles everyone wears." She clunked soup bowls in front of us. "But you will never understand." She picked up her beer bottle.

Steph's students understood her fine, repeating back her every word, unlike my keg fillers who had begun bringing bottles for the whole class. In the afternoons, I sat in Jan's office and listened to the State radio play the low tuba and accordion. When the one station started the calm, slow news, Jan's eyes slowly rose.

He furrowed his brow. "Miners in Romania," he said, "they've beaten the revolutionaries with pipes. Right there in the square." We sat in a pause which seemed to ask, could that happen here? Jan shook his head, his eyes sure. We listened.

"Yugoslavia," said Jan, "their army is dividing up for war." He discounted this too, it wouldn't happen there or here. Again his eyes cornered toward the radio. "Poland, no pipes, no war. Instead they plan to switch the factories and currency overnight. Shock therapy, it's called. I suppose they'll be France by spring." The quiet music started again, and, soon after, Jan lowered his eyes back to his numbers. At night, I biked down the broken, cobblestone lane to join Steph in our tiny home. I closed the tall, red, courtyard fence. The winter breeze blew Ivana's white sheets hanging on the line. I tiptoed up the steps, keeping the dark, not to disturb the family.

"Come," whispered a voice behind me. Thick Yarda stood in his open doorway. To get into their kitchen we had to duck a low frame, as if entering a mine.

I sat down at the red table and Yarda uncorked a great green jug. He poured two glasses of wine. Elbows on the table, we stared into the bottle's thick distortion.

"And the building?" I asked. "Who will own this building?"

Yarda said, "What? Oh, no one knows. We all will own it, no one will own it. I say leave it simple." He leaned toward the table. "The hard life, that's what they taught us, the Reds. The hard, hard life." And his hand tightened an imaginary belt. "The hard, hard life." His face was proud. The girls were asleep just a reach away. Through their dark little room peered a streetlamp. When I climbed under the covers toward Steph, she awoke and held me and told me she had tried to wait and told me about her day. "I really like it all." We smooched. In the morning, we sat with hot tea at our small table by the window. The winter sun struggled over the rooftops to briefly color our lane. In one corner we could see the onion-shaped spires of the church. At times we noticed their iron chimes. We bicycled through the snowy forests, then ate lunch at the workers' hall. We went home to prepare our lessons. Steph said, "I think we have everything for dinner. Noodles and carrots for soup. The bread and salami."

"We have each other."

"Oh Smoo," she said. I tried to coax her over to the bed. She said, "It's still sort of strange." At night, we took our bowls to our table and ate by lamplight. Steph said, "I want to bake brownies for my students."

"They love you."

"They're so smart."

"I love you."

She said, "You're smart." We caressed each other's fingers there at our table. It felt good. "No really, Reks. You are very smart." She looked around the flat. She asked, "Isn't it weird how all their little homes are the same size?" I answered, "It's weird how you think you can bake brownies when they barely have chocolate."

She said, "I'll just melt a whole bunch of those dark little bars." I said, "You'll have to go to every shop."

She said, "We'll go to every shop."

I said, "You're great." When she was invited for a weekend trip to a family's cottage, I encouraged her to go.

I woke up alone and I jotted my little story scenes. I was thinking clearly and calmly. In the quiet I could hear things like my own breathing, which I noticed after long intervals. When eventually I thought I heard a voice in the hall, I walked slowly down the stairs—I stood silently outside the family's door, considering whether to knock.

But a voice called me in for breakfast. I ducked into the kitchen. "I didn't want to wake you."

Ivana said, "Thank you. I awoke at four and baked cakes."

"That's crazy."

She said, "I'm bringing them to babychka's cottage today." Ivana's eyes, I noticed, were not gray as I'd thought but the same green as those of the daughters. "Yarda, oh Yarda," she called, not quite seriously. She requested wine from the hall cupboard. Yarda was on his way out with a hammer and shovel to work in the courtyard—first he brought in one of his wine jugs. Ivana put it in the rucksack. On the table sat the fabrics she was making into his ski suit. The other babychka came up from her flat below.

"Oh Reks," she moaned with a smile, "they're retiring me, all of us, retired at sixty. They must make work spaces for the young. So I go for a month to the mountain spa. No more newspaper stand for me."

"Newspaper stand?"

Ivana explained, "Just this year—she wasn't quite sixty when the fabric factory needed her space."

Yarda said, "Last year she served as a lifeguard." He was still standing beside us with his hammer and shovel. "Do you understand? A lifeguard at the big pool. She can't swim. Never could." And babychka's smile alternated between Yarda and me. "She was worried every moment," jabbed Yarda. "Worried they'd find out."

"I worried about the children," refuted babychka. "I cautioned each one very strictly, avoid all and any trouble." I returned upstairs and sat again at the table and worked for another stretch. I was able to spend a long time alone in my mind. At dark, I diced up salami and grilled it in garlic and added it to eggs. When I lay down in bed, I felt the deep night around me, out the window and beyond. The quiet was incredible. It was as if some great machine had been shut off. Deep in the night, I dreamt about jumping across the city's slanted rooftops, black and red and green, above its stone streets.

The next evening, I walked across the square and knocked at Jan Mraka's. "He's at the brewery," Jitka said grimly at the door. We stood there for a moment, then she turned and walked away across her little foyer. I followed her into their living space where she stooped down and wiped a cloth across a record. Soon a woman's sweet soft voice blended with horns and flute and the record crackling.

"My favorite, when I was young," said Jitka. She flipped her hair aside but kept her eyes on mine. She charged, "Then they forbid her. They sent her to the factory, because she had signed the list for more rights, she signed with the few artists brave enough to speak out. What she sang was just sad love songs. But to me they held all the feeling of those days.

"And now? They make some ceremony for her at the castle? It's too late, do you see? Those stolen years, should we just live as if it never happened? Those thieves still walk the streets. The president—I know he's good and fair—but he simply pardons them? Forgives them? They forbid us money, travel, truth." Jitka's face was pale white as if bloodless. "Yes I'm angry, but I was always angry. Not like others, that when I hear them now I think I'm dreaming. Yesterday they were all happy Communists, suddenly today is great and new." She poured us coffee in the porcelain cups.

"I came to learn."

"So you think you are some soldier. But where were you when we were scared? Where were you when we couldn't show fear and pain, couldn't let our neighbors know our thoughts? We kept it all inside. Yes, you come to learn, you come to help, but it means nothing if you don't know where you are. And soon you'll be gone, I know."

When Steph and I we were back sitting at our table she told me about her trip. "We cooked, ate, cleaned, read to the children, put them to bed, then drank. Then we cooked, ate, cleaned, and drank again." She shrugged. We smooched. That night, I rotated her onto all fours and tried to make love from behind her. She said, "It's uncomfortable." Her stiff sincerity made me uncomfortable. I wanted her to enjoy it. We gripped hands and drifted off to sleep.

The next afternoon, I refrained from asking her to nap with me. Indeed I thought it would have been really nice to roll around here in our little flat while townspeople did their tasks on the lane below. And though I held my tongue, Steph asked from the table, "Why do you always want that?" I said I didn't know what she meant.

I walked downstairs. Ivana gave me soup. "Potatoes," she said. But my spoon found much more, mushrooms and carrots and leeks. She said, "Yarda's working in the courtyard. He says one day he'll build some new little shop, when it's allowed. Really he just likes little labors to keep him busy."

"And you?" I asked. Ivana shrugged. She nodded. In the evening, Yarda poured us wine. Ivana sat by the open window and smoked a cigarette. "I never do this," she said. She raised her chin and asked Yarda, "You'll meet the girls?" Yarda nodded and closed his little newspaper. The little girls, returning alone from gymnastics, would be met at the night bus-stop by their father. Ivana said, "Oh Reks, I do need one little labor from you."

We walked down to their stone garages and lifted up a great sack of potatoes. "From the cottage," explained Ivana. "To help us through winter." We carried the sack up the stairs. She asked, "Have you heard of the American beetle? Sent to destroy our potato crop? They said you sent over a beetle to destroy our great socialist life." She smirked. "They said things like that."

"Things?"

"Crazy things. That you sent this beetle to kill our crops. That you mix salt and sugar on your foods because your tastes were so perverse. Crazy things. That sex and killing were all that was talked of and written of because only this remained for enjoyment." She shrugged it away. "That some there cannot even read. Or that you could be killed just walking down the street—you just walk down the street and they might kill you. I don't know, crazy things."

Back in the kitchen, she said, "Welcome home girls, your math must get done." The girls were playing their little piano and they said they'd done their math. Ivana turned to me at the table and said, "They also piled on these hours of homework each night, it was too much. We would sit here together for hours." She picked up her sewing. I went upstairs and climbed into bed and Steph awoke and said, "I was really waiting for you."

I said, "I'm truly sorry." But when I made hints the next afternoon, her face again took on that dark frown. I said, "Remember when you said your neighbors smoked weed and you automatically thought there was something dirty about it? I think that's how you look at sex."

"That's so not true." She was standing by our bureau, her face even showing despair. She repeated quietly, "It's not true." We both sighed. She asked, "What is this, Reks?" I answered, "Well, I didn't come over to this place simply to be with my girlfriend. That's not totally why I came to this place."

She was crying. She stepped out into the cold hallway and closed our door. I stayed at our table. I shook my head. I looked out the window at the rooftops. Steph was likely at the hall window with the opposite view, to the snowy courtyard and red fence. I scribbled some writing notes. I cleaned the dishes. I went into the hall and stood with her by that window. I stroked her back. She wiped her knuckles across her eyes. She said, "Geez, I didn't think you were even going to come out for me." I got her a towel. She said, "I came to this place to be with my boyfriend."

The next morning she biked off to the school and I to the brewery. Jan handed me a note from Lenka Rosolova. She had finally received a response from the

American hiring the nanny. In the afternoon I walked my bike down the square toward her.

An icy wind was blowing out from the lanes and pulling at her long tresses of hair. She tried to gather them in. She held up the air-mail letter. I read it. She said. "I don't quite understand."

I told her about the climbers' magic phone. Maybe it really worked. Lenka followed me silently to the top of the square. She gave me a single coin. It had to be dropped in the slot at a precise instant during the dialing, or no service.

My coin clunked through the iron phone and the silence became a smooth far-away ringing. I stared into the corner of the old booth. "Hello," said a man's voice. It was the magical sound of America. I yelled, "Can you hear me?" Deep quiet followed. Then the local pulse blared in my ear. I tried again, turning the cold dial many turns. Three times I heard the voice—at first it was curious, as if also sensing the space between us, but as we were cut away each time it grew angry. I stepped back out to Lenka. She was looking off to nowhere. Though she had those cheeks of rose, the wind exposed her winter paleness.

She finally said, "I expected nothing more." She looked up at me and added, "I even told you this."

I said, "But you had a chance. It was the mail's fault, your Posta service." Lenka blinked, trying to comprehend. I explained, "He wrote that your first letter was late, your second never arrived. It means he never got your photo. He chose from elsewhere. He says he was waiting, trying for you."

She asked, "Do I understand, our Posta, my Posta, they failed with my letters?" Lenka was crying. That there'd been a chance and such dark forces had prevented it, this made her blue-black eyes glare at the wind and at her passing townspeople. "It may have been better to not have hoped."

The sun broke in and out of the puzzle-piece clouds. I walked Lenka toward her flat and we stopped in the park outside her gray building. This was the park where my young economist character received Lenka's invitation up to her velvet couch. Lenka and I sat on a park bench and looked off down the different paths. This wind was withering off the top layers of snow.

"So, I will be here. Right here. Always here."

Yarda took his dream cross-country trip and returned and said, "It can't be expressed." He kissed his fingers into the air and went to work with his hammer atop the stone garages in his courtyard. In the morning he bicycled to the agriculture school. In the evening he walked to Steph's class.

A heavy rain began to fall. I gazed out the morning window at the opposite roofs. The rain pattered the slates and gutters and ran along the cobblestone curbs. "Smoo," said Steph, "let's travel this summer." We smooched.

I wanted her to be happy. But this great thing here was finally getting ready to start. Travel Western Europe with my American girlfriend? I wanted to bike out in the gray morning here with Yarda, I the lone westerner, and I wanted to be in that capital city with all the new possibilities on its endless dust-colored lanes. "Reks," she said, "don't look so worried."

Soon again I sat with fair-haired climbers Karel and Andre on a flat, high peak above the woods. We sat for a long, still moment. I could see the huddled huts of a village collective. I felt like I could walk right down the treetops, into the damp fields.

Finally, Andre picked up the rope for our descent. He looped it around a tiny tree and a jut of rock and Karel. He tossed both ends of the rope over. Then he gripped one end above him and one below. He glided easily down to the forest floor. I looked back at Karel here atop.

He nodded, sending me. Gone was the sitting and reflecting. It was time to step backward over the edge. This first twisting step, this was the true task—the work would then become the rhythmic releasing, but only after I took that seemingly wrong step. Now the treetops seemed a forever distance away. "Trust your hands," said Karel.

Down on the ground below, we calmly walked the trail back. Our steps cracked icy puddles. We entered the knoll in front of the climber cottage. Over the fire cooked our lamb. The brewery barrel stood by the wood pile.

Benjamin Wallace from Georgetown had moved to a little flat in the city, and he invited me by postcard to visit. Still in the black of morning, my train braked amid the station mists. On the corner, coal cubes were stacked like sugar—a worker stood with his foot on the pile. No need to shrug off anyone's judgment of his task, he had no doubt about his place on these streets. I saw so in his eyes as we shared a quick glance. His work clothes whipped in the wind, which slowly pushed the low clouds above.

I rode the subway, through stations made of giant columns and dome ceilings and not a word. Across town I rose above ground and walked the quiet streets. And there walked the worker, a different face than from the other side of town but here again blue-eyed and blue-capped, mustached and stained. At his side, his woman wore the same clothes and boots, they walking to the nearby pub, where they had a space on the benches, just as they had a warm place to return home to tonight. So they'd never been a threat, never questioned the Party. Yet they'd come out on those days in the square, come out for what was missing.

Ben's window looked straight out at that tall black presidential castle, aglow in purple-white above the rows. We stared. "The flat belongs to a former dissident—he moved in with his mother. I teach him some things, we go to the pub, he let's me live here." The toilet closet was in the chilly stairwell, pigeons cooed in the building's shaft, the tiny fridge was empty, and there was one coal-stove for the two rooms. Ben said, "But where again will I have such a view?"

The Foreign Ministry had hired Ben to edit their new West-bound communiqués. "There was no one else to hire," he said as we strolled past his ministry building tucked within the city's dark maze. We passed tiny windows and stone faces and chipped arches. I said, "We've walked into a place of strange feeling, unknown feeling, enchanted feeling." Each next corner produced a stone fountain, or ladied lamppost, or sculpted drinking spout, all in intricate detail. Ben looked around as if for what to assess next. "I do like how some forest is always nearby. It seems like the Party ensured this one thing, trees could always be reached by foot." We stepped off a tram elsewhere in the tight rows. I said, "Trains between towns are kept cheaper than the gas to drive by car. It actually makes some sense."

The remaining Georgetowners had also moved to the city. They kept a key beneath their doormat. Their firm State beds couldn't be seen beneath their thorough strewing of clothes. "I can't believe I'm still here," the first to awake might emit. I looked over from my seat at their table. I was supposed to start graduate school but this was the place to be and these guys just didn't see it.

They did have a phone though. The first time it rang, they handed it to me. I heard Steph's lovely, lonely, blonde voice.

"Reks, we're in Amsterdam, you'd love it! My sisters want to see you. We're having fun. I miss you." I responded, "Wow." She said, "Come, Smoo. I checked the trains—you can leave tonight and be here tomorrow. I checked the trains for you, I went to the station." I looked out at the evening street and I looked at the Georgetowners leaning on pillows and re-reading books. "Please come," said Steph.

I said, "Steph, I don't know."

I took a bus back to town instead and strolled across the square. The church clock chimed its two iron tones, high then low. A tiny bell chimed in the door of the food shop. As I approached the brewery, the air was scented with the beer cooling in the attic pools. Lenka Rosolova was approaching from the other way. She wore the poor, sad jeans and shoes. At the brewery gate she said, "I have a surprise for you."

I nodded. She said, "My father received a phone call. I am wanted in America. The man received my second letter. He received my photo. There is work for me." She smiled. She asked, "Did you understand? I've been awaiting you. It's coming true. He arranged the visa. I have the flight. I go now or not at all. I know, I know," she motioned around her. The brewery's little truck pulled up between us toward the gate. We stepped back. Beneath the truck I could see her shoes. The scraggly-haired driver jumped down and opened the gate and then drove in.

Lenka said, "Goodbye is better if it is quick, if it is just a quick decision. So goodbye for now," she said. I watched her walk back down the long lane. I went to my room above Ivana and Yarda's. I looked through the drawers. I stared at Stephanie's clothing. She had brought her little socks and underwear and shirts across the ocean to be with me. She had washed them in Ivana's slow old machine, and dried them on our lines, and then folded them. Downstairs, I sat with Ivana and Yarda at their kitchen table. Soup simmered on the stove. *Dallas* was beginning on television. This old show was brand new here. Yarda glanced at it and then went out to work in his courtyard. I walked out through the courtyard and crossed the near meadows and entered David's cement building and stepped gingerly past a woman scrubbing the stairwell floor. She said, "Tell him I hung his laundry."

David opened his door wearing a robe. In his bedroom a young woman lay in another robe, her legs winter white. As I passed she raised an eyebrow. David directed me to his square little kitchen. When I handed him a bag with rolls and ham he said, "And we were sure we were going hungry tonight." He had that squint again as if he understood something I didn't about what exactly was happening here. We then sat there for a while, long enough that I forgot about the girl.

"The ministries, the institutes," scoffed David, "forget them, they won't do anything real. They don't get it."

I said, "There's the president and his Civic Forum."

David said, "No, no. It's not time for ideas anymore. We're talking real lives. If these factories were on our side, not one would survive. They have ten men doing the work of one. And the women, they're still the computers. The floor is dropping out." He paced.

"And what did it all produce? The only milk comes in a small plastic bag. If you can find it and it doesn't drip out on the tram, then it's rotten by Monday, when the bread's stale too. And their refrigerators at home?" He opened his. "I guess you don't need a light in them, unless you want to see. School staff took me to lunch the other day—we finished our pork and emptied our beers and sat silently, the waiter's only customers. We waited for fifteen minutes. Half an hour. An hour. For sixty slow minutes we sat there alone. Finally I asked, 'What the hell is going on?' They shrugged. I walked into the back and there was the waiter, smoking a cigarette with the cook—he was leaning against the wall and he just kind of looked over at me. Did he forget about his one table? We would've waited there until nightfall. And to pay, this was to pay. Think some poet president is gonna fix that? You and I know what to do. You're in the city some now—I'll be there as soon as I finish this."

In the city, I lay by a sunny window on one the Georgetown beds. They'd now fled home for the summer. Ben was still here, reading and maybe writing in his flat on Iron Footbridge Street with its once-in-a-lifetime view. The phone rang. I stared at it across the room.

The Johns Hopkins School of Advanced International Studies was offering, based on my experience here, a scholarship to their Bologna Center. Graduate school was unavoidable. There was a knock on the door. I opened up to see Steph's pink and white smile. "I am so excited to see you," she said.

I said, "I am so excited to see you." We spent cozy days in this flat and then were all smooches and hugs as I put her on an airplane for Chicago.

IV

I had this city flat all to myself and at night this drove me near to crazy. I had to get my Czech girl in here. There were so many, so much eye contact. They were pretty and slender and feminine and natural and whatever else that made me want to ride the tram home with them and do it in their East-Europe kitchens while speaking their language and then lie in their quiet beds.

But now I couldn't find her. I walked the lanes. The pubs and bars were closing. My time here was expiring. Where was that sultry sweaty smart girl with the poor but neatly ironed clothing and that candy voice?

I ordered a final drink and sat on some outside steps. I couldn't bear the long night-tram across the city. I watched the dark river flow by and I burned inside. A BMW pulled up to the curb. It had to be a westerner—in fact the car had diplomat plates. The guy at the wheel was looking at a map and meanwhile he edged open his passenger door.

Maybe I could get a ride home. Maybe I could get a hand job. From these steps I stared motionlessly out at the car. The door just hung open, there at the curb. I was wearing khaki shorts. I drove with him toward my side of the city. He was French Canadian. He switched gears with his left hand and his right hand went to my thigh and eased upward and somehow he was steering too. He asked, "Where did you get those legs? I myself am a rower." He was desperately serious about advancing this situation. I let him feel me. He parked in a dark spot. I felt his chin stubble against my skin. I got out of the car.

He said, "C'mon." I said, "Sorry." He said, "C'mon." I walked through a city meadow and climbed a fence and crossed the next road. There he came, speeding up. He opened the door. I said, "Sorry." I shut it. At home I took an icy shower, because each building lost hot water for two summer weeks. I was shivering. I should have punched that guy in the face and stolen his BMW and gone for my village girl. But damn, I didn't like being so controlled. Look at what just happened. I didn't want to need it so badly that I would do any crazy thing. The nighttime summer air slowly warmed me back up. The next day, Karel picked me up in the old auto. We drove down the long, gray road toward the country's border. We watched the chipping old towns approach and pass. Karel said in slow thought, "It's a simple country, a hopeful country, but very damaged."

We approached the Czech border post and then the Austrian border post and soldiers stood on both rooftops. Then we were out, passing bright white houses with neat wood embroidery. Here were this side's homes, cars, shops, fields. I had been in a place long untouched, a place whose gate had only just opened to its dark kingdom inside, and now it was behind me.

"Mountains," I said to sleeping Karel as we entered the Alps. On the range's other side, we entered Italy—so said Karel, nudging me awake beside him. "Si, si," I said, my eyes unable to open. At dawn, we crouched beside the car and Karel stirred up a breakfast mush in his camping pot. He sprinkled some cinnamon. I cooked tea on another tiny stove. We sipped slowly. We returned to the Italian highway.

Entranced by the sun, we turned our heads at times toward the whoosh of a passing car. Faces stared at us each time. We felt how the eyes would have had us feel, strangers in a strange land, like we had just been released from places unimaginable. We pushed onward through pink villages and past doorsteps where men sat and stared into the buzzing heat.

We drove into Bologna, where students buzzed on mopeds across the red piazzas. We negotiated our way to the Johns Hopkins School of Advanced International Studies and Karel turned off the auto. I wanted to go back. The other new students stood around the SAIS entrance. I looked at Karel. "You'll like it," he assured me. I was led upstairs to talk to some Salvatore, who didn't look up from his desk, but said he would, when he had a minute, show me places I could live.

Karel wouldn't approach the building. He gazed at the gathering of students on this Italian side-street. I stood beside him and the little white auto and we mumbled. Two passersby stopped because one was Slovak.

But he seemed comfortable in his dull clothes. And the other wore round glasses and was a Europe-living American and was calmly mature about that. He had been working for the U.N., and his Slovak boyfriend was simply dropping him off—they were looking into my and Karel's eyes to gauge whether we were the same thing. Salvatore finally drove me around while Karel waited with the car.

One apartment was narrow like a train, with seven bedrooms and one bathroom. Another had bedrooms with no windows. I was definitely returning home with Karel. I told him so while awaiting the next Salvatore trip. I would be walking out on a scholarship. I would have to write. I would be a writer in Prague and during the winter I would pull up the collar of my coat and walk off with my locals to some pub. I would sit at Ivana and Yarda's table in the town and write while they did tasks. If I didn't return now, their lives would go on without me.

Salvatore took me up another building, and there stood an American who had already chosen a room—again the apartment didn't have a piece of carpet or a single lamp but one of the rooms had wood walls and a brown desk and I thought maybe I could get something done here. With Salvatore waiting at the front door, I stepped in to greet this guy.

He was slightly taller than I—he looked over at me. I asked, "Party a lot?" He answered, "I'm here to do what we were sent for." I left—I didn't know what the hell I was saying. I paid Salvatore for the room. I shook hands goodbye with Karel and gave him money to fill the gas canisters and I hugged him and went back and slept in my new room.

In the morning, I walked toward the bathroom sink and the American guy was standing there. He hadn't seen who ultimately moved in, and by his expression he didn't much seem to care. He left the sink and walked down the hall. I rinsed cold water on my face.

He said looking back, "Wanna get some groceries?"

So, I had a friend. The apartment came with two very old bikes—new bikes would apparently be stolen off the street without fail. Mark Quinn had taught English in Egypt. I assembled and rode my black Apex. I had my black kryptonite lock. As we rode, I thought about Karel still traveling back to his land. Mark and I filled our grocery cart and then filled our backpacks and pedaled home. The U.N. guy would be living with us. For dinner, Lars Larson cooked us eggplant parmesan. He said a Czech girl would be studying here. I said, "Oh?"

For breakfast we ate muesli. So far we were just doing intensive Italian. We kept the textbook in our bathroom. I was planning to take "Transition in the Soviet Union" and I had begun looking through its books. But that week, the Soviet Union ended. With some more flowers handed to tank drivers, seventy years of forever were done. And here I was, stuck in Italy. I didn't care how excited the other Americans were about the new fashions and old rooftops.

Bologna had one little park and Mark Quinn and I jogged the circumference several times. I was still thinking about escaping back to Eastern Europe. During the hot days of the Corso Intensivo, I daydreamed out the classroom windows. I was mostly in some Moravian meadow. Maybe some little Lenka was with me. At times I was with my bike. My Steph thoughts were about her sad little underwear drawer. Eventually, the students who couldn't pay for the Corso arrived.

This included the Czech girl, the Russian girl, the Bulgarian guy, all firsts from their nations. Lars Larson pointed out Jana Stefackova leaving the building, and I hurried my bike alongside her. "Hello."

She said she was living in one of the flats with eight others. She was not a little Lenka, instead thicker and taller. For this first day of school she had worn her nice dress-suit. "My mother made it," she said as we walked. I told her I was happy to meet her. She looked at me and smiled.

I read Roy Medvedev's, *Let History Judge*, in our bathroom while daytime buzzed outside our open window. The book took me into dark prisons for Soviets who had thought the wrong thoughts. Medvedev described lying on the bench of his bright cell and being assaulted if his eyes dared to close. While enduring this deprivation he listened to a woman moaning in torture in the next cell. "What could they possibly be doing to her?" he asked during his sleeplessness.

Mark Quinn and I met in the kitchen to cook lunch and discuss the odd little "European History Since 1815" professor. I said, "He builds up these sweeping, conclusive statements with irrevocable ends. Then revokes them."

Mark imitated him. "And in 1815 the European balance of power was suddenly as peaceful and orderly as ever. Or was it? Metternich had masterfully and single-handedly created entirely new politics. Or had he? One could travel across the whole of the continent without even needing a passport. Or could one?" We laughed. Mark would be selling international satellite insurance—his future employer had sent him here. He said toughly, "How much can this history really matter? I mean, c'mon?" We talked about the curvy Danish girl. Mark said, "Judge as if putting them on a scale. She stands there and you just place them right on the scale."

Mark wouldn't be weighing them, because his longtime girlfriend was coming over at Christmas, and also he was doing this little eyes-closed religious thing before we started our meals.

"Napoleon was nobody," orated this Professor Schoenbaum. He stood at the podium, head not high above it, yet proudly nodding and dashing. "He came from nowhere but harbored deep ambition. Why not strive to ascend and overtake all? Why not? So he risked it, he acted himself out, Napoleon acted his inner self out. In a disorganized France within a distracted Europe the lone man clamored to the complete top and ruled without pause or doubt. Or did he?"

"Last winter I wrote to our president," said Jana Stefackova at the cafeteria. She had worked as a journalist in Communist Prague. "But I haven't mailed it yet. Actually, it's right here." She showed me the letter. We ate our pasta. She said, "Actually, I heard the Italian mail is even more unreliable than ours. I heard they burn half of it here. And my mattress is very soft. And the walls are surprisingly thin, no?" She was surprised. She seemed happy to address my questions. "After the revolution, he said we were all guilty, we all shared responsibility for those decades, because we each had accepted our own little place while knowing that bigger things were wrong. We had our little hobbies and collections, our small gardens and small groups of friends. We made this our freedom. And that was the exact person the Party wanted us to become, with our eyes kept to ourselves." Her hands made quick blinders. "Only a few dared fight it, only a few were dissidents." And this was a precious word, here in the quiet cafeteria.

"As an approved journalist, they let me study English, and so I translated western news for them. It meant I read forbidden things and no one could inform on me. That was our society, people informed for the police, they reported on one another. We even had some strange man visiting our little office and watching my boss. The man pretended to be, I don't know, just stopping by, each time. Maybe he would ask a few grinning questions about this person or that. My boss would calmly respond. Then we never mentioned it.

"My boss was a drunk anyway. And he was having an affair. The woman was in the building right across the lane. I think they communicated in the windows while I was right there. But likely he had been drinking, so he didn't care. There was no reason to care, other than his being married. I suppose lovers were a hobby for many. People needed something to do—they couldn't get promoted, couldn't make money. So they found other tasks." Jana laughed. "But you know? I found out that my boss was informing too, he was working for them too. He had been offered and he accepted. It could get you ahead a little bit. But now I wonder what those two were really speaking about in my office. Luckily I never spoke against the system. I never thought to, really. Most didn't even realize we weren't free. The boys were soldiers, the girls were students, and they met and took trips to the woods and campfires. When they married, they went as couples. Soon they brought kids. It was just life. We sang about our sad little flats and our sad little rides on trains. Again then, I wonder what motivated those who did speak out." She shrugged.

"Anyway, in my letter I thank him. For he was truly among the few—he had stood for more rights, more care, for us. But mailing it does seem a bit silly."

I biked home. While I sat studying at my desk, Salvatore came in to fix a light. His dead silence spoke volumes about disliking managing accommodations for international students. I said hello and he didn't respond. When he finished the task, I said goodbye and he didn't respond. The next time he came to fix something, we had the identical dialogue. I wanted to say my part regardless, though I wasn't sure why. Maybe such efforts did good. At night I lay in bed and listened to the television show playing in the apartment above me.

It was louder than I would have played it in my own room. Mark also had one beyond the wall next to his bed, playing the same game show. Our kitchen wall had one. In the daytime they blared soap operas. I said to Mark as we jogged, "I don't have time for my writing. And it's urgent." Mark said, "Well, I'm certainly happier with you here." He said it with his tough, satellite-insurance voice. I sighed.

Medvedev had spent a while in our bathroom now, because there was much history judging Stalin, and I figured Mark and Lars had been glancing through the pages, though they said nothing. I said no to the SAIS Thanksgiving Dinner. "C'mon," said Mark, as he donned his dress shirt and readied to pedal to school. "How can you skip this? C'mon."

I wrote instead. But soon I had to switch over to the economics, history, and Italian. The next day, I told the dean that I was foregoing my scholarship and taking leave. I was not a grad student.

Mark and I prepared for finals—we navigated through the hundred and fifty years of modern Europe. "The Russian Foreign Minister at the 1908 Summit? How in the heck are we remembering that?"

"Alexander Izvolsky," I said. "So when he walked in to the summit they said, 'Who is that? Izvolsky, Izvolsky.'"

Smiling Mark said, "It's Volsky. Who is it? Izvolsky. Yeah baby, we got that one." We turned the pages. Mark said, "Someday, I want to live in Silesia, wherever that is."

"You?"

"Me. The dark forests and villages of Silesia. And I'm thinking of becoming a historian."

"You?"

"An Interwar Europe historian," he said. Interwar was also our label for the type of curves possessed by that Danish girl. Mark said, "Maybe a few too many Interwar curves."

"Women were more womanly then."

"Then let me tell you, she was asking about you at the Thanksgiving Dinner."

"I wish it were Interwar Europe now."

Mark said, "But life was in black-and-white then. No I get it, you want life simpler. Hey, maybe you could've prevented the second war."

"I wish I'd been in it. I wish I'd been on that snowy front."

"With the Danish girl of course."

"In the snow, at the front, in our cottage." At night, I lay in bed and thought about Steph alone in Chicago and I felt sorry for her and I missed her and I listened to the Italian television blare through the ceiling.

These were everyone's first graduate school finals. The library doors swung in with last-minute entrances for a tidbit from someone better prepared, and swung out with exits toward the waiting bluebook exams. I glanced at Schoenbaum's questions.

Okay, Metternich's role in creating the post-Napoleonic balance, I could answer that. No Izvolsky, but here was Mark's and my Alfred "Fight-to-the-death" Blanqui, who vowed to do just this in the effort to instate a fair society. In three hours I stepped into the darkening lobby. Salvatore stood among the students and wasn't looking at or talking with anyone, and when he did talk to me it was barely audible. But the dude gave me back my two-month security deposit, though the scholarship rules said I should have lost it.

I had a big chunk of western currency. I thanked him. Jana was in the lobby too. "Reks, this is very strange. My roommate Antonia had, well, during her exam, I guess you call it a stroke perhaps. Half of her face froze."

Jana's brow was wrinkled with confusion. I liked her sincere tones and sympathy. She said, "I'm going to visit her at the hospital. Is it possible that you might come?" I agreed right away.

The problem was that Bolivian Antonia was unattractive and unfit and I didn't want to be associated so much with this girl who now also had some sort of half-face paralysis. I rode Jana there and locked my bike and considered how it was wrong for me to disrespect Antonia.

But the hospital was crowded with people mostly not as misfortunate as our patient, and I still didn't want everyone to think it was my misfortune. Jana told her a lot of encouraging words and held her hand and Antonia struggled to be hopeful, mumbling that she would try not to cry. Jana helped her eat her soup.

Jana and I walked out to my bike and it was gone. I had locked it to a chain, not to the gate. I had known that it was wrong to think that way about Antonia and I had known clearly not to lock my bike to a chain, but I had done it. It was a lesson, I had no doubt. "I am so surprised," said Jana, "I am so sorry." My beautiful bike was gone. Jana and I stared at the spot for a long time.

After exams, we took a train up through Vienna, and then transferred to their east-side wartime station, which now again had the connection to Prague. Jana said, "So, you are spending Christmas in my country. With whom will you be spending it?" When I didn't have an answer, she wrinkled her brow. "Of course you can stop by my parents' flat anytime." I had decided to connect with no one. I had used Salvatore's money to buy a Toshiba laptop computer. I set up the laptop at Benjamin's flat on Iron Footbridge Street. Benjamin was gone for good. A tram passed on the street below, with all its wonderful lonely clickings. The goal was to be alone. I would succeed with this story.

But I ate on the other side of the table while looking over at the laptop. I looked through the few drawers. Some remnants remained from Ben's having lived here. In a small notebook he had written a list of Czech words. He had left a box of pencils and a copy of *Tess of the D'Urbervilles*. He had a recent *Time*, featuring this city, even dubbing it, "The Soul of Eastern Europe". In a bottom drawer was a *Playboy*. Goddamn I was happy. It had a spread of Marie Antoinette-types doing things with each other that evidently caused the French Revolution. I utilized the magazine that evening. Then I sat on the bed for a long, silent time. I again looked over at the laptop. Had I really just left grad school in order to write fulltime? I had a whole unwritten novel before me. My hands seemed heavy. I picked up *Tess of the D'Urbervilles*.

On Christmas Eve, I proudly walked the empty streets. The only other guy out here was selling the Christmas fish in the big tubs. Back at the flat, I picked up a pencil and I leaned over my first scenes. Then I looked up at the walls. The flat was silent—I never heard one noise from another flat—and this writing was terrible, juvenile. The description was trite, the dialogue choppy. I slunk down at the table. I had been trying to paint out the deep mystery, even magic, of the climbers, the Jezek Brewery, the new president, the feeling.

This wouldn't do. My pages had too many adverbs, too many adjectives, too many sentences starting with "It was". I looked over at the magazine.

I picked up *Tess of the D'Urbervilles*. I read in bed and then watched the periodic shadows of the night trams cross my ceiling. In the morning, I picked up *Tess* again. I read it slowly, not wanting to miss a word. I wanted to understand what a sentence was. I wanted to believe in green-meadowed Wessex.

I was falling in love with Tess. The story had opened with the good news that we knew of course would lead to tragedy. Of course too it would fall on slender Tess.

> ***'It was a thousand pities that it should have happened to she, of all others. But 'tis always the comeliest! The plain ones be as safe as churches, hey, Jenny?' observed the woman in the red petticoat. It was indeed a thousand pities; it was impossible for even an enemy to feel otherwise on looking at Tess, with her flower-like mouth and large tender eyes, neither black nor blue nor grey nor violet; rather all those shades together.***

I was falling in love with Thomas Hardy. His sentences were often long and winding but a re-read always made them vivid and worthwhile.

> ***Doubtless some of Tess d'Urberville's mailed ancestors rollicking home from a fray had dealt the same measure even more ruthlessly towards peasant girls of their time. But though to visit the sins of the fathers upon the children may be a morality good enough for divinities, it is scorned by average human nature.***

I began to think my way back into my paper scenes. Perhaps I could climb into those moments again and still capture it all. I began entering them into the laptop. What else was there to do? The tram traffic outside was a backdrop. At dusk I stood up and walked down to the street for a cool stroll.

On a springtime stroll through this capital city, I saw new cranes. They stood over the black towers and gold domes and fading chimney smoke.

New scaffolding was erected, with new planks and pipes. The old planks and pipes, also meant for fixing and building, but instead rotted and rusted, were removed. The single State radio station was removed.

A new station was heard, and it might play, amid its British and American rock, the musician's voice welcoming the station, the country, to Europe. Springtime birds were heard, in the city forests, where fragrant flowers budded at the ends of branches. Funds arrived. The ministry divided up the works into shares for each citizen and new funds vowed to grow them. Harvard professed ten-to-one return on money given them.

This fund was introduced by a local man who had once escaped and now returned—he said he had studied at Harvard University, though Harvard said they didn't know him or his fund. Everyone here knew, because they heard about it hourly on the new rock-radio. And they saw it on giant billboards now on streets and bridges. And they heard and saw it before and after *Dallas* at eight o'clock each Sunday evening.

At a shadowy café on a crooked little square I turned toward pleasant Jana Stefackova arriving at my table. She was on break from Bologna. She sat and watched as other patrons entered wearing colorful clothes and wearing gazes as if seeing a strange wonder here among the unlit walls. The waiter, in the State tuxedo, took their order.

Jana said, "As a little girl on the train to Babychka's, I remember seeing the little plaque, 'It is dangerous to lean too far out the window.' It was written in four Iron-Curtain languages and then, surprisingly, Italian. So I pretended I was allowed to travel out to Italy. I repeated the sentence many times. I spoke it while walking around babychka's village. I never expected to find myself, one day, studying in that same free and exotic Italy.

"And you know, now that I think about it, their towns are just made of shops with big windows and lights. Yes, there are sites amid. That's if the cars don't drive over you while you're looking. I like our towns. I never would have imagined so, riding on that train." She looked over at that other table. "And now they're coming here, people like it here. I can be proud."

These newcomers were German and they had already finished their coffee and the waiter was there to close their bill. "Excuse me, sir-waiter," said Jana. "Is there some rule that Germans get served before we?" The waiter's eyes bulged. Such tones had never been used on him, his rank never questioned. Jana suggested we try another place. We walked up the sidewalk. A tram approached and we watched it slowly pass—Jana said, "Actually I think they're pretty, the newly painted trams that everyone is speaking of. The new colors are pretty."

Her mind was working, figuring. She said, "They won't all have cigarette names or banks." Still she was thinking. We slowed down on the sidewalk. She said, "I guess it's not really a painting, actually."

Satellite dishes bloomed. On city strolls I saw them amid the chimney pipes and balcony laundry. They were a sign of new channels possessed inside. In the metro passages, new lights were hung, ridding previous shadows. The lights were for illuminating ceiling billboards—shingle after shingle of mottos now met the eyes of escalator riders, down and up. These blues and reds and yellows were designed to grab the eye—they were a mastery perfected in other places, over time. They were sprung upon this gray town. The same breeze still blew up from the metro tunnels, and up it came past an appeal to try the new insurance company, read new *Blesk* newspaper, buy Janet Jackson's new album, use Compaq computer. If riders instead chose to look down, they could see new ads painted on the old iron escalator stairs.

"The president," said Jana at our next café, "he says that as a child he was small and unhealthy. So when other children were playing outside, he stayed in and read and thought. I wasn't quite like that but I remember much time with books. My brother and I might sled all day on the town hill, and at dark I would come home and sit by the fire-stove and read. Because my father caused no problems, we were allowed a rare visit west, and I would seek out a book in English. It was something special. I would keep it beneath my pillow. I would read some pages when my parents thought I was sleeping and then I'd wrap it in the paper again—the next trip could be far off, or never.

"Once, we bought a package of German candies which my mother then refused to open until we'd arrive home. But the ride was long and finally father just took the bag and said he was eating one. So we each ate one. Then our mouths were empty and silent. We had tasted nothing like it. So mother handed out one more to each. And still, like children, we couldn't stop desiring them. We were laughing, our eyes wide. Soon the bag was empty. For days, mother walked around complaining how she had never done something so weak, and never would again. My brother taped the bag on our wall—such a thing couldn't be thrown away. Today these candies are in each of our shops." Jana sipped down the last of her coffee. "Strange," she said, "we had our own candies and today I feel silly eating them. Just as I feel silly riding my bicycle now since such new models have come. Even bicycling itself feels different today. Plus there's not so much time. In fact, I must go, I have an interview. There's such a need for translators now. And I'll need a summer job. You understand."

Benjamin's former dissident was raising my rent—up the street lived an old babychka who said she needed a bit of money, as her pension wasn't rising with the prices. She cooked me tea in her unlit flat and she showed me which room could be mine. I said I needed time to decide, but she gave me a key anyway.

With the summer heat came a flood from the West. They had heard that things were happening here, which they were. I heard on trams, "You saw your sorority sister? Yesterday I saw another Ohio State sweatshirt. I talked to the guy for awhile—we knew a lot of the same people. Some of them are here."

"It really is the most beautiful city in Europe—I read it in the *L.A. Times*. I also heard there're a lot of artists, like in Paris between the wars. This is the new Paris."

"Wow, I didn't even know. I just saw a brochure on campus. I wanted to live in Europe so I joined some program."

"The border security was nothing. We drove right in."

"Oh I didn't even think about the border, I was looking out the window—the fields and rooftops are like a fairy tale. And these trams and cobblestones, so romantic."

"Guess what I saw in a shop, Colgate."

"I know, it's not as backwards as I thought. But still I get homesick. I live with my college roommate. I tell her how homesick I am but she doesn't care, her boyfriend moved here."

"Jenny can go out alone after dark, any time, any place, without even thinking about it. We're almost used to the idea. Hey, did you hear Jenny had a lobster dinner tonight?"

"This city wasn't even in last year's guide."

"The coins still have the five-pointed star."

"We're waiting for our Jeep to arrive."

"We're selling a chemical that cleans buildings."

"I'm selling alarm systems."

"Why go to Paris? We were crossing a street there and were maced right in our eyes, and by girls, normal French girls."

"The language here really is strange, and they yell it in the streets—what does 'Ragazzi, ragazzi' mean?"

"I left home when on the same day two different mailmen went on shooting sprees in two different places, with automatic weapons. 'Goodbye,' I said."

"Blacks and Whites hate each other. We don't realize how ludicrous it is until we're out for a time. Then you look back and see."

"Here at least they can be content biking together to plant potatoes in a field." On trams the old faces saw the new faces too, when they themselves weren't reading the fresh new *Blesk*. It was in every bag or pair of hands, as if it had to be read—its poster said it did—unless one wanted to be attached to the old, accused of past thinking, wrong thinking. The color pages revealed soccer salaries in Italy, Madonna's doings, someone's divorcing. Page five each day showed different bare breasts.

When I returned to the old babychka's, her door had a new bolt. "A colleague was robbed. These gypsies, they now break into people's flats. How is this?" Here at the table in her small kitchen her deep-ridged eyes considered. "He is weak on these things, our president, things which I know he opposes. Civil Society he asks us to build." Sitting here, we weren't quite sure what that meant, though we both approved. "And another colleague, she'll now own three homes. One family, three homes? That's not democracy."

I explained it to her. "Oh," she said, blinking. She cooked up the pork and sauerkraut and dumplings. Each forkful warmed my stomach. Her old friend visited from the opposite building—she crossed the courtyard in her flowered smock. She brought cakes for tea.

"I also rent rooms now. To Germans and Iranians. One hundred dollars per month," she informed us. "But I hear others get twice that."

"Thieves," said my old woman. "Money, money, it's all I hear."

The friend confessed, "It is the new talk. But I'll tell you why." She had our attention.

She said, "It's the new products in the windows. Haven't you seen them? Plus, we have that *Dallas*. Oh the money you have," she said to me. My old woman groaned back, "Oh, every time I watch that I get angry. I think it's not even true, it's a tale." Her smiley old friend was still fixed on me. "We knew we didn't have much but we didn't know all this. The electronics, the clothing, and oh, the new fruit shop—I didn't dream I'd ever see it in my life." She said to her friend, "I can send someone for your other room. I've got extra people, with Deutsche Marks and Dollars." The doorbell buzzed.

"Oh, it's that fellow," they chimed. "He likes to just stop by for coffee."

He was slightly their junior, and he told us more local talk. "These new Germans, they drive around in those cars. Those are now their tanks."

"Oh stop," said the friend. "They bring the needed money."

The fellow responded, "They brought money last time they invaded."

"But now we've invited them."

"They brought invitations last time. They said they were helping."

"Well, it's better than those who were just here."

The fellow said, "Those Reds also said they came to help."

"But they brought no money."

"You're right. But we'll see how I eat under this new way. I'm just an old worker." He turned toward me. "And talk of armies, I heard there are twenty thousand of you here now." He said to the women, "It's some sort of exotic living to them, that's what I hear. Some are even millionaires. But some of us must be millionaires too—our men who buy up factories? I thought we all had no money. I hear we can be put out on the street, simply if they choose it. We now have freedom to do what we want, and freedom to be kicked down by these others."

My old woman asked, "Can't we have this first part, and not the second?"

I explained it to her. Her smiley, smocked friend said, "Yes, if you choose the first, it determines the other."

"Oh," said my old babychka. I went home and jotted notes and then lay on my bed and fell asleep to the sound of the trams slithering by. On Sunday I went to tell her my decision. Heat seeped up from the city streets. I boarded the Peanut M&M tram and I stood by the driver's booth. His worker's shirt was unbuttoned to the heat. His rolls and salami sat in a bag in the shadows. He had no steering wheel, only a pedal. He stopped to pick up another driver who waited at an unmarked spot. "Inferno," the two agreed on the weather. They talked with low voices in the driver's booth. They shook their heads. The driver dashed sour words to his colleague, who was standing, listening, nodding, looking outward at the traffic, until at a further point he departed. A group of youths walked right across the tracks and the driver rang his bell and no one reacted except one youth who, without looking, without fear, cursed the driver with his finger.

When I rose up the old woman's stairwell, she was there outside her door, holding her collar tightly. "I gave them to him, my Deutsche Marks from a rental, I gave it to the fellow, the man, who visits for coffee. I didn't want to go change them myself. But he disappeared with them. He's gone. The man is gone."

"Maybe he'll return," I said.

"No, the man is gone." I was standing on the steps below her. She looked down at me with new clarity in her eyes, and she said she couldn't rent at our agreed price, she would fill all her rooms in the style of her friend across the courtyard.

I found David in the lobby of a fancy white building once belonging to the Party—the old secretary calmly handed him his mail. Whose mail had she handled before, in this same building? David told me, "I'm at lunch but then driving a classmate to town with us. He's getting his MBA too."

"Yes, I've heard of you," said David's classmate at lunch. "I was an economist knowing your Mr. Mraka." He shook my hand. The thin strand of his gray tie hung longer than the thick. When we sat down, David picked up their previous discussion. "What exactly was their offer?"

His classmate shrugged. David clanked his fork down. "Vrata, what do you want? I got you an interview with Digital." The classmate blushed. He answered, "I just don't know whether this is what I would choose to do. Perhaps something not so narrow, not so small in its good."

"Oh please," said David. "Don't you understand? Digital wants you—it's what everyone else is reaching for. What are you going to do instead? No, please, don't tell me. First get the job, then worry about whatever else you're planning."

The classmate knew what to say to this too. But he said nothing. I said nothing. We were too few. We were too weak. We couldn't speak up. And there was shame on this day for anyone thinking something else.

We walked to David's car. Soon it sped down the thin road. I watched out my side window. With each weave of the car I leaned the other way, slowly, unpreventably. "Yes," advised Vrata the classmate, "you can run that database on your laptop, but it makes no sense without Intel—it would be too slow." David's eyes were squinting, listening. Along the road walked a young woman wearing her village dress. She saw us through her falling hair. Oh I wanted to keep her here, preserve her, not for myself, I would give that up, just to keep her what she was, here in the village. Vrata said, "I finished the budgets this morning. Accounting makes sense to me. Marketing & Advertising I find most difficult."

David said, "Just get it before their eyes as often as you can, so they think of your brand without even knowing why. TV's best because they're not doing anything else, just sitting and staring. But roads, trams, walls work too."

Vrata the classmate listened. He said slowly, "I've just been naive. For so long, naive." A new crane stood high over our town too. We arrived at the outer wall and faced a great Benetton billboard on which a black preacher kissed a white nun. I met Jan Mraka on the square beneath the crane. He said, "Oh, they're painting the church tower, finally." Up in his stairwell he rang his bell and then dug out his key. His boys were in front of the television. It was playing *Mutant Ninja Turtles*. Jan asked stiffly, "You didn't answer the door?"

"We didn't hear."

"Turn it off." The phone rang. Jan picked it up. In his ear he received a loud, brief chewing out. He put it down.

"The zoo director," Jan explained. "I organized some lessons for Anne, and some zoo workers came. The director wants money." Jitka arrived and banged her shopping bag on the kitchen table. "Something new and healthy," she showed a bag of soy meat. "And they immediately throw the price as high as possible, these privateers? How do they know to do that? Where do they learn that?" She placed it in the cupboard. Jan handed her the *Blesk* newspaper and walked out of the kitchen. Jitka looked at the paper then looked at my glaring.

She snapped, "You weren't told what you couldn't read, couldn't know. You can't understand." She flipped through the bright pages. Soon I tapped on Petr's window. Mirka pulled open the curtain. She motioned me in. "Petr has gone for food." She sat me down on the couch. "The climbers, they've split," she said with the half grin fitting such a statement. She filled the tea kettle. She said, "Some have joined new contractors, with no place for my Petr. Andre is doing business with Anne but I believe he is using her. Karel walked away, he didn't like any of it. So Petr and I, we were arranging to buy one of the State bookshops. But our partner took the whole thing—she knew the banker, she dropped our share." Petr entered carrying their little daughter and the bread bag, and he placed them on the table. He shook my hand warmly. "It's true," he said, to confirm what Mirka's eyes suggested. "Unemployed."

He stepped closer to me and said, "Don't worry, we can still go to the pub. Though truly, the beer costs double what it was just last year." Mirka cleared her throat, and Petr apologized. He said, "So, American boy, yes it was something special when you came. We had waited so long for you. You were something of a height." He sprang up and measured high with his hand. "We saw you as something higher." He patted my shoulder fondly. At dusk, I turned more tight corners and came to Ivana and Yarda's flat.

But no one was there. The door was a crack open. I walked in and stood motionless in the quiet dark.

Out their back window, their new fabric shop shone in the courtyard. Ivana walked in behind me and clicked on the light. "Oh good," she said, as if expecting me. "And it's Anichka's birthday." Ivana removed scissors from a drawer and left a handful of cash, and she dipped back out the door. She said, "We close at eight, but I think we will first sell out."

Soon the family was sitting at their little red table. Lunch's soup went back on the burner, and Ivana served bread with cheese and peppers, and she quieted everyone for Anichka's gift-getting. Yarda said, "A horse."

"Ne," smiled Anichka. Her mother gave the gift. It was Pert Shampoo, in a green bottle. "Wash and Go," said Anichka, her eyes and smile wide. She took the gift with both hands. Wise Ivana said, "That's what we got you. It's just a little thing, that's all." Ivana shrugged, and she kissed her daughter's forehead. "You're a big girl."

And everything seemed to make sense for a moment, everything was alright.

In the morning, the courtyard bell buzzed through the little hallways upstairs. I stepped out with my rucksack. Karel drove me in the little auto up the tree-lined road, across their meadow-filled countryside. "Stranger," said smiling Karel, "I have news about a traveler to your country."

The sky was silver-blue, the trees white-flowered, the thin road empty. It could really seem that this was the place. I looked at Karel. I said, "You're going." He said, "Tomorrow. I have the visa, I have my flight, I have my pack. I'm just dropping you by the cottage." We met eyes again. He said, "Can I tell you? These who are my friends, they now envy me." Karel stressed his words. "They look with anger, not joy, at the special chance I have. You know, Reks, people are now talking about victims of the revolution, victims of the believing. This is how some are seeing it." He stopped the car and we stared out the front windshield.

"Goodbye, my friend, I thank you for your coming. Truly it meant something."

I stepped out and strode toward the woods. Karel brought me here and left. I approached the little cottage. The electrician and the teacher were here. They were basting the pig over the fire. They nodded to where the others were collecting wood. I walked there. The sun flashed among the tree trunks. Igor shook his head—no one else was coming. It was just a gathering under a lonely sky, a small retreat for the forgetting. What it was an escape from was never spoken of, though it hung in the air and the surrounding forest. The next day, I strode back through town. Yarda sat quietly at his table. He didn't look up at me. Ivana said, "Today I receive fabrics for the shop."

No one reacted. Her sister was at the table too. I jotted a letter to Steph, telling her the important things happening here. The bell buzzed. Ivana ducked out the door.

She returned up with David. She said, "I thought you were the fabrics. Sister is here to help when they come. Relax at the table. I'm just baking little cakes." She worked at her stove by the open window while her sister drank coffee. Yarda went out to hammer on the unfinished roof of the shop. And David and I talked at the table, at times with coffee and cakes, at times slouched back, at times alone on this long summer day.

"It's the Finance Minister who needs to take the reigns here," said David. "And the people want him finally. He works well with the Bank. He understands."

"Understands?"

"Understands a rational economy. Understands you've got to convert all the way, let the market iron out the kinks, let the money guide things right. It's the only way."

"But wasn't there another view?"

David narrowed his wry eyes. "Listen," he said. "Listen. The problem isn't the new methods, it's the old minds. Broken minds, and bad hearts. They still think someone's going to use something against them in order to climb up, higher than they are. In fact, they've lost sight of everything else, if there was anything." He clicked on the radio and said, "The Sales Station, she talks all day, brokering everyone's crazy selling. A cottage, a shovel, a shoe. My classmates can get all the MBA's they want, they'll still never understand business. They think I'm a walking wallet. It's all they see now. They won't even smile—half the western firms are coming out to ask me who to hire, I'm going to be a broker on the new exchange, and these people won't smile with me?"

"What about Vrata?"

"Vrata's different. That guy is truly talented but he'll never succeed. See, that's the difference between a youth and an adult. A youth thinks money is the most important thing. An adult knows it is. I told you before, the school would take you." I tried to hold his gaze. And now David smirked, here in this little kitchen with its lacey, breezy curtains.

"Fine," he laughed, and his face showed both sympathy and impatience. "Fine. The president's a playwright, great. Tell me where that's going to get anyone. Tell me where that gets Vrata or anyone. I'm listening." He looked deeper into my eyes. "Fine, fine, I've seen it. The Italians come with full wallets and they wander around the capital starving. They can't figure out how to get a meal. So they stand in line at the new pizza place, a hundred Italians standing in line for pizza on the square of the revolution. They take some photos, show us their fancy shoes, and go home and tell their friends they have to come see it here. And the friends come. And they stand in line for pizza. For a slice they're paying what's half a day's salary here.

"So is the owner going to lower the price for the people? Of course not, he'll raise it, he'll build more now. For the Italians. The Germans pay the same thing just to enter the old underground tavern. Now it's a German beer-garden. And why the French have to drive all the way here to line up at the new Indonesian restaurant, I don't know—and no they don't know who they're giving their money to, who did the torturing around here and who did the suffering, and they don't care. I talked to one of these Italian girls and she complained, 'Few shops here.' That's what she said. At night I saw a French car speed across the old walking bridge. At home his penalty would be a month's pay—he wouldn't even consider it. Here, why not? The Germans play on the trams as if this is their backyard. It is, suddenly again it is. So what do you tell the bearded worker standing in the corner of the tram? Do you tell him not to worry? No, if he's smart he is worrying, he's thinking how do I join up, what can I produce, what need can I sell to? That's the way. If you're not greedy, the greedy step on you.

"So what am I saying? I'm saying that if there could have been another way, yes this seemed to be the time and place, there was a humanist in the castle. But that doesn't mean it could've worked."

Ivana peeked out the window for her fabrics. Frowning Yarda hammered rhythmically on the roof. David left. The sister brewed more coffee. She was a city version of Ivana but with the same work hands, come to fold and pin fabrics for the day. She said, "I too just put my girls on the train. They met Ivana's little ones at babychka's village."

Ivana at the window said, "The man will come. He came last month. We've just been selling it all." Yarda came in for dinner and he lounged back in his stiff chair and poured his wine. While eating he wanted to watch *Dallas* but Ivana kept the volume down so she could hear out the window. "Plus, I don't think I understand your shows and films," she said to me. Her sister would barely sip the wine, in case the fabrics came. Yarda shook his head, saying, "There'll be no fabrics. Sister hens just want to gab all night." The bell buzzed.

Ivana ducked out of the kitchen and opened the door. In the hall stood David, gazing through at me. "I've just been thrown out of my flat. The owner said he could get twice the rent. So I told him to go get it. He threw me out. I used to be the king of this town." We explained it to Ivana who said, "Stay here when you want." Harvard Investment Fund said its profits were highest. The news showed a mugshot of a pale-faced rapist of a twelve year-old girl. In the summer evening, frowning Yarda returned atop the fabric-less shop, and David and I walked across the meadow to his little cement building.

He said, "It was just for visits now anyway." He repacked the boxes that he had brought down from the army in Berlin. "I guess I'm done with Jihlava town."

I said, "It's too bad." His neighbors stood in their doorway—on each passing David spoke with them. They recalled things they had done together, such as learn to communicate, and eat soup on cold days. The husband and the boy helped carry David's loose books and pots.

"It's too bad," I repeated. David shrugged. I said, "It's sad."

David said, "Life is sad. What'd you think?" We unstopped the building's old glass door and it closed behind us, though we could have still been seen through it, walking away this final time.

Yarda was walking up his stairwell—at the sound of my footsteps he turned around. We stared for a moment. "I'll need that room," he said. I nodded. Night came and Ivana was still peeking out her window.

She looked back at us and said, "They're here." She led our march through the courtyard. The driver opened the canvas flaps of the old truck, and there were Ivana's little business items, piled neatly by color. The driver helped us carry them across the courtyard. The women set out to calmly fold all night—Yarda curled up in the girls' bunk a reach away because he wanted to hear what the women said about him, but instead they heard him snore though they didn't listen. They chatted and folded and I sat with them, and I stood against the wall, and I stood in the hallway, and I looked up the stairs at my and Stephanie's floor. I walked into the courtyard and I slept in my bag on the little grass plot.

"My bicycle was stolen," I heard at my table. I looked up at Jana's disbelieving eyes. "They broke into the building and then the basement sheds. Isn't it the strangest thing? My old bicycle." She sat down and settled in at our table at our new café.

She said, "Our Finance Minister, the creator of the investment funds and the selling off of factories, he who is sure we can't slow this at all, he has taken charge now. The president is just a symbol. And I never sent my letter." Her smooth expression was flat.

"Some say he was weak."

"Yes, for he didn't punish the leaders of the old way and he made no laws against exploiting the new. I suppose he thought we'd finally be good to one another. We thought that's what we had. But friends are turning upon friends. We're stealing from each other. It's true. Families are fighting in court for land that a year ago no one wanted. Then the winner sells it right away to some sort of developers, a thing we didn't even know of before. There've been five rapes in my quarter this summer. And now a murder by the bridge, a shooting, right by the old square? With a gun? During the winter, I think we all feared having even less than before. Now it seems we each want more than the other." Her gaze was distant. She drank up and stood to leave for work. We arranged our next coffee. She looked down at me and said, "I hear there are fifty thousand of you here now. But you know, some of us have now been to your land. They say you see only cars, no people. That's just what they say." She shrugged. "They say you drive to the gym to walk on a machine. Oh well." When I resurfaced she was gone.

In the rushing, running, shopping city, I drowned. I walked down cobbled sidewalks blocked by Coke signboards. From a stone balcony hung a blue banner advertising German cookies newly arrived. The old theater lane, with its sculpted roofs, now housed the Daitsu dealership. Its billboard blocked the view to the castle. Wrigleys was offering "True American Quality", Renault was offering "A View to the Future." The old Grand Hotel was erecting a tall lot for valet parking. I tried to pull my eyes away from the candy stands, the detergent wall-painting, the Proctor & Gamble bus, the meaninglessness, the worry, the bustling, the street lamp pole that wore a placard crying, "STOP!" It was calling for a citizens meeting to STOP the destruction of their culture.

Laughable, a citizens meeting—I was surprised that a few were still making the plea. One signatory was a singer who had strummed his guitar on that great day in the square. They had sung about the "Greatest Thing". They were singers returning from exile to sing on the big square about freedom, which had just been seized and secured by the chorus of people, who then sang on and on at their campfires. The songs still played in my head. I watched the little placard flap in the breeze, here in this capital city that had quickly become the whore of Eastern Europe. Jana never made it back to the new café. But its tables were filling. In came a shaggy local with a cast on his arm—he spotted the empty space at my table and with a nod he sat opposite me. We both looked at his cast lying on the table.

"Auditor. That was my State work, taking shop inventories. But now we're supposed to fine the businesses not paying the tax. In one shop they broke my arm. Right there in the back room. I just lay there on the floor." He shrugged, his eyes comically sad. The waitress brought him a whiskey. I asked, "So you're on leave?"

"Leave?—what kind of leave? I'm unemployed. And what are you, Polish? You talk funny. What do you sell? I haven't met a Pole who isn't selling something."

I shook my head. He said, "Or your parents were from here? They escaped and now you've come back to cash in? Makes sense."

I shook my head again. He asked, "Then what? Why the fake accent? Who are you?"

"Spy."

"You're no spy, that's all gone. What's there to watch?"

"The happenings."

The auditor smirked. I asked, "No point?" He answered, "Of course not. There's no point watching this."

"A waste of time?"

"Complete," he said.

"And you understand it?"

"Completely. We were full of proud Bolsheviks, now we're full of proud Capitalists. The Bolsheviks grabbed it all up, and now the Capitalists take it. They're the same person, same heart. You've learned something here, spy." Night had dropped down on us. The new neon buzzed through the city. The auditor melted off into the streets. My own tired feet took me past the *New York* combat-video gambling bar, where each machine was patronized by western clothed youngsters, though not from any west but this. A white mountain-bike passed me going the other way, its rider spinning calmly. Two men wearing ties stepped from their western sedan and entered past the fatigues-wearing bouncer at the *Malibu Klub*. Had any of them been there on the square on those cold nights? Where was everyone who had?

Or maybe it was me, maybe I had the problem. Indeed these streets could seem quite fine—so many strangers had come approvingly from afar, that it was no longer far. They had rushed over to build their lives here as if this were just the next, needed frontier. They came here to open chains, build suburbs, make movies. They published a restaurant guide to disclose the hidden taverns in quiet cobblestone coves, where a local author might have come for twenty years to sit with a beer. And they sold this information as many times as possible, because they had to grow their newspaper, no choice. So they advertised how next week they'd reveal another hidden tavern, for the thousands of American readers who had also come here to grow something.

Or were they in fact fleeing? What to be made of fifty thousand Americans come here to have this be their fairy-tale city because in their ruined New York, L.A., or even their Paris enough people had used up all the space they could and enough others had been elbowed out with no place at all, so that now one could be killed just walking home at night?

So they came here to make this their clean safe city. And they brought the same mind they were leaving behind. And someone let them. Or was it me with the problem?

But I had in fact discovered something on those misty lanes that first autumn—now it would be gone, unlearned, untaught, covered up by footsteps and paint. It had been a time of grayly busy days, in simple courtyards, with quiet tasks, followed by time together at the table. It had been a simple walk in sweet nights, before time had become money. Clearly now, no new age of thought had come.

Yet, hadn't anyone else thought America was going to say more than, "Come to Marlboro Country," which it said with a giant sign in the grassy park beside the castle? The Canon Copier tram picked me up. It was painted an immaculate blue and white on the outside. Inside, it stank of the dirty grease-faced bum slumped in a seat. The smell filled the tram. Nobody cared. Everybody cared. Nobody said a thing—their eyes cornered to one another with shame for being on the same tram. The driver threw him off.

When I stepped down, I continued past a manhole hissing white steam, and past busy workers preparing the EuroBank sign on this Sunday night so it could open tomorrow, and past an old woman staring at a rainbow-colored fruit display in a large window. A thing came out of the shadows, moving low and swift above the ground. It passed me with a bearded appeal, mumbling, aching. For whatever reason, this coatless thing needed help this night.

From the manhole hissed warm steam and so this thing stopped there and crouched there and lay down. Its eyes left mine as we both now looked at the coming headlights and then watched his body being hit by a car.

The thing slithered off the road, even less a person now. The driver stopped, and stood, and stared. Her concerned eyes and silent mouth seemed to say, "I didn't see him. I didn't mean it."

And I wanted to hug her, console her, this poor woman who had just hit a man and who was to blame. That was the point, that was the message—even though he had been lying in the street, she could have prevented it, if only she had seen.

Now she saw. I returned to the flat and I felt it right away—someone had been here and my laptop was gone from the drawer. I walked into the tiny kitchen and walked into the living room and then stood in the empty stairwell. Someone had simply used a key. The next night, I took the bus to town and stood outside the tall red fence at Ivana and Yarda's corner. I stared up toward their warmly lit window.

Ivana appeared beside me, her old canvas food-bag in hand, and her unsurprised hello on her lips. I followed her through the courtyard and up the stairs. I sat with her and the quiet daughters at the kitchen table. Yarda was sick and asleep in their closed and cozy bedroom. Ivana put on tea. She asked what else I needed. Yarda came out and said, "Reks."

I said, "Hello, Yarda." He was in his pajamas and we stood in their little foyer. He said, "Come here." I stepped toward him. He said, "Did I kick you out?"

"Yarda," I answered peacefully. He asked, "Did I kick you out?" We stood in a triangle with wordless Ivana. "Did I kick you out?" I answered, "No." He looked bitingly over at her and said, "You see?" He looked back at me.

"Now I'm kicking you out." He picked up my pack and placed it in the hallway. I stepped there. I said, "Goodbye." Ivana followed me down the stairs. She tripped painfully into a large pile of new cobblestones stacked for fixing of the courtyard. I waited for her to recover, then I walked on. She said, "You think you know someone, so long, yet then you realize you don't know them. How is this?"

"I don't know, Ivana." I took the last bus to the city. I flew out to Frankfurt, and then boarded a trans-Atlantic plane, on which the American guy beside me started up a conversation. When he heard where I had been, he said, "Oh you've got it made—employers will eat that up." He had just spoken at a global corporate conference.

"The new systems they've put together for decision making, it's unbelievable. It's all in these new books. You can now gain great know-how for precise decision making." I was watching out my window, and then I looked at him and nodded politely. He smiled, seeming to understand.

In America I went to the pizza buffet with old high-school friends. The pizza was rich and juicy and saucy and sweet and hot and salty and did not exist outside this continent. After lunch I stepped out to the sidewalk and stared at the faces and voices and words. My old high-school friends stared at me. I went into my old room and set up a computer. There was no stopping it. That breeze had blown through me in my first days there, and though it had gone onward, something had lodged in me.

The laptop with all the scenes had departed but I had saved the paper scraps. I slept in my sleeping bag beside my bed and before dawn I awoke and typed. I could hear the quacking of ducks that lived in a pond across the suburban street. It sounded like laughing. At night I dreamt of Russia. I was arriving there and its changes hadn't begun yet, hadn't yet been done incorrectly. SAIS was expecting me at the DC campus, but I now used their career center to discover an Iowa man aiming to go deep into Russia and teach collective farmers how to buy out and manage their own farms. It wasn't too late back there in that giant frontier that had only just opened its own long-locked gate.

Steph called. Though I agreed to visit, I would sadly have to keep us long-distance for a bit more. Waking up in these dark mornings and sitting at my desk was what I supposed to be doing. She picked me up at the Chicago airport, and there was my college blonde who had come over to live with me in Jihlava. She wore her Levi's and she was thinner, in fact not only free from that cheese-meat-beer diet but also training for a marathon. I was surprised, back in her bedroom, that she pulled me atop her. And soon we were lying naked by candlelight. I felt right back at ease with her, and she was calmly silent.

Her sister took us out with her new boyfriend, who told us how his being cool-blooded allowed him to be a successful stock trader on the stressful Chicago exchange. He then confirmed it by sparingly telling us about sailing off the coast of South Africa when a storm so big hit his yacht that everyone fled below, but he and his brother strapped in on-deck and calculated that turning the boat into the storm on every seventh wave for the next two days was how they would avoid drowning. Only when they drifted into port and saw houses and horses drifting back out to sea did they hear that it was the worst storm ever, or something. The few details, downplayed in the telling, gripped me, and I wanted more. I wondered whether, indeed, I knew how to tell a story.

I had brought *Dr. Zhivago* for Steph to watch the next afternoon—she didn't feel as deeply about all the history and meaning, and in fact she sort of wore a frown about it all. In fact she went and sat on the other couch. "I was really hurt when I came home from there. I wasn't into all that fuss you were into. I came home to Chicago and I just thought you hadn't really treated me right. Then I wrote those letters looking for some acknowledgement from you, and I didn't read anything satisfactory back."

"You're right," I said, "I got caught up in the possibilities. I got the priorities wrong. I'm sorry. Keep the film. It explains it all. I'm not saying it's so important but just watch it again and we'll discuss it later."

"You need to take the movie," she said. I was starting to feel a twist in my stomach. I looked at her more closely, there on the opposite couch. I joked, "Am I not going to see you later? Or something?" Steph stayed silent. I asked, "You're saying I'm never going to see you again?" She had some sympathy in her eye, watching it dawn on me.

I was back typing in my DC room the next morning. I had so much to do still. But at midday I searched through my unpacked bags and I collected Steph's and my little trinkets, coins and photographs and a tire-patch that I had used to fix her bike, and I mailed them to her, to remind her, to re-stir her.

V

I felt guilty about writing her out of the story. But I typed onward. I went walking in the local park. Every plastic bottle that I saw in the creek made me think how such an item hadn't even existed in that other society. Here, the plastic newspaper-bagging that was caught throughout the brush, and that allowed deliverers to toss their papers from moving cars, reminded me how much less waste and driving existed over there. I typed. At night I was visited by another Russia dream.

I would arrive there, be there, no longer worrying about the changes going wrong. Relief would descend through my whole body. I walked and talked around Moscow. It could still be saved. I breathed in peace. Then I would awake. I would blink for a moment. I heard the ducks in the pond. Well, the Iowa agriculture guy had written me back saying he was coming to DC, so maybe I had my chance.

But what about America? Someone had to deliver the message about our flawed path. Plus I needed to finish this book—that was the main duty. And I had to get Steph back. How could I go to Russia?

I took rare breaks to see those old high-school friends. Some were couples living together. One girl talked about television shows I'd never heard of. I criticized her weekly anticipation of them. She said they relaxed her. Another said, "Reks, what happened to you over there?" Another said, "It's so good to have you back from Russia." It would all be cleared up by the book. I wanted to go home and type. Another said, "Reks, you should call that girl, Debbie."

It took a moment but I recalled her being part of our group the night before I had left. She was the cute practically-married gabbing little brunette at the other corner of the table. "She thought you were cute."

"I didn't even speak with her."

"They're completely broken up." We walked outside and some friends of friends were standing against a car and we all smoked a joint. I went home. I pushed my story toward that winter of impossibility, an entire society seeking how to dismantle itself, how to cross over to the other side. The phone rang. It was Steph. "Wow," I said, "I'm surprised."

"Maybe I shouldn't have called."

"What? Did you get the things I sent?"

"I got them. I probably shouldn't have called. I was feeling sorry. I thought I could just call."

"Of course you can call."

"No," she said, "probably not." I pictured the teeny blond hairs at her browline, and how her skin became even more golden when she was upset. I could feel her scowl through the phone. I implored for her reversal.

"No."

"But don't you feel sad? Don't you feel empty and awful without us together?"

She said, "That's how I felt when we were together." I stared at the receiver.

In the quiet now, we seemed to be breathing in unison. "You get it now, don't you, Reks?"

I said, "I get it now."

She said, "You see?"

"I see."

She said, "Goodbye, Reks."

I said, "Goodbye, Stephanie. I'm sorry."

Lars Larson was in DC for a conference. We met at Starbucks at Dupont Circle. "A bright youthful neighborhood," he said. I said, "And I'm the voice of the generation." Lars said, "Uh, self-professed." In any case, I knew he really meant that the neighborhood just seemed safe. As we strolled over toward some grad-school party, Lars's youthful nook fell instantly behind us.

The air tightened. Faces were mostly black. They looked at us meanly. The Institute of Science on Sixteenth Street had tall, impressive columns between which lay bodies wrapped in sleeping bags and cardboard. The party hosts complained about living here—one was German and he simply couldn't believe

America looked like this. "You can't walk most streets." My blood boiled. Shame was on the faces of his American partygoers, briefly. But no one would admit it, no one faced it. Facing it meant needing to fix it, and fixing it meant a whole system admitting its failure and stepping down, of which it had no intention. First, hundreds of thousands would have to meet in our city squares. Uggh, I wanted it expressed.

Lars and I saw the same sights on our walk back, people living in dark corners. I saw the tension on Lars's face. A woman called us white-ass mother fuckers. Then we waited twenty-five minutes for a subway. How could I go back to school? America was sick. We were suffering from wasted people and a wasteful economy. But it couldn't be turned off. Lars and I shook hands goodbye. On Sunday I called Debbie.

She said, "I guess I know who you are. But I can't really do anything with you. I have to study. Sorry."

I said, "Okay."

She said, "But maybe in a couple of hours."

I laughed small. "Okay." I bicycled over to her apartment. She came outside and she still had that short little brown haircut. We walked down a bunch of side streets and met up with the city's long, thin park.

"I don't know how you even thought of calling me. That was like a million years ago." We walked among the bare trees. I told her some things about those years. She said, "Tell me dates, I like to know dates."

"November seventeenth, the revolution."

"Cool. Any others?"

"August first is probably when I decided I would go to Italy. Then November seventeenth I decided I would leave it."

"No way!"

"Roughly." I told her how hard it had been to tell Mark Quinn I was leaving. She asked, "Why?" I said, "I didn't want to hurt his feelings." She said, "Oh, I know a little bit about that."

I said, "I hate this trash." I pointed to the tires and cartons in the creek. She said, "I try not to notice." I told her how that other society had manufactured far fewer items. She said, "That's really interesting."

I told her the Thomas Hardy quote from Chapter Twenty of *Tess*, "'Dairyman Crick's household of maids and men lived on comfortably, even merrily. Their position was perhaps the happiest in the social scale, being above the line at which neediness ends, and below the line at which the conveniences begin to cramp natural feeling, and the stress of threadbare modishness makes too little of enough.'"

"Wait," she said, "did you just quote that?" I said, "It's my favorite novel." She said, "I know, but you just quoted it, and it's like not even English." I said, "I've been spending a lot of time alone." She said, "You're kind of weird. I should read that book though."

I said, "It might make you weird." She said, "I'm learning to spend time alone." We strolled back up to the avenue.

Debbie said, "There's a pizza place here called Cugini's and I think I'm the only one in the city who goes there but it's really good!" I said, "We had pizza the last time we saw each other." She said, "We didn't even talk that night. I don't get why you called me." I said, "That was August first."

She said, "Okay, you're weird." She had a cute little nose. I asked about her breakup and she asked about mine. At her front door, I asked whether we could do something again, and she had anticipated this and with her happy, curious smile she quickly responded, "As long as you understand. A relationship that long has things that last."

Meanwhile I was arriving in Moscow regularly. I would ask myself whether it was a dream and the answer was no because I was still there—I was seeing the long rectangle buildings and not a billboard on them. The city was not yet filled with words. The old words, far fewer and duller, were still there. I sat with Russians in their little kitchens. But I awoke in my own bed. I heard suburban cars. I heard the quacking ducks, laughing maybe.

Ivana and Yarda visited me too. They were strolling on the town square and I was walking right up toward them—Yarda and I were going to reconcile. He was going to apologize. This too was deeply real, and I regretted waking.

The Iowa agriculture guy was here to address Congress, and I called him and he said it was indeed worthwhile to discuss my helping him privatize Russian collectives as employee owned, but could he find time on this quick trip?

He had to—I was wrestling with the book urgency, the need to refocus America, and this Russia thing. He had to help me. After a patch of writing, I biked up to Debbie's. I turned onto her street and right there her little car zipped away. Where to on a Sunday evening? It suddenly mattered so much. I stared after the car. I went home and typed and then biked back up and she hadn't returned. Someone else buzzed me in and I sat on her lobby stairs. I had brought *Tess* for her. I had brought some writing pages and I looked them over.

Debbie walked through the lobby door. "Wait, are you like just sitting here waiting for me?" She had a little jump in her step. I said, "It is a little weird."

She said, "I mean, you know?" She was shaking her head, standing there before me. She said, "Well, do you want to come up?"

"Do you think it's right?"

"I didn't ask you to move in."

"I brought you a book."

Her cute, thick-carpeted apartment was just above the outside awning. The book on her table was some acclaimed new novel, *The Shipping News*. I envied the author, her book was out and was being called special—the cover was nicely gray and melancholy. I picked it up and I hit all these sentences that weren't sentences. They had no verb. Or they were one word. If it was an attempt at style, I considered it the inability to find style, inability to write. Many disagreed with me evidently. But by page three I had to put it down.

> ***Quoyle shambled, a head taller than any child around him, was soft. All stemmed from his chief failure, a failure of normal appearance. A great damp loaf of a body. At sixteen he was buried under a casement of flesh. Head shaped like a Crenshaw, no neck, reddish hair ruched back. Features as bunched as kissed fingertips. Eyes the color of plastic. The monstrous chin, a freakish shelf jutting from the lower face. Foraging in a box of excursion momentoes, he found photographs of his father beside brothers and sisters at a ship's rail. That sly-looking lump in the shrunken sweater, hand at his crotch, his father. On the back, scribbled in blue pencil, Leaving Home, 1946.***

Debbie said, "So I was watching this movie, we can watch it together." We sat on her bed and watched *Singles*. It was about dating and breakups. We sat separately on the bed, our legs hanging over.

On the next visit, she read and I wrote and I proposed that we kiss. She asked, "Oh you want to?" I said, "Do you have a sleeping bag? I sleep in a sleeping bag. We can just get in."

She said, "I do have one, but can you first explain why you sleep in a sleeping bag?" We kissed in her bag on her thick carpet. I said, "I guess I'm traveling." She said, "Oh are you? Where exactly are you traveling to?"

"I guess, homeward still. But then, I don't see how I could stay here. Yet, I do have to finish some things here. I'm thinking about starting a movement." The next week, she took off my clothes and put me in her bed.

"Should we?"

"I don't know," she answered. "It could be fun."

"Lots." I stood up out of the bed. "But it changes me, it changes my whole thinking. The male orgasm changes everything. When it occurs, all thoughts leading up to it instantly dissolve away. I will see you completely differently." I was pacing. She was lying under the covers, only her little brown-haired head showing. She said, "God, who thought you'd turn out to be so complicated?" I said, "I'm just trying to be honest." I considered this. I still planned to sleep with her. I was standing in the middle of the room. She said, "Come back to bed." I obeyed. We laid there. She said, "Is it bad if I just sort of jerk you off?" I said, "Deb, you're cute."

We walked up to Cugini's for lunch the next day. Her ex had made the same mistake I had—I had stopped appreciating Steph and then she left and then I clearly saw that I would never get a girl as good, and that's what Debbie's ex was telling her. So Debbie told me she was in no mood for anything serious. We decided to have fun.

One problem with fun was my rush to implement those other tasks. Debbie and I woke up to her radio news and it was about pedestrians being shot with guns by black people in cars. The next morning it was about people being pulled out of cars by similar gun wielders. I explained to Debbie that the suburban mother who was carjacked by this black person and was dragged holding onto the car because her baby was still inside was to blame too, because she wasn't trying to change her country though she knew about its politics of negligence. Debbie blinked.

She was amazed when the next morning had similar news. It was as if such words hadn't really been reaching her ears before. Of course, these blacks were shooting plenty of each other too. And we had no intention of selling them fewer guns. We were built on selling. There was no halting it. America had to wake up first. The trick was to walk into the ghetto and apologize. No one had ever apologized for slavery—all the feelings still needed to be reconciled. Hate was still crumbling our cities, and so we were paving away elsewhere. The United Waste of America, that was us. After the apology, the new economic message would be delivered and the fixing begun. Debbie listened quietly.

We got stoned and lay in her sleeping bag until three in the morning. She moaned, "I have to teach second grade today." I told her I would work the whole day while she worked too.

A big snow fell that weekend, and the couple responsible for my meeting Debbie was throwing their engagement brunch. I told Debbie we should walk the five miles. She agreed quite quickly. "I'll just dress warm." Along the way, I told her more about that society.

"Like, for drying your hands in a public bathroom they have a towel on a roll which you turn to get a clean spot. The bathrooms might be old and cracking but they wash that towel good and put it back in. They weren't trying to save the world, just who can afford to throw out all that paper?

"They had trees everywhere. Trees without trash. And you didn't have to pay a fee to see them. Thick full forests and the people loved them and walked in them and built little cottages in them and didn't know what they had. They used the land and lived on the land—they had never left the land, you see? Humans still lived on the land. You could see it. It wasn't like seeing patches of grass. A town sat on the actual land—you stood in the center of town and you could see where the town became land. Even from the city, that sacred city, you could just walk out into the land. You could feel it." The day was bright from the snow and sun, and we walked in our boots on the unplowed avenue.

"If someone found a jar with a screw-on lid, they saved that thing for life. For life. They pickled in it from the garden, they ate from it that winter, they washed it good and maybe preserved fruit in it the next year. The garden wasn't a hobby, it was a need, they needed the land. And this is Europe I'm talking. Sure, the tyrant leaders were inventing ways to be irresponsible, but the citizens made life work, actually work. Their food scraps went to the hens, the hens then fed them back. If you could buy a car, you fixed that thing up for twenty years. That was your car, simple. It was a simplicity which came from a poverty. And it gave them a richer life. Their leaders forbid them the world, so they simply had time to get on the well-funded bus and visit their friends in the next village. Or walk there."

"That's how you got like this?

I said, "I'm just saying I learned some things." She said, "We walk to Cugini's." I said, "And that's great." She said, "And the pizza's good, isn't it?" I said, "There's no better." Her smile was bright and I wondered whether she was my little brown-haired girlfriend. We were walking up and down the snowy roads of Bethesda. Deb said, "Now I remember, I took a train to New York once and there really were a whole bunch of slums on the way. Oh and once this other teacher said she moved to Crystal City so she could get to her stores and gym and car without ever having to go outside. That's one, right?"

Each time one of the brunch guests questioned whether we had really walked, Debbie squinted at their bewilderment. Myself, I could see deeper now, I could see their instant realization that their lifestyle was flawed and thus they felt judged by our walking. But the guy who had said, "It's so good to have you back," now repeated it as he walked in with his red-haired wife and his big, intent eyes. I happened to be standing on the stairs above them, and everyone in the hall heard it. I felt proud. I was surprised that broad, blond Ted Woods was still saying it.

He was sharply dressed despite having been our lousiest student—he had moved to Greensboro and painted a neighbor's house and from this made a small business. When we now toasted some champagne, he said, "I can't even imagine what you must've seen over there." He still didn't know where over there was. Yet I was drawn by the rugged seriousness in his gaze. Ted Woods said, "Let me know if I can help with anything." I thanked him. Deb and I walked back. "So are you never going to live in the suburbs?"

"It's a prison created by the car and television. Yet you have to work non-stop to afford it, you mortgage your life away. Money is time. Creating expenses steals your time to think, figure, craft."

She said, "I teach elementary school, I'm not really allowed to create expenses. But so you're saying I have to live in the city? With roaches and rats. And black people who want to hurt me? No rapes here please. That's a little goal I came up with."

I replied, "Our cities are unlivable. And of course we have no villages." She said, "I could live in the mountains. I like snow. I like to ski."

I said, "You know, our mountains do have villages. They're not real, but you can indeed walk places. And some buses are free. People know each other too, they pass in the street. There's also employment. You should go."

"I'll just quit my job and pack up."

"You can."

"Oh I can?"

"You're free."

"You're a fool," she said. Now the road was plowed and we had no space to walk in the speedy lanes—we had to labor on the sidewalks where the plows had piled the snow. Deb said, "It's okay, we'll just take a hot bath. So, I heard your friend became some born-again since you last saw him."

"Wow," I said, "I think you're right. But that was just a phase." She asked, "Did it change him?" I answered, "I think he stopped cussing. It also might be why he married what's-her-name." Debbie asked, "Yeah what's up with her?"

I said, "They say he might not be happy." We arrived at Deb's place and we lay around to the light of her stereo. She played me the album *Language of Life*—I had missed its coming out—and it was essentially a relationship album, replete with breakup tunes.

> ***Still can't believe you two are now just friends, you've got no lover and he's free at weekends. Why don't you get back, try and get back together? Matches aren't made in heaven, they're made right here on earth. He searched the starry skies, ended up in your arms. Now you're two years on a losing streak. Some people search their whole lives through, and never find what was shown to you.***

It had a Jack Kerouac song too. "The seven seas you roam and who's waiting at home?" Deb was already finishing *Tess* so we decided *On the Road* was next. We again talked past midnight and now she wanted to have sex. "Isn't it late?"

She answered, "But if we do it tonight we can be ready to do it again by morning." In the morning, I filled out the paperwork for summer Russian. Then I lay on the carpet and moaned about having to finish my writing and start a movement. Deb was reading on her couch. We listened to her funky-smooth Toni Childs, who sang, "Stop your fussing boy, you're time will come." Deb said, "See?" I stood up and sat down next to her and read her *Washingtonian Magazine.*

The main article was about Christian Prince. He was a white senior at Yale, and a black guy about his age walked up with friends one night and took Christian Prince's wallet and shot his heart and left him bleeding onto the empty street. Christian Prince had gone to private school here in DC. He had played lacrosse. His sister worked in ecological protection. She was filled with anger, according to the article.

According to me, her anger would find no home. No one was planning to do anything about this. It had made the local magazine—and there were probably similar articles in most cities' Best-Of magazines—but there was nothing his sister could do. In fact, the magazine was over a year old. I hadn't once heard about this, even on our radio violence every morning.

We needed a full re-building, re-teaching. The black guy, though he hadn't been employed, had driven a white BMW. He was in jail now. He had those sort of vacant eyes which never really look at you, said the author. He meant the uneducated, undeveloped eyes which belonged to that type of urban black who didn't care, but the author didn't say it. The black guy's mother said he had always been a nice boy.

I would need Colin's help. We had to get deep in the ghetto, and we would need a microphone. The group that I had seen at Colin's hotel meeting, they had color and spirit, and I would lead them into Harlem. It was time to speak out.

Ted Woods came up to DC again. Debbie led some party games and was bouncy and energetic. She wore a jeans outfit with short sleeves. Ted played although he usually had short attention for things not his painting-and-construction business. He and I went to the kitchen to fill our drinks, and his wife followed and asked the question I could see others thinking, "How's that relationship going, Reks?"

I said, "She and I are just, I don't know, I can't explain."

"Fucking," said Ted.

"Ted!" exclaimed Betsy. Ted said, "I sure as hell hope so." He high-fived me. "Reks, if you ever need anything, just say."

I said, "I may need a place to write. I'm getting kicked out by that older couple upstairs unless I return to school or work." Ted said, "Come down. It's that simple." Deb and I went back to her apartment. She said, "Let's try to go for an hour. Think you can last an hour?" I said, "I can only try." She said, "Okay, you try." She got out the clock. For the summer, we agreed on no air conditioning. We would sweat it out naturally. Out the open window was the awning and below that the phone system for buzzing up to the different apartments. We could hear talk from people phoning up to their friends. We were too busy to listen.

But I wasn't living, wasn't really here—I was supposed to be doing those other things. In the morning I biked to SAIS and asked for a leave of absence, again. I pedaled back on the park road. Though its sign read "Bike Route", the constant car-flow was inches from me, and honking. Some drivers spewed their venom out their windows. I was responseless, because they were immediately gone. It made me want to get home even more quickly to write.

A white van, adjusting none for me, clipped my pedal. I pulled up to the van at the next light. I was right at the driver's open window. He didn't expect a human to be anywhere near this spot. He turned his head very slowly as I said, "You almost hit me. Please be more careful when passing bikes."

He said, "Man, I'll kick your mother fucking ass." I said, "I'm just asking you to be more careful." Surfacing further, he reached for his door handle. The light turned green. I saw his indecisiveness though—did he actually want to confront me standing right here? His passenger said, "Buddy, why don't you go about your business." And the driver used this to drive onward and talk tougher out the fading window. What I shook my head at most, as I started forward again, was that my country sucked.

Deb and I sweated on the couch and Toni Childs crooned, "Stop your fussing boy, your time will come." Would it? Toni Childs was a white girl who had lived in Africa and crafted her funky art, successfully. I was trudging through my scenes, one by one. I was also reading a Solzenitsyn Interwar book.

> *For several decades political arrests were distinguished in our country precisely by the fact that people were arrested who were guilty of nothing and were therefore unprepared to put up any resistance. Almost no one tried to run. You weren't gagged. You really could and really should cry out that you are being arrested! That villains in disguise are trapping millions! If many such outcries had been heard all over the city in the course of a day, would not our fellow citizens perhaps have begun to bristle? And would arrests perhaps no longer have been so easy? As for me, I kept silent because those Muscovites thronging the steps of the escalators were too few for me! Here my cry would be heard by 200, but what about the 200 million? Vaguely, unclearly, I had a vision that someday I would cry out to the 200 million. But for the time being I did not open my mouth and the escalator dragged me implacably down into the nether world.*

By the light of the stereo, Debbie and I looked into each other's faces, until, stuck to each other on this humid DC night, we drifted off to sleep.

I made it over to Moscow. I met with people and conversed. They walked me around town and—my dreams had been accurate—the buildings still bespoke the old era, the new words not yet come. I sat at my host's kitchen table and reflected for a long while. I even joked with them how this still could've been a dream but I was glad it wasn't. The airport had been dark, gray, lovely. Home seemed very far away. I felt such relief and joy.

When I awoke, I felt the emptiness of discovering it a dream. Emerging from it felt like the actual journey away from Moscow. No, whatever was happening there, I was not a part of. I lumbered over to my desk.

"Reks," said Debbie that evening, "you've been right, I need to make a change."

"Winter in Aspen."

"I probably should."

"You're on the road," I said. We left for Cugini's. In the lobby a neighbor smiled at us. The building had a young crowd and we got lots of smiles. In the morning, Debbie's alarm went off to the local news. A DC student had walked into the cafeteria and shot a schoolmate five times. The shooter's mother called it self defense. Next the news discussed a car chase—the radioman said police had chased a gun-shooter through the county. The driver, while shooting, rammed several cars, injuring two policemen. The driver was named Leon. The next story was about a sexual assaulter of a pre-teen girl. "They report it," said Debbie, "as if they don't realize there's something really wrong." The next story was a poll about America's least safe cities for pedestrians. I said, "They don't know they live in a sick society."

That night it dawned on us. "Oh my God, we can hear them talking beneath our window, so they've been hearing us too, all summer."

I said, "We hear their every noise." Deb said, "We're not quiet, Reks, you know?" She shrugged. We decided to leave the window open. She said, "We totally don't care what people think of us. I think it's because we're happy." She shrugged again. She said, "Maybe it's good for them to hear." She was moving to Aspen. I was headed to Greensboro.

I arrived by train. From the Greensboro station, zero modes of transport were offered. No bus, tram, train, anything had ever been considered, I was sure, and not another face was considering it now. A person could only be picked up by car. Ted was working. I walked on with my tall rucksack. The town was mostly fast-food restaurants, with looming signs. I saw no walkers, zero.

"I may never see her again," I told Ted, as we held beer bottles at night in his kitchen. "We packed up her little car and she drove off." The words sounded heavier than I'd expected. Ted said, "Sucks. But you like doing that to yourself, don't you think?" I was surprised when he made the occasional insight into me. He said, "Man, did I get home at eleven again? I gotta go to bed, I gotta be at a jobsite at five. Make this your home. It's so great to have you down here." Betsy was long asleep. I set up in their newly carpeted attic. I pasted all my scenes into one computer file. I would polish it all up here.

Good God, it was a thousand pages. No wonder this was taking so long. I would now have to travel through this enormous document and craft it down, a lot. I took the rare break maybe if a postcard from Debbie arrived. She described her beautiful drive.

I took my last break each night when Ted arrived with beer bottles. "Hell yeah I left college," he said in the attic while making me watch *Blood Sport*, in which Jean Claude von Damme karate kicks all into submission. "I had to go door to door with a paintbrush." He told me he had read one book, *The Firm*. "It might have been trash but I couldn't put it down." He said, "It was a guy in karate who told me about the Lord. He was just one of the many studs on the team but then he got all peaceful and he talked to me about it and I got saved. I would've made it too, I mean all the way, I mean really shining for the Lord if this one girl from Bible group hadn't invited me over and insisted on giving me a blow job. I was so bummed afterward. I thought if that can happen when you're really trying, if that shit gets thrown in your path, then it's not worth fighting so hard, not right now. I'm sure it was just a test and I failed. But I'm still saved—that's the great thing about what the Lord did for us. Oh, it was also during that time I met Betsy."

He was no longer knocking doors but managing his own crews. He had built the attic that was now home to my desk, though I was tenting in the backyard. It was the tent that Colin and I had bought after bailing out from Bakersfield. I was striving to make it to my desk at the same early hour that Ted left each morning. Sometimes we saw each other, he hurrying out with a giant cup of Coke.

When he came home I tried to still be typing. Sometimes I jumped up from a carpet nap and returned to the desk as he strode up with our beers. He would say, "It's so great you're here." He had dust on his clothes and a pencil behind his ear. We might drive down one of the pikes to get Jamaican Wings or Chinese. We came home and practiced kickboxing.

I did have my rantings, against the greed and guns and ecological damage and the corporate conspiracy to continue earning from all of this while pretending all was fine. Ted listened. We sat in his big Mercedes. I said, "First we need racial reconciliation because all the violence distracts us from our real agenda, to stop greed and denial from plowing through our limited resources. We need to march into Harlem and make peace, speak up, and tell society that it's time to halt the destructive thinking, time for a new dream."

Ted said, "I'm in." It was midnight in Greensboro and I now had someone to march with me. It was Ted. He added, "Someday I want to start a charity to find lost kids." We were in his driveway, staring at his big backyard. He had an apple tree. The apples were falling to the ground and rotting, all of them. When I complained, Ted smiled. He was out the door at five in the morning. I rescued some of the apples and sliced them up for the household. I sat at my desk.

When Betsy arose, she talked about her plans for working on the garden and helping Ted's accounting, then she slammed shut the window I'd opened and she fiercely objected to my having turned off the air conditioning. Then she napped. One day, Ted actually came home at dinnertime and he said at the table, "Reks, what's wrong with this room?" He was looking at me but Betsy was now smiling cautiously, bracingly.

Ted had added this room and installed the windows and assembled the dining table. "What's missing, Reks? The one thing someone else was supposed to take care of. I'll give you a hint—I also hung the curtain rods."

"I know, I know," said flushed Betsy, "I said I'd buy curtains." Ted said, "A year ago." She said, "I'll buy 'em, I'll buy 'em." She put a forkful in her mouth. Over midnight Jamaican Wings, Ted told me they hadn't had sex for over a year. "What?" Back at home he made me watch *Blood Sport* again. He had me nearly appreciating it, because to him the plight of the tough pretty boy was meaningful, was art, and I hadn't caught that. Betsy had felt sick and drunk Nyquil and retired. I gave another late-night speech about the march to overthrow the system, and Ted repeated, "I got your back. But you gotta admit, there are black people, and then there are niggers."

"Ted!" I exclaimed. He said, "When I die, you can at least say someone called it the way he saw it. But I totally appreciate you trying to make peace. It isn't gonna be easy. We did a paint job down at the college, and across the street were some projects and we saw those people every day, and they fucking hate white people. No doubt about that." He opened two more beers.

I said more quietly, "Ted, you know you've got the right to be happy, don't you?" He looked at me. He said, "I know. You're right." I said, "If someone's in a situation that is making him unhappy, he's allowed to speak up and make a change." Ted said, "I appreciate that." We went out back and kickboxed.

Ted bought a little warehouse in town, and he built out office space and hired an accountant, a small brunette named Debra. She lent Ted her favorite album. Ted had no time but I listened to it while consolidating scenes, themes, even characters. It took me twenty listens before I realized that this Peter Gabriel instrumental was profound. I reported to Ted that we needed to rent the *Last Temptation of Christ*. He said, "Fuck yeah." He enjoyed renting films just not returning them. They sat in his Mercedes for months. He had no time.

I began collecting them up and I biked over and paid the fee. Debra the accountant asked our opinion of the music and I said it was a journey into a mysterious past and she smiled at me and said, "I thought you might like it." I thought about my Debbie, getting settled in Aspen. At night, Ted came upstairs with beers and put the film in. We watched it again the next night, and the next, eventually muting it while the soundtrack played and we smoked Debra's weed. Then Ted went down to sleep while I typed a bit more. Then I again watched William Dafoe walk across the hard desert two thousand years ago. I gazed at the song list. One was called, "Of These, Hope." I gazed down the album's broad list of musicians. Here were more artists who had succeeded in their craft. My heart was sort of pounding from the weed and exhaustion.

I tried to pace away the fast thump in my chest. I sat on the couch. I sat at my desk. I went outside, then back in. I was sort of trapped in it. I curled up in my tent, fearing the worst. In the morning, I was working to that ancient energy again—these rich beats and hums lifted me high up. I was sharing something with the artists—it was right there in the first song, "The Feeling Begins".

I put the film back in. Jesus was striding to that same music. But he wasn't quite Jesus, he was the author's expression of the struggle to make the sacrifice. This Jesus got married and stopped his revolutionary street talk and later regretted it. I nodded my head—it was true, you had to give it up. If you really wanted to improve the world you couldn't live your life. On the way home from Jamaican Wings, Ted said, "We should drive out to Colorado and see Debbie."

"I've been thinking about her."

"You're going, that's a no-brainer, but I think I need to get out there too."

"You need to do what you need to do, Ted."

"And I suppose I can."

I said, "You can." He was deep in thought. We pulled into his driveway and he said, "You do see whose car is sitting in front of the house?"

Little Debra was waiting on the front steps. Ted asked her, "Why didn't you go in? Where's Betsy?" We found her asleep upstairs, the Nyquil bottle and wine glass by her bed. Debra said, "I didn't mind waiting." I slept in the plush attic that night, and brunette Debra was still there beside me the next afternoon when Ted returned surprisingly early for a trip down the pike—I called out, "You might not want to come up right now." His head was already appearing up the stairs. Grinning Ted turned around. I regretted missing an afternoon with him.

His company began removing asbestos. "They're gonna pay someone, so why not me? It'll help me start that charity to find lost kids." He bought a big house on a Greensboro hill and he knocked down walls and carried up sheetrock and fixed the plumbing.

At home he yelled, "Betsy, how did we get all this crap in the house and garage?" Betsy yelled back, "We bought it." Ted said, "Well, it's history." He began emptying it out for trash pickup. Betsy helped. I watched them build a mountain by the curb. It included unused binders and notebooks and lamps and clothing. Ted said, "It's easier just to buy more later." He and I, somehow, had unrecognizably opposite thinking. He got a call and he sped off, super-size Coke in hand. I took some of the unused notebooks to carry around with me where I might.

One night in my tent I suddenly heard the highway. I hadn't known it was close enough to be heard. Afterward, I couldn't unhear it. It wasn't the cold weather but this sound that had me pack up my tent. But I could hear it from the attic too. I'd just never noticed.

The next afternoon, the kitchen phone rang. I was alone in the house—I hurried down from the attic. The voice asked me to guess who it was.

I said, "Colin." He said, "Very good. Guess why I hunted you down." This required a longer pause. "Yes, I will participate in your wedding. I've been meaning to talk to you."

"Come up early," said Colin.

"We're going to Aspen," said Ted when he marched upstairs that night.

"I'm packed." I zipped up my black-and-green square LL Bean bag in which I could fit all I needed for such a trip. I tingled for leaving. Betsy said, "I suppose I'm not invited."

She stood in the doorway and waved. I said to Ted, "Our dream trip, it's coming true." I imagined how great it might feel to lay beside Debbie again. Ted looked very happy. In Kansas he lay across the back seat, while I drove and explained why our currently broken system couldn't fix itself but would instead pave its way to two oceans. We gazed dully at the straight path of Interstate Seventy, and we gazed back on those long workdays back in Greensboro. Finally we were winding up the snowy mountains.

We ate at the Aspen Tavern. My girl worked here. She had a hot waitress friend with short blond hair. It was snowing outside. The disc jockey was trying to start some fun but the dance floor was empty so he asked whether anyone knew the full 'Patty Cake' and a couple of people failed at it, shyly. Ted said, "C'mon Debbie", and out she went, her hair a bit longer than our DC days. She knocked out the full Patty Cake. I was proud at her calm cool unafraid spirit, and how light she looked in her white outfit. Ted and I went to her house to unpack.

Atop Debbie's covers I fell into a deep slumber. I stirred when she came home and fiddled in her closet. In a waking, yawning motion I took her comfortably down onto the bed, and she said with cautious sarcasm, "Oh you think so?" In the morning, we went up the mountain with the blond waitress. She was eyeing Ted cautiously. At night we drank with her and Debbie. Oh those mountain margaritas, they added to our fresh laughs, emitted from our sunned faces. Ted went to the bathroom and blond Leann moaned, "He's married?"

"Not for long," I answered.

I went to the bathroom and returned to another pitcher of margaritas and Debbie said, "I can't believe you're here." I said, "I came to see you." We all sipped. "Unfortunately I have to go back for Colin's wedding."

"So who're you gonna sleep with there?" asked Debbie.

"What are you talking about?"

Ted said, "So which ski instructors you two sleeping with?"

Leann said, "You mean that hot-tub thing?"

I said, "Wait, what are you talking about?"

Debbie said, "She's not talking about anything. It's probably her fantasy. But Reks, be honest about your fantasy?"

"Fantasies, bartenders, I like it," said Ted.

I said, "What bartender?"

Debbie said, "You've been fantasizing about being with that Lenka girl one day."

"I'll be fantasizing about her in about one hour."

"There you go," said Ted. A young family sat at the next table and I regretted that they were hearing this talk, though they didn't know I regretted it, and likely they thought the opposite. That night, Debbie curled up beside me and said, "I moved here, it was your idea." I stroked her cheek.

I said, "I think we're in love. But I have to get to Russia."

She sighed. "Well, how long do you have to go there for?" I briefly considered the large unlikelihood that I would ever return early from there for Debbie's sake. Yet, time with her felt so good. I answered, "I can't see ahead." She stayed lying here comfortably beside me, and I was glad. In the morning I asked, "You were with someone?"

"Nothing happened." Again that night we lounged around the couches. We drank bottles of champagne and then Debbie and I forgot to even shut our door, and she was no quieter than those days above her awning. Then we lay around in the night. She said, "We're happy together."

I needed to get back for that wedding. And I was due at grad school, no leaves allowed. We went to the Tavern. The bartender leaned over and chatted with us.

He was strong and confident. He was the only one who had never come skiing with our group. Debbie was looking at me.

"Did you do something with that guy?"

"Nothing happened."

"What is this 'Nothing happened?'"

She said, "I'm telling you. Nothing." Her shift began and Ted and I walked home through the snowfall. We called the airline and booked flights back here for March. At sunny dawn Debra stood on the stairs and Ted and I got in the big white Mercedes and zipped east. He said, "I heard you two last night and it drove me nuts so I went in and got a blow job from what's-her-face, her fat roommate. She wanted more but I said no. So she wanted advice or something."

"What was that bartender thing?"

"Oh, that blond whore Leann said she and Debbie were in a hot tub with two of the bartenders and that clothes came off."

"That fucking sucks."

"You like Debbie that much?"

"I don't know about that, but I don't need her fucking around with that bartender." As we approached Iowa City, I called the agriculture guy. Ted was willing to go off course.

But while I held a gas-station telephone, Iowa guy told me, "You and I have been trying to discuss this Russia opportunity for a while, and I am going back over there soon, and I do need help, but I just cannot meet today, I just cannot." I was simply being prevented from getting over there. I peered around to see whether this might be a station where Colin and I had stopped on the way home from Bakersfield. Soon Ted and I weren't returning from the great West anymore, but dropping south, as if from any little eastern hill. Soon he dropped me at the DC train station, he off to Greensboro, I to New York. "We both have a tough year ahead."

Ted said, "At least we're back there in March."

VI

A tuxedo was waiting for me midtown. I buzzed Colin's door in the Village. He said richly, "Rekstein," with his slight mock. His handsome smile welcomed me in. In his long-halled New York apartment we passed several rooms, and then we sat at his sleek gray table, in the center of which stood a photo of a young woman.

Her skin wasn't so smooth and I felt that Colin was showcasing how he was marrying a plainish girl and was too humble to care what people thought, and was showing us this, or something. The phone rang and the doorbell buzzed and his church members began emerging. Some would be bunking here. Some members were out-of-towners whom Colin had met at conferences along the way, such as the one I had ducked through in Newark. They had returned to celebrate with Colin.

The front door opened, and down the hall came a tall girl with reddish-brown hair tucked behind her ears. She placed down her many bags as people approached with hugs. And while crouching and handling these items and people, she looked across the room and said, "Rekstein, it's so good to meet you finally. Is there anything you want or need, anything I can do for you to make your stay better?"

She seemed to be trying too hard but I didn't mind so much. Arriving at the rehearsal ballroom, I automatically caught the gaze of Colin's father—Sue's father must have been the other tall gentleman in the suit and he watched Mike greet me warmly. I felt special. Jordan walked in. This mixed-race artist, I had envisioned him in my march. "Reks, man, I was looking forward to chilling with you. I don't know if you remember me from the Regional Missions Conference. We gotta grab some time this weekend."

"The sooner the better."

"That is awesome." He looked around the gathering and said, "Man, I knew I'd be underdressed. I simply had nothing." I took off my sports coat and let him wear it. Jordan said, "Man, I knew God would hook me up. I had need. I knew he'd meet it."

After the dinner, some friends put Colin and Sue in adjacent chairs and took turns expressing pleasant thoughts about them. It became clear that all the speakers were church members, declaring the couple's great practice of the religion. Members were blond women and sporty black dudes and Asians and Africans and just about everyone. Colin's dad seemed to feel obligated to say something. He looked a bit uncomfortable but to me he was always dignified, Mr. Mike Vonn, Goldman Sachs partner. He touched upon Colin's seeming happy with Sue.

Then I stood up and insisted that God wanted us to help society and not just go to church, and that this was actually the value of the crucification, which was the word my mind finally located. One of the blondes laughed. During dessert, Mike Vonn took me out on the balcony and said, "So how've you been, Reks? Really, how's life?" We were standing in the dark outside and he had drunk some but I felt by his tone that he really cared. I felt, maybe due to Colin's straying, that I was like a son to him. Mike put his arm around my shoulder. I didn't know quite how to respond. I told him life was great.

I did know how to respond to Jordan when we were walking together, behind his group, up the avenues. "Jordan, do you know what the biggest problem with humankind is, the biggest problem with people, why they don't oppose the destruction around them?" Jordan was smiling forward—no he wasn't really hearing me and I needed these guys. The others were a gap ahead of us. I said, "Do you know what the biggest problem is?"

"Greed," said Jordan. I exclaimed, "That's it, that's exactly it. So I'm starting a movement, I know it sounds funny, but we're on the wrong path and there's no plan to get us off. So we're going to march into Harlem, make peace, take the microphone, and start a new effort to use our resources right, use our people right, live life right."

He was at Colin's the next day with his tux, and some of the party hadn't seen Jordan in a while, so he reclined at the table and answered questions. "My goals? You wanna know my goal? I'm looking to chill. Just chill. I am looking to chill the heck out." He had them laughing. "I am so serious," he said. "I could not be more serious."

Colin seemed strained by the crowd in the apartment and by the planning and packing too. He asked me to cab over to the wedding site with him. "Reks," he said. "Today is a big day for me." He wanted me to understand something. I nodded. I had the duty of seating Mike Vonn's second wife and her now third husband. Colin's mother had her own third husband—I was glad after that lonely summer in Bakersfield. Mike and his third wife had a new son. I stood by the altar with old Patrick Pearsall in front of me, then Mike, then Colin. The young minister told us why this night was special.

For example, Colin and Sue had fallen in love and were marrying and only then would they share themselves and become one. Most people, the minister contrasted, came together and gave themselves away and then waited to see whether it was love. "That's how people get hurt, that's how people get divorced. It's because they're living opposite to God's plan for us." I could see Mike's shoulders tightening, here at his son's wedding. To me though it made some sense. I was surprised I let it in. I compared my life to Colin's since our sidewalk goodbye five years prior. I was proud of Colin. Patrick Pearsall and his new wife had this same thing.

My first class was scheduled for Monday, and on Sunday I again found a pipe in my mouth and regret in my mind and extra pace in my heartbeat. I broke away from this high-school group and pedaled home to type—I combined more characters and deleted more villages and more the next day, and then I bicycled down to school, all the while contemplating my urgency to get to Russia but first speak out to America. Clearly Colin and his group had to help me.

Biking daily to the SAIS meant passing Cugini's Pizza. I would look away and pedal harder. When I pulled a chair to face right at my Russian teacher, I still couldn't hear a word she was saying. Ted drove up for asbestos business and we went to his favorite Chinese restaurant. He said he aimed to earn a million dollars this year, nothing would stop him. He said he was leaving Betsy. I reminded him about our Harlem march. "I'm still in," he said. "But I'm sure you're moving to Colorado." I stared at my food. He said, "Or maybe not."

I biked homeward again to type—I wasn't the only one who had seen the wild transformation in those parts so I was bracing to hear of some new novel that captured it. I legged hard up the avenues but then cut through the last section of that long park where Debbie and I used to walk, and now I coasted a moment among the gray trees. The creek, despite its trash lining, made nice water sounds. Finally I sat down at my desk to hurry my slow writing.

Instead I had to open *Management & Employee Buy-Outs in Central and Eastern Europe as a Technique of Privatization*. Then I tried my Russian homework. When I sat again in front of teacher Ludmila, I stared at the impossibility of my situation. I had to be writing but it meant leaving a top grad school, for good. Ludmila was explaining the extensive weekend homework and I was dropping out. Class broke and she stared at me. I slowly stood up. I took a train to New York City.

Colin met me at Penn Station. He wore a warm smile. His dark clothes and backpack fit with the City. "Let's walk down to this jazz club and get a beer," he said. "I actually have the whole weekend free for you." Later we met Sue at a restaurant. Colin declined a second beer but Sue ordered one with me. I said, "Beer-drinking girl." Colin said, "This is my wife, my other half."

We had agreed to swap an hour discussing our respective positions. So in the morning I told him how humans were doomed because they swore by a system of ceaseless consumption of limited resources, and he quietly listened.

That afternoon we again sat at his sleek, Manhattan table and he placed before me a brown, leather Bible. He had another for himself. He had me turn about two-fifths of the way through it, to an Isaiah chapter from which I was to read some lines. They discussed how our trouble was not due to God refusing to help us, instead our bad actions separated us from him. Colin had me turn ahead a chunk of chapters, which he said was a chunk of years too. In some Luke section we read John the Baptist saying, "One more powerful than I will come."

And when the crowd asked what they should do, Mr. John the Baptist answered, "The man with two tunics should share with him who has none, and the one who has food should do the same." I was impressed by Colin's literary prowess—he knew this book well and it did have historical and philosophical meaning. In the morning, we drove his jeep uptown. We parked atop Manhattan and rode the subway to the Apollo Theater in Harlem.

As we funneled in for the service, here again was that every-color mix, greeting one another. We sat in a back section and I recognized faces from the wedding night and I received pats on the shoulder. I looked across the sea of heads toward the stage. The speaker, much applauded by the audience, was a fit black man in a suit. His voice filled the Apollo, and he said, amid his hour, "I was talking to a friend I've known for years, who isn't living our life, but living the life, if you know what I mean."

The audience did. The speaker said, "He thinks he's living good, or he thought so but now his wife left him. So he came to me. I asked him, 'Joe, honestly, would you let your daughter date a guy like you?'

"And Joe didn't think very long, because finally he's getting open, and he said, 'You know, I would not let my daughter date a guy like me.' And I said, 'Then Joe there's something wrong with your life.'" The audience cheered with agreement.

When the gradual exit began, there was much stopping for talk and hugs. When I stepped out to the trash-blotched street, the passersby were black and tired—I felt filled with the same energy as the church audience, this huge colorful group that possessed a power that the passersby clearly didn't. Jordan put an arm around my shoulder. He had purpose in his eyes.

We stepped into a dirty Popeye's. I felt so positive. We ordered a big lunch and I treated. Jordan looked hungrily at the food and said, "Man, we are blessed." We had big windows to the Harlem streets. Jordan said, "Reks, you need to study the Bible. I mean, you need to get deep into it." I said, "I'm open." He said, "We need to hook you up with DC brothers. But this is no small decision. I mean, I'm looking at my life, I'm feeling so blessed, I've got the fellowship and I've got the Word and now God is hooking me up with a girlfriend more awesome than I could ever pray for. And I prayed, dude, I prayed for years for the right girl, I'm talking years, you hear what I'm saying? You met me in Newark way back. I've been single, you read? And I'm still single—I don't know what God's will is with this sister, he might just take her away from me. You never know what he's thinking. And I mean she is like perfect. She's from freaking Israel. A sister from Israel who wants to serve through Christ. And she's pure. And she's beautiful. And she digs me. She and I are just thanking the Lord. It is intense. I don't know if you can understand. But I'm saying we have to be committed. Committed. To being in the Word, to being out of our selves, to being on the street, serving, giving. Sometimes the Church of Christ is the last place in the world you want to be." I said, "I think I understand."

I decided I would stay in graduate school. If I studied this Bible and really learned what this group was doing, then I could allot some time away from the other movements. Jordan called a DC member and he coincidentally lived two blocks from the school. I had been a day away from quitting. After Russian, I walked toward this strange apartment. In hand was the leather Bible in which Colin had jotted his spiritual notes for these years since our parting.

Steve Cannon opened the door and of course he looked like Patrick Pearsall, black and handsome and happy. He switched on a lamp and opened his Bible and I read aloud, "'For the word of God is living and active, sharper than any double-edged sword; it judges the thoughts and attitudes of the heart. Nothing in all creation is hidden from God's sight.'" I looked up and nodded.

The thing was, the words were rising off the page—the letters seemed separate from the paper, and light was essentially coming from them. I said, "Of course God knows all."

Steve said, "'But it's about the Word. Do you hear what it's saying about the Word?'" I stared silently across the room at him.

"I hear." In a moment I read, "'Watch your life and doctrine closely. Because if you do you will save your self and your hearers.'" It made complete sense. You had to do right. Talking it wasn't enough—those guys made no sense. Ted talked it. Also we had to watch for *what* was actually right, of course. And then live it, life and doctrine. "Watch 'em."

I hadn't wanted to, of course not. But I had dragged myself to this day and now something was happening. "'Knock and the door will be opened to you.'" We met the next day.

I read, "'To those who believed, Jesus said, "Follow my teachings, and then you'll be my true disciples, and then you'll see the truth, and the truth will set you free."'"

Again, believing wasn't enough, of course not. That was why this group was different. Steve Cannon and I sat by lamplight on his couches and studied for hours. "Wow," he said, hearing about my Europe experience. "The pressure you were under—you wanted big change. But why just clean up the guy's greed? Why not clean it all out, the divorcing, cussing, lying, laziness toward God, the temptation to steal at work, to seduce the babysitter, to do drugs, to drink and drive and kill someone, why not get in there and clean out the whole mess? Get in there with the power. Cut him open with the sword—Paul writes that the Word of God is a sword. This is surgery we're doing here. On you. This is a scalpel." He held up the book. Today I had come by subway and now I knew exactly what to do.

I stood up in the front of a rush-hour car and announced, "God is real. It's actually all real. I mean really real, not just an idea. He's right here, waiting for all of us to reach out to him, if we dare. I can't believe it's actually true." Faces were mortified. I said, "I know it's tough, so if anyone wants to talk more I'll be in the next car." My heart was pounding—when the door opened I spun out to the next car and I waited there.

No one came. The next day, a white guy was sitting on the couches with Steve Cannon. Of course he reminded me of Colin, clean-cut and brown-haired. We read about this Paul guy spying out and executing the first converts. On one such murderous mission he had been hurrying through the desert when evidently Jesus appeared. Paul asked, "Who are you, Lord?"

"Jesus."

So Paul walked a different direction to a different town and confessed all to some surprised disciple and led the new movement through the first century. "And that is what repenting means," said this guy John Goodman. "It means to turn directions—your life is going one way and you turn and go the other. In your case, what do you think it's going to take to repent and begin living the right life?" I was supposed to visit Debbie next month. Stopping the marijuana now felt easy. Done, finished. Cussing was out the window too—people didn't need to hear those words. As for sacrificing time, I had already slated a revolution on the schedule, so I could free up Sunday mornings I supposed. Masturbation was slavery and I was happy to free myself. But why drag Debbie through this? I said, "I'll just bring her to the Colorado church."

John said, "But what will really happen? Why put yourself in that situation? In the Bible there're no negotiations, there's no saying I'll stop this but not that and I'll just go visit my non-Christian girlfriend and sleep in the same bed with her."

Wait, who were these guys? Steve Cannon was sitting in one corner and John Goodman the other and I couldn't quite see them both at the same time. Now the lamplight seemed too dim. Steve said, "You need to cancel the trip." What did they really want? I didn't even know them. I stared at John. I said, "You're right."

The study had lasted unexpectedly long and today I had come by bike and soon I was biking without a light into DC's crowded dusk. I tried hurrying along the park road, but the darkness was dropping too quickly—I would be caught tightly among the cars. I had sacrificed extra time for God and now I was in trouble. Cars were sweeping past me, angrily. Worse, my mind was distracted by that whole repenting thing and by the phone call I had to make.

But no, this week's feelings had been too powerful, I wouldn't let go of them. Wasn't I supposed to trust? This dark road was curvy and the car lights were blinding. But suddenly everything changed.

It was Saturday, and the weekend barrier forbade cars, and I zipped through it and I had miles of park road to myself. Peace, peace, peace, I pedaled through it, all alone in the forest night. I looked up and I was connected to the sky and I was connected to these characters from the first century—they were real—and they had seen the same sky. They had known the same God. I would give everything.

What about my writing? I was conversing aloud with God. "Okay, I'll put you before the writing." I would obviously remove that scene with Lenka on the velvet couch. Gone. I was pedaling through heaven. Peace and nature were all mine and they were gifts handed down to me, Rice Rekstein. Person by person, that was the real revolution, I was simply joining it. Live righteously and teach it to someone. That was the formula. I could exhale away my attempt to fix global economic doom. Deer were feeding in the grass and raising their heads with a calm glance at my passing in the night.

And get married, that was part of it. Colin had done it, Patrick had done it. That Apostle Paul guy had not. John Goodman and Steve Cannon had. I quickly pictured my wedding night. We would come home and she would be in her dress.

Maybe it would be Debbie. She was so special, now I could see. She liked skiing and did Patty Cake and had read *Tess*. And she was a teacher and she liked talking to strangers. And we fit together. Plus, she had been devoted to me, except for this hot-tub thing. See, that was why it hurt so much—a pain that couldn't be imagined until actually occurring—because we had already joined together, as if married.

Or maybe she would be Russian. They said the Moscow church was growing quickly. Oh no, my empty road was ending. I biked out from the barrier and was about to merge with the evening traffic. My taste of heaven was over. Of course I had to return out and face the ugly world and its gritty roads and do my part, God be with me.

Before entering my house I stared one last time at the night. I could see Christ, in the sky, in my mind, looking down at me from some ancient, high, dust-walled window. He actually existed, I was getting it. The fairy tale was somehow fully true. I felt completely clear inside. "Peace I leave with you; my peace I give you. I do not give to you as the world gives. Do not let your hearts be troubled and do not be afraid."

I was filled with peace when I next walked—or danced essentially—into Ludmila's class. I was so unburdened. I could still see Jesus in that high old tower window or whatever. In the elevator, I shook hands in introduction with a classmate—the school year was three-quarters over. "Are Christians allowed to have fun?" Debbie had asked on the phone. I so badly wanted her to understand.

She called again that night. "Let's go camping together."

"But I'm not coming out there." Yet the camping image was floating around my head—I imagined us in a tent. Ted drove up and we again went for Chinese. "Reks," he said, "what you're doing, this is the greatest thing. Man, when the Lord wants back in your life he just knocks, he just comes. Man, am I feeling it."

"Actually," I said, "it's we who are supposed to knock."

"Listen to you," said Ted. "I always hoped you'd see it someday. I need to get back into it, you're right." He had been planning to visit a girl up here. But he slept on my couch instead. In the morning, he called me from the road back to Greensboro. "Wow, I've been praying the whole ride, I've been thinking about that charity for finding lost kids, I've been thinking about meeting God some day. I'm just rejoicing."

"Ted, we should get into the Word together. It's like food, it calls itself food."

"You're absolutely right. Give me a call."

Sunday service was at George Washington University. Through tall side windows poured sunlight, and the DC group was as colorful as New York. Here came John Goodman, hopping off stage to give me a hug. Back at the podium he introduced today's preacher, a strong, well-dressed, articulate black man like at the Apollo in Harlem. He fed off the audience's energy. Its source was the thought that God was moving during these days, parting clouds from the clarity of the message.

"'And when the people heard it,'" read John Causey, "'they were cut to the heart and said to Peter and the other Apostles, "What should we do?" And Peter replied, "Repent and be baptized, every one of you."'"

Thus the first church had been born. This at GW was meant to be that church again, right out of the book. John Causey roared, "They asked what they should do. They wanted to know. They were open. And what was the answer? 'Repent and be baptized. Everyone of you.' Could it be any clearer?

"But in my hand I have a list from the *USA Today*, asking what people want from a church. And the people responded, 'We want to be with members we can relate to. We want our privacy. We want to be comfortable.'"

John Causey tossed the newspaper far away. "They want to be comfortable? Jesus said, 'If anyone would come after me, he must deny himself and take up his cross daily and follow me.'

"They want privacy? *Matthew 4* says, 'Peter and his brother were casting a net into the lake and Jesus walked by and said to follow him, and at once they left their nets and followed him.'

"They want people they can relate to? Look around this room. Can we relate to each other? Absolutely not. We have people from every corner, every color. Such people, in this world, do not like each other. We come to church so God can teach us *how* to relate. That's not how we *pick* a church. That's called playing church. If you're visiting, I'm sorry if you don't like this message. But I know a church you can go to." He went and picked up the newspaper. "All of them!" The aisles soon filled with mingling. A group of black members ushered a white member many rows to meet me. They were delivering Daniel Bertholet from Switzerland—they wanted me to know that DC had a European brother.

Daniel Bertholet, with light in his smiling spectacled eyes, was interested in my story. We walked under the winter-morning sun on empty downtown Sunday streets.

Ahead on the sidewalk, a hooded man waddled away from us. He was homeless by his attire and, despite the hood, I glimpsed that he was black and rough. Coming toward us all was a well-dressed black woman, and to avoid him she leaned toward the buildings. But still he roared right into her face and alarmed her.

She continued past us without glancing. I turned and said, "My love is stronger than that." She took a few more steps, then angled on her heels and looked back at me and Daniel Bertholet.

"I believe you," said the woman. When we passed by that homeless guy, somehow a big white woman was actually under the hood—Daniel was surprised too. We descended the escalator, and below us a small white man in a bow-tie and prim suit turned his head toward us in hello.

His decent demeanor then became biting words, "Riff raff above." I opened my mouth to assuage this, and the man let out the most supreme profanity and it was meant right for us actually. "Reks," said Daniel Bertholet, "do you see what Satan is throwing at you this morning?"

I was to be baptized in the Reflecting Pool in front of the Capitol, to symbolize the public road I would make of it. It was March 1994. John Goodman led a prayer as a group of us shivered and circled, I wearing just shorts, Colin soon dipping me below the water.

We gathered at the late-night diner. I was proud to be in the University Ministry of the DC Church. Daniel Bertholet was here with recent convert Bill, a black grad student. Rosemary was here, an attractive African girl in glasses, with a handful of years as a disciple already. She had good handfuls on her chest too, but I forced myself not to stare. I wanted no dark images in my head. Kelly was here, a somewhat pimply white student from the Midwest. She was simply always smiling. "Baptism is burial. It's a coffin. You died."

We were sitting here talking about the movement, the faith, the reality of it all, and I felt high. It was physical, the elation. Colin said, "Jordan says his conversion was visual like this too. God is reaching out to you strongly." Rosemary said, "I heard how a New York sister was once threatened by a stranger in Central Park—they caught the guy later and asked him why he hadn't touched her and he said it was because of the person standing next to her. But she'd been alone."

Harlem

'litost'

I still had Debbie's bestselling *Shipping News* beside my computer, and because the story would now be a film, I picked it up again.

> ***At last Quoyle dropped out of school and looked for a job, kept his hand over his chin. He fell into newspapering by dawdling over greasy saucisson and bread. The saucisson, the bread, the wine, Partridge's talk. For these things he missed a chance at a job that might have put his mouth to bureaucracy's taut breast. But Partridge, dribbling oil, said, 'Ah, fuck it.' Sliced purple tomato. Changed the talk to descriptions of places he had been, Strabane, South Amboy, Clark Fork. In Clark Fork had played pool with a man with a deviated septum. Wearing kangaroo gloves. Quoyle in the Adirondack chair, listened, covered his chin with his hand.***

I had written like this in early drafts, thinking it cool and creative. But then I determined that it was a failure to write a sentence. Yet I had no readers to agree with me. Instead I read *V* by Thomas Pynchon, which hadn't earned bestseller status but something better, cult, according to Benjamin in Prague. I had seen it in his book box, now I saw its old poster framed in the library.

How could I be hitting the same non-sentences? They were on every page.

He could hear a party on in the background. New Year's night. Where he was there was only an old clock to tell the time. And a dozen homeless, slouched on the wooden bench, trying to sleep. Waiting for a long-haul bus run neither by Greyhound nor Trailways. He watched them and let her talk. She was saying, "Come home." The only one he would allow to tell him this except for an internal voice he would rather disown as prodigal than listen to.

Somehow this church towering Gothic and solid over their heads, the quietness, her impassivity, his confessional humor. He was talking too much, must stop. But could not.

So I never found out what his V meant, never heard his message. This choppiness might work in dialogue—I was trying it. But otherwise I wanted my story to be clear. Kerouac had managed to use subjects and verbs.

Flat on my back, I stared straight up at the magnificent firmament, glorying in the time I was making, in how far I had come from sad Bear Mountain after all, and tingling with kicks at the thought of what lay ahead—whatever that would be.

It was a fine night, a warm night, a wine-drinking night, a night to hug your girl and talk and spit and be heavengoing. We never budged from those crates. We were alone and mixing up our souls ever more and ever more till it would be terribly hard to say good-bye.

I typed away each night, even if just one paragraph, one step closer. More often I was studying in a quiet carrel at SAIS library.

The diplomat Van Moltke had the ability to understand the significance of events without being influenced by current opinion; the ability to make quick decisions without being deterred by a perceived danger; the ability to be silent in seven languages.

Young Hitler was working as he had never worked. But it was work which suited him: his hours were irregular, he was his own master, his life was spent in talking.

Unpleasant as it was, the seminary still left young Stalin with enough time for arguing, dreaming, and reading; and these he would not easily give up.

At home I picked up *Jude the Obscure*. Just as he had done in *Tess*, Hardy portrayed people allowing themselves to be trapped by tradition.

> ***People go on marrying because they can't resist natural forces, although many of them know perfectly well that they are buying a month's pleasure with a life's discomfort.***

But his Jude did eventually recognize how his lust had steered his bad decision.

> ***What a wicked worthless fellow he had been to give vent to an animal passion for a woman, and allow it to lead to such disastrous consequences; then to think of putting an end to himself; then to go recklessly and get drunk.***

True to tragic Hardy, Jude, only after marrying, found the woman he did love.

> ***Jude, in his light-grey holiday-suit, was really proud of her companionship, not more for her external attractiveness than for her sympathetic words and ways. That complete mutual understanding, in which every glance and movement was as effectual as speech for conveying intelligence between them, made them almost the two parts of a single whole.***

And in Hardy's bleak world, it was too late to be with her, ever.

The Bible was like no book I had read. Yes, every sentence had a verb, but it was the colorful characters that elevated it, in that the gospels felt too real to be fiction. They were alive with urgent walking and talking. The Jesus character spoke like no one I had heard. I read the critics. They said that the Jesus character was either exaggerated or amalgamated. But about Paul they could only say he must have somehow been mistaken. No one doubted he existed, and that he ached for his cause, Jesus. To Paul's mind the gospel made complete sense.

John Goodman read to us in a sunny park. "'They devoted themselves to the apostles' teaching and to the fellowship. Everyone was filled with awe, and many wonders and miraculous signs were done by the apostles. All the believers were together and had everything in common. Selling their possessions, they gave to anyone as he had need. Every day they continued to meet together in the temple courts. And the Lord added to their number daily those who were being saved.'"

After the sermon, we played volleyball. At my park table sat Mabel, big boned and big lipped, and she was my "sister" and I was elated. The cause had brought us together. We were on the same peacefully fighting side. It was the obvious solution to so much. Mabel talked to me about how great she thought God was, and how she was studying to be a medical receptionist, and how warm the day felt. A mustached little Mexican walked by on the grass. He passed by with his head pointed down. He was not in our group. I recalled that he didn't see with our sureness, didn't know that the sunshine indeed had a source, and that the source was reaching out from heaven, truly, with hope and help for us down here. I saw that I no longer had those bleaker, finite eyes, wherein the grass was just grass. I was smiling wide.

I was deep in a Virginia suburb but one bus did actually operate on Sunday, once. I could take it to the subway and travel home and write. Daniel Bertholet said, "But you should stay." I was already wearing my rucksack, and that lonely bus was due. Daniel said, "We're supposed to spend time together, build the fellowship." I laughed. I said, "Daniel, I've been here all morning and into the afternoon." He had a very concerned expression behind his glasses—he was worried that I didn't get the concept. I put my hand on his Swiss shoulder, and I left. We met for lunch that week. He said, "I was so challenged by what I heard you did on the subway." We were sitting on the grassy quad of American University. He said, "We should all be doing that."

"Aren't you?" I cocked my head. I asked, "So, what about your own conversion, did you feel a lot of changes? Did you actually see Jesus?" Daniel's eyes analyzed me again, still not knowing where to place me. He answered, "I didn't actually see Jesus. I don't think we actually see him. I felt many changes through the Word. I see Jesus in the Word. I see Jesus in you," he said brightly, as if solving the issue. His eyes got serious. "No, I changed directions completely. I had been completely selfish, thinking only of me and my ambitions, and pursuing pleasure with so little satisfaction that I was considering becoming gay next. I was so empty and didn't realize it."

I nodded for a moment. I said, "The evidence was so strong in my conversion, there was so much evidence—and it grows every time I pick up the book—that even if this feeling fades, I will never have an excuse to forget."

At SAIS I sat on a courtyard bench and prepared for Russian and said hello to more fellow students—I was aiming to show each of them the Word and the fellowship. I gazed up at the sunny edge of the rooftop and I was amazed that sophisticated SAIS had a crazy evangelistic born-again in its student body, and that it was me. I shook my head.

In an upstairs carrel I studied silently. I took breaks and leaned out the window and looked down at Happy Hour in the courtyard. This was how my schedule could succeed, by studying on Friday and Saturday evenings. Happy Hour attracted most everyone else. They massed together in the courtyard and they held their beer-bottle necks and their voices reached up to my window. I sat back down and read.

Ted no longer took my calls. He was divorcing Betsy. Debbie called again to invite me camping. She just didn't get it. "We were happy."

"No," I said, "I didn't have the power to love you. And there was cheating."

"I told you that was nothing."

"No," I said, "I cheated on you. With a girl named Debra. I was lost but I didn't know it. I was blind. Come see love with me." Now she said nothing. Scripture couldn't get through the phone, it didn't reach her, she didn't even react. She said, "You were always an extremist. You always want to live an extreme. It just isn't immediately obvious about you."

At the subway stop, a homeless guy asked for a little help. The city was dotted with these guys but I was no longer analyzing the whole unmovable mind that allowed it. I just knew I had to give this guy my tuna sandwich. "It's from God," I said. He thanked me. I wanted him to understand—"It's from God." He looked blankly back at me. He said, "It's always from God. Just last night I was reading how man can't survive on bread alone, but on the very word from his mouth."

I chatted with him the next day. I gave him a sandwich—I had made two this time. I gave him a Jesus scripture. "'Come to me all you who are weary and burdened, and I will give you rest.'" He had one for me. "'I am the bread of life. He who comes to me will never go hungry, and he who believes in me will never be thirsty.'"

I went to our little university sub-sector, where John Goodman read one too. "'Every kingdom divided against itself will be ruined.'" He had a slight southern accent. "Yes it's Jesus Christ who actually said that. And today, Christianity *is* divided against itself. But God is unifying the movement through us, the evidence is overwhelming."

John discussed other denominations. "The quick emotional decision is not a conversion. Find one 'altar call' in the Bible. Find one infant baptized. No, the book of *Acts* is filled with people who hear the message, then believe, then change, then get baptized. Repent doesn't mean to feel sorry, it means to turn, to change. Look around at those who weren't properly converted. Of course their lives are still filled with sin, they never repented. Likely they were converted based on one scripture, and even that they probably didn't read. Ask them." He was training us to teach others. ""I used to go to so-called Christian camp and there'd be a campfire sermon and none of us cracked our Bibles once and we'd sing Kumbaya and call it a night. No one taught righteousness, so no lived it. Luckily I was met in college by a true disciple." Jesus says, 'Suppose one of you wants to build a tower. Will he not first sit down and estimate the cost to see if he has enough money to complete it? For if he lays the foundation and is not able to finish, everyone who sees it will ridicule him, saying this fellow began to build and was not able to finish.'

We had smaller units called Bible Talks, for inviting friends to. My Talk was at Bill's, that black grad student who lived among the row-houses above Georgetown. I was knocking doors again, now with Daniel. His face was serious—people could not afford to forego our message. Most people closed doors right on us. One tall guy opened his door and just walked away into his apartment, leaving us standing on the step.

"Sorry," he said, promptly returning, "I had to check my computer. You guys live around here? What denomination?" He looked like some country-club type, with wavy sandy hair. This was a singles area and walking it reminded me of Debbie and thus the sacrifices I was making. Sure, we had a disciple living in this cool neighborhood but Bill was obviously living differently. I sighed. But I recalled that I was avoiding breakups and drugs and hangovers and selfishness and loneliness and even politics. This tall guy, Wade Davis, brought his own Bible to the Talk and he agreed to study with Daniel and me, and I was glad.

I was glad that Colin's Bible Talk was filled with artists. Someone knew a Sister at Random House—I got her phone number on my next visit. Colin took me up to his rooftop. We gazed at the sunny skyline. The breeze blew through our hair. We were here to pray, and Colin began. He thanked, conversed, wished, asked.

Then I looked up and looked down and looked where I wanted and spoke to him who was actually listening, and I spoke like he was a friend, like he was a father, like he cared. Then we went downstairs and walked to the end of Colin's long hall, where he pushed the button on his message machine.

During the next half hour of our listening, Sue came home and stood beside smiling Colin and the machine—Colin had a long series of requests from other members. They wanted help with a temptation, a conflict, reaching out, building faith, keeping faith, moving apartments, encouraging a Sister, finding a date, planning a wedding. Each time the machine beeped, another voice, black or white or Latino or Asian, asked something of Colin. I asked, "How is this possible?"

Colin said, "My life is not my own." I stared at his wise grin. Sue went in to listen to her own machine. On the subway, Colin leaned close to me but said with an open tone, "You know, when I was breaking up with that black Sister because of our impure act, and I asked my leader's advice who he thought I should marry, he suggested Sue. And I thought, 'This really is a cult, they're trying to steer me to Sue because she's a loyal member and a way for them to control me.' But I prayed about it, and I sought more advice, and I searched the scriptures, and I saw that she was beautiful."

"Colin," I said, "when I came up for the wedding, you were different than those earlier years, when we had tried to live together in Harlem, with Patrick." Colin responded, "Do you mean drinking a beer at the jazz club? Yeah, I wanted to show you that I could be a disciple and be real too. But I orchestrated that whole weekend, of course. I had everyone positioned for your arrival, Jordan and the groomsmen and Sue and the minister and your tablemates. I coached them all, 'Be gentle, be subtle, this guy's very intelligent, very prideful." He smiled again. He said, "Move to New York, Rekstein. Sue and I could make up a room for you, though technically you're not supposed to know what married people do. But move up here. You have that zeal that I can't always find in myself so easily at present."

He took me to see a new film. Walking out from it and back into the sunshine, I berated him. "All that cussing, all that stupid shooting, what were you thinking?"

"I just thought it was creative, different."

"A meaningless story isn't different. Is it creative to say 'fuck' every five words? Every one of those Reservoir Dogs—so cussingly cool—was two-dimensional." I felt I had been fully polluted, and by Colin no less, a five-year disciple.

He said, "You should never say that word. No matter how many times you hear it in a film, you should never speak it." It was the first time since repenting that I had said any such word and I decided instantly now it would be the last, no problem. We arrived at his apartment and he closed his bedroom door and talked with Sue. I sat at their table and drafted a query letter, which evidently had to convince publishers in two paragraphs or fewer about my story and style. I also read through some scripture, which was all God-breathed, according to Apostle Peter, but still seemed to vary in quality, in my opinion—the Old Testament seemed a bit wordy, and violent. Perhaps it was all a setup for Christ to free us with true light. I lifted my head as Colin now returned to the table.

I had really ripped into him—his face was still heated, and he'd come out to respond. "Reks," he said slowly, "I want to say that I felt hurt when you criticized my tastes and efforts. I understand that you have different opinions, but the way you negated mine hurt me." I was amazed. He had clearly boiled over inside but he controlled his voice entirely. He said, "I wanted you to know that." I could only apologize, and deeply. Back in DC, Wade Davis met with Daniel and me on a park bench.

I shared with them about the homeless guy quoting from *Matthew*: "Man does not live on bread alone." Daniel said, "*Luke* quotes it as man 'cannot'." Wade said, "Cool." I said, "Wait. Why is it different?"

They both calmed my worry, saying that Jesus probably expressed these concepts many different times, in many different ways. Daniel added, "He said he was the bread from heaven which gives life to the world. So the people asked to eat some of this bread. They still didn't understand."

Wade added, "They wanted food." We paused, and then laughed.

"Anyway," said Daniel, turning fully toward Wade. "So do you know this bread of life? I see that you go to church and you have a Bible, but can you feed yourself? And importantly, can you feed others? Are you making disciples? Do you even know how?"

Wade said, "Oh, you guys are toughies, I knew it when I saw you. Especially you"—he pointed his Bible at a slightly embarrassed Daniel. Wade continued, "You're going to tell me that accepting Jesus into my heart was not sufficient? Right? Okay, I'm open." He was tall and he spoke cleverly. He said, "Let's hear what you have to say."

Smiling Daniel said, "Well, it's not us saying, it's the Bible. Maybe that's the problem, maybe you've been listening to people, and not the Word. That's why I asked whether you even know this bread." We sat through an impasse, because Wade Davis was a part-time teacher in his church but was still not attempting to show us any doctrine. It was a bit like Electrolux—we wanted them to use their vacuum first, and then we would run ours over the same spot.

Wade said, "The famous one is *John* 3:16."

Daniel said, "Let's go there."

We turned to the New Testament's fourth book. Wade read the sixteenth verse. "'"For God so loved the world that he gave his only son, so that those who believe in him would be saved."'"

"So what does it mean?" asked Daniel.

Wade answered, "It means that all you have to do is believe in Jesus and you're saved."

Daniel said, "Really? That is still how you interpret it?" Though I knew Wade hadn't meant it, I kept silent. Serious Daniel said, "If you go to verse one in the very same chapter, a teacher named Nicodemus comes to Jesus and says he does believe Jesus is from God—and Jesus's immediate response is, 'No one can see the kingdom of God unless he is born of water and the Spirit.' So then what does that mean?"

Wade answered, "It means you need to get baptized to be saved."

Daniel, getting it now perhaps, wearing a slight smirk himself, said, "And not just baptized, but born again. Which means die first, end your current lifestyle, repent. But in this same *John* chapter the people are arguing with Jesus. This is why he explains that they must believe. He ends it, 'Light has come into the world but men love darkness because their deeds are evil. Everyone who does evil will not come into the light for fear that his deeds will be exposed.'"

Wade agreed to meet with us again. I went to SAIS and read my Trotsky assignment, and then I mentioned to a schoolmate that I had changed my life. SAIS people had traveled and explored and experimented but still I tried to be gentle. "Weirdly I'm a Bible follower, yet I think it can all make sense."

"Are you really so closed-minded?" Their responses showed they had suddenly found themselves with an intolerant person, intolerable too.

One girl who asked it then added a little laugh. "I'm just kidding. I mean, I totally entirely disagree with you. But you're allowed your opinion." She and I sat next to one another in Russian. Ludmila the teacher came to church with me. I handed her a pocket Bible. She met John Goodman's wife and big lively black Mabel who said cheerful things to Ludmila on the subway and got Ludmila talking, for example about her husband, who was also interested in attending but then didn't come the next week when in fact Ludmila came again, whereupon she and Mabel set up a study. I had to quickly pedal over to the Wade Davis study.

"Please turn to *Acts*," said accented Daniel. "Jesus has just left the new doctrine with the disciples, and Peter is preaching it for the first time."

And Daniel read, "'And when the people heard it, they were cut to the heart. They asked, "What should we do?"'" Daniel paused. He began answering it himself, "Believe? Accept? Pray? No, Peter's answer was, 'Repent and be baptized, every one of you, in the name of Jesus Christ, for the forgiveness of your sins. And you will receive the gift of the Holy Spirit. The promise is for you and your children and for all.' Wade, these are the steps to becoming a Christian. And they make sense. People firstly need to bring their lives into the light."

Wade silently read through it again here on the bench. Tall, slouching, reading Wade finally asked, "What about the countless Christian people who think that believing is how you get forgiven and get the Spirit?"

"What does the Bible say?"

"So all these people are just wrong that they're Christians?"

"Are they open to looking at the Bible?" We sat in more silence.

"I have to leave," said Wade. He stood up. "Relax, I can meet again. I just have to meet this girl. Relax, I've never even seen her, and it's nothing physical. I met her on the internet." We stared at him. He said, "You guys don't know about that yet, but it's going to connect you to everything, including girls, or I mean, people."

I knew that Daniel was concerned about Wade doing anything that would close his heart. "You should come to church on Sunday."

"You know I'm a Seventh Day Adventist and I attend on Saturdays."

Daniel Bertholet groaned. "You are not with the body, as Paul describes in *Corinthians*. You are with a group that does not teach discipleship, does not teach repentance."

On school days I was giving tuna sandwiches to homeless Perry Morgan and he said, "I heard they need someone to hit some nails uptown but I don't have my tools no more." The next day I gave him five dollars for a hammer. The following day, he wasn't there. I received back my "Politics of Change" paper, and the professor had agreed with me that Hitler and Stalin seized power during a time of weak centers—Interwar citizens were on the extremes, bitter soldiers were about, and alternative structures lurked in the shadows. The professor did not agree with my use of 'indeed'. He wrote, "To be used once every fifty pages. At most."

I invited him to church. He said, while donning his professor's satchel, "One morning I was driving with Catholic friends and they said that Protestants weren't truly Christians, and precisely that same exact day I was driving with Protestants and they managed to mention how Catholics weren't truly Christians." So what? But he proudly left me that. I took it as a "No." I wished

I could have studied the scriptures with everyone in those two cars. I went home to my story and did an 'indeed' search through the large but decreasing number of pages. I deleted a few 'indeeds'. That Sunday, we had a guest preacher from the London Church, and though my "Politics of Change" professor would never hear this sermon, I was very glad that a pretty, freckly girl who had visited our Bible Talk was hearing it.

Fred Scott had that sharp and articulate British self-deprecation although he admitted having been a supreme scholar, athlete, and musician. Then one day he let himself entertain his secret curiosity about the Bible. "In fact, I actually bought one. With money. No, I didn't read it, but I had it in my pocket, my smallest pocket, because I had bought the pocketiest version possible. Nonetheless, I soon had that embarrassing situation many of you have had, orchestrated I'm sure by our sniggering God himself, when I was sitting down with friends even less spiritual than I, and guess what happened when I took off my coat.

"There it came, spinning out, ever so slowly, everyone staring, the scene unfolding with horrible suspense, waitresses dropping plates, dogs barking. And my friends, my mates, the pals who were supposed to support me—right?—they reacted with sincere mortification that a Bible had been dropped into their presence. They criticized me. They mocked me. And you know what? I was ashamed. I was silent.

"Jesus says, 'Blessed are you when people insult you, persecute you, and falsely say all kinds of evil against you because of me. Do not be ashamed. Rejoice and be glad, because great is your reward in heaven, for in the same way they persecuted the prophets who were before you.'

"You in the audience, you will be criticized if you want to be a Christian. In fact, I understand they are going to write an article in your newspaper any day now." The audience shrugged this off. Fred Scott said, "Expect to be criticized. In fact, if it isn't happening, you must wonder how closely you are really following Jesus.

"His language gets stronger, 'Be on your guard against men; they will hand you over to the local councils and flog you in their synagogues. Brother will betray brother to death, and a father his child. All men will hate you because of me, but he who stands to the end will be saved.'

"And these are the words of a man—and I'm talking about me, not Jesus—whose London Church was written up fifty-four times last year. That's more than once a week, folks. There were photos of me with captions reading, 'Evil Cult Leader.' I asked my wife, 'Honey, are you sure you want to be married to this man?' She answered me, 'Yes, I do.'"

And the audience cheered. I was glad the freckly girl was learning that while the life was indeed difficult, we responded with commitment. Fred Scott said, "That's who you want to be married to, by the way. Anyway, I called up Mike Fontenot, your own evil cult leader, and I confessed my discouragement. He reminded me about the *Acts* disciples. They met daily. Yet we get criticized for meeting a couple times each week. Those first disciples shared everything. Raise your hand if you've sold all your possessions yet. Raise your hand if you've been beheaded yet. They beheaded John the Baptist. First-century disciples were executed. They stoned Paul to unconsciousness, regularly. We are nowhere near that life. But the *Washington Post* plans to call us a cult."

Wade Davis, Daniel Bertholet, and I met with a sense of importance in the park. "I don't think it's wrong," began Wade.

Daniel read, "'I tell you that anyone who looks at a woman lustfully has already committed adultery with her in his heart. If your right eye causes you to sin, gouge it out and throw it away. And if your right hand causes you to sin, cut it off and throw it away. It is better for you to lose one part of your body than for your whole body to go into hell.'"

Wade responded, "You know of course that some people, because of that scripture, have emasculated themselves."

Daniel read, "'For I tell you that unless your righteousness surpasses that of the teachers of the law, you will certainly not enter the kingdom of heaven. Wide is the gate and broad is the road that leads to destruction, and many enter through it. But small is the gate and narrow the road that leads to life, and only a few find it. Many will say to me on that day, "Lord, did we not prophesy in your name and in your name perform many miracles?" Then I will tell them plainly, "I never knew you. Away from me, you evildoers."'"

Wade didn't say anything. I read, "'When Jesus had finished saying these things, the crowds were amazed at his teaching.'"

Wade sat up straight. He said, "You guys are right." He closed his Bible. He stood up and walked away across the park. Daniel and I sat there quietly. We had driven Wade here in Daniel's new Honda sedan, which was a gift from his parents for having graduated and found a job in global marketing. He drove me to McDonalds and bought us twenty McNuggets. "I love these things. You don't? I remember when I first came to the States, ordering food is when I noticed how weak my English was. It was during those first months that a disciple invited me to a Bible Talk. Hey, you've got to start dating some of the Sisters—why don't we go on a double date?" After my pause, he said deliberately, "Even if you don't like someone romantically it is crucial to encourage the Sisters, protect them from the world. But I don't know, maybe you do like a Sister in particular, huh, huh?" He was elbowing me. I was really enjoying his grin and his friendship. I said, "Maybe some New York artist someday. Or maybe I'll have to go over to the Moscow church and go on some dates." We drove off to midweek service. I asked John Goodman's wife about the freckly girl who had been studying with her and Kelly. She had stopped answering their calls. "She just didn't want to give it up."

At home that night I had a letter from Random House. Editor Ashbel Green was purist enough to type on an old Smith Corona, but not enough to appreciate my cobblestone story. How much he had read, and was I even close, I couldn't know from his two sentences. Well, I could keep trimming and tightening.

Also in the mail I saw a lingerie catalogue. Obviously the thing to do was not remove it from the pile. Were I to do so on this night, I might not battle strongly. In fact, soon I was sitting and turning a few pages. The photos were incredible. The women, the beauty, my desire, such a conflict of powers burned in me that my face reddened and my breath shortened. Soon I was done. Now the photos meant so much less. Yet I had fallen from that high-towered joy.

Was God still here? I sure didn't feel like all was okay between us. Nor did the scriptures feel the same. Nothing would until, well, I biked back up to Daniel's.

I told him while we stood on the grass outside. The words were humiliating but I pushed through. Daniel said, "How could you damage what we are working for? God is relying on us to be pure and obedient so that he knows to move the hearts of these guys we are reaching out to. They are completely lost. We are their light. It is true though, that I had to tell Brothers in my household that, while shaving my face last week, I considered shaving somewhere else and did begin so. I fought it off, yet I still confessed. Reks, we are in a battle. *Ephesians* says, 'Our struggle is not against flesh and blood but against the rulers and authorities of this dark world.'"

Filled with relief and peace, I walked the bike home just to be outdoors for longer. I descended through the suburbs and looked at the trees standing from the ground. Their branches blew like arms. Christ used so many metaphors about trees. The whole earth was probably just a metaphor. Seeds, seasons, harvests, weeds, fruit, he used it all for teaching. These are the things he chose to craft and then discuss. True, Bill the black grad student had said he was quite sure that if Jesus were here today he would instead drive a car, and a Taiwanese Brother had stood beside us, nodding. But Christ and I knew the truth.

My "Economics of Change" professor divided us up to negotiate a factory dispute. A French student named Philippe suggested that some labor be allowed on the board. I applauded. Philippe agreed to read some Bible with me. I brought Daniel.

Daniel said, while we waited in the SAIS lobby, "You convert one of these guys, and he can go lead a whole country of churches. We're in nearly one hundred countries now, and Kip McKean wants us in all by 2000."

"Who's Kip McKean?" I asked. French Philippe arrived, carrying a briefcase and wearing red shorts and high blue socks. As we walked up the street, Daniel said, "Reks is still a new disciple, so I'm telling him a bit of our history, which began in 1979 when a young preacher gathered a small group in Boston and told them if they're going to do this they should do it right, do it with their whole hearts. So he showed them scriptures that they hadn't understood clearly until then, though the words had always been there of course. We want to share it with you."

Philippe said, "That is quite a history." We sat down for a bite. Philippe said, "The Catholic Church reaches back two thousand years. The power has been passed directly from pope to pope until this day. Strange that you would believe it all was changed by some little man in 1979."

"You're right," said Daniel, "our faith has absolutely nothing to do with this man, it has to do with the Bible, and if you don't happen to have one in that briefcase, we have brought an extra." Daniel passed it across the table. Philippe didn't touch it. Daniel said, "The real question is whether our lives match the standard of the scriptures."

Philippe said, "And if not? Then two thousand years of Catholic tradition is meaningless?" Daniel read, "'The word of God is sharper than a double-edged sword.'" But Philippe was set on his stance, as if debating profit-share in "Economics of Change". He said, "And I do not believe we should be making sarcasm and jokes. This is one thing Jesus never did."

I asked, "How can you know if you won't pick up the book?"

He said, "That is the job of the priests at church, not boys sitting at pizza places."

Daniel said calmly, "If you would visit our church we would be happy to visit yours and truly listen."

Philippe said, "I do not go to church." He struggled not to grin. "And I know what you are thinking, but one need not go to church to be a Catholic. That is the power of tradition. It covers you through the generations." Why had he agreed to meet today? Even Daniel was willing to quit before it began. With a handshake we left.

Kelly from Wisconsin began appearing at my lunch table in the SAIS cafeteria. She would open her marked-up Bible and read some wild psalm. "'My heart is steadfast, O God, I will sing and make music with all my soul. Awake, harp and lyre! I will praise you, O Lord, among the nations. For great is your love, higher than the heavens.'" Isn't it great? She wanted to study with SAIS women.

The director of SAIS's Change Department was Grace Goodell. "Dr. Goodell," I asked, "is anyone employing the homeless?"

Dr. Goodell answered, "I know you've been doing some thinking. And even though our curriculum offers only international grassroots study, I know you want to focus on grassroots here. So you're asking me whether any local NGOs are attempting to put our homeless or disenfranchised DC residents to work? I don't know. Go find out."

At lunch, I looked up to again see Kelly, bike helmet in hand. "You can feel the stress in this building," she said with a giggle. "I walk in and feel it right on my body."

I wasn't very interested in her body. I felt bad about this. I sensed that she thought I could make a good honest boyfriend, leader, husband. She read, "'If you accept my words and turn your ear to wisdom, and if you call out for insight and cry aloud for it as silver and search for it as for hidden treasure, then you will understand the fear of the Lord.'"

"Thanks."

"'Fear of the Lord is the beginning of knowledge.'"

"Thanks, Kelly, you read that last time too."

"I know," she said, covering up her giggle. "But the Bible says to spur each other on, and that our faith is refined by fire. I think you just need to be humble."

"Thanks," I said. She said, "There are thirty-one Proverbs. And you probably figured out, since you're a lot smarter than I, that there's one for every day of the month. Today's says, "'Do not be wise in your own eyes.'"

"It rhymes."

"Yeah," she said. "But not in Aramaic, which is what Solomon wrote in, which I'm sure you knew. Everyone knows God can do great things with you, Reks, but you have to let it be *him* doing it. He says the more talent he gives, the more he expects. I just want you to be careful. Oh, Solomon also writes, 'With much wisdom comes much sorrow." I knew she did care. And I did want to be more loving to her—I could feel that muscle aching and strengthening.

I uncovered a Bible Group at a SAIS professor's apartment, and Kelly and I visited. They welcomed us with smiles, to soothe any embarrassment we might feel in having revealed we were believers. They were proud to not be ashamed, here in this apartment.

But none wanted to repent. None wanted to read about it. One said, "You're the ICC, aren't you?"

Another said, "The group from the *Post* article?"

Another told Kelly, when Kelly visited her at the cafeteria, "My parents repented for me."

Kelly and I sat quietly while they divided up the book of *Galatians* for presenting—I was waiting to pick the conclusive chapter five. Kelly likely knew where I was headed.

II

Dr. Grace Goodell sent me to the far corners of the city and in one I encountered a new operation called Ready, Willing & Able, indeed aiming to put handfuls of recovered street alcoholics to work. I found the Water Ministry, outside of which I saw a crew-cutted white guy digging through the trash. I offered him my tuna sandwich. He shyly declined, drifting off to wherever.

I told this to the Water Ministry office girl. She was white and young and experienced and she pop-quizzed me, "Do you know why he reacted like that?" I couldn't quite articulate why, and she seemed to think I was some suburban dope naively trying to do good.

She said, "Because he's mentally ill."

"That's what I meant."

"And society requires him to live on the street, without a roof or bed. And the Water Ministry has funding only for them to wash their selves and their clothing."

A church Brother, Olivier from Benin, cooked a monthly dinner at a little shelter. I helped them stir the beans. I asked Olivier about his goals as a disciple. While he considered his answer, I interjected, "I'd like to see it change DC so you could look around and say that disciples had made the city noticeably better."

Olivier was wearing an apron over his bank suit. He said, "That's exactly what my goal has been. I come from a poor country but, dang, children at least get some reading and writing there."

While most of DC was ghetto, the piece across its river was pure destruction. Trash was strewn layer upon layer and fear filled the air—an Asian-American girl had just come out here on a Housing Department assignment and had never come back. Missing, then discovered multiply raped, and dead, she took the city's attention for a few days.

No one did anything. In my search I walked the Anacostia streets and passed the hateful glances—I had an address for the ABC Development Corporation. Upstairs in a boarded-up row, the thin black man who worked there, alone, smiled when he saw me. He seemed to think that my walking up his stairs, with my notepad and satchel, meant he might get some of the help he'd long awaited. It tasted of being the American arriving in post-revolution Czechoslovakia to bring new spirit and new insight, though there hadn't been the trash-strewn streets there, not a one. All I had accomplished, it turned out, was to write a never-finished novel and become a victim of a revolution. Otherwise I had proved to be powerless. Would I ever get back to those peaceful distant lands that suddenly didn't exist anymore even though I'd just been there? Of course it had been not just a different place but a different time. So, no, there was no returning to that brief Brigadoon. The ABC guy told me, "We ain't got no jobs, we ain't got nothing happening—there's lots of people doing nothing." I walked down the block to a pizza place.

It was flanked by check-cashing and liquor establishments. Each had barred windows, some broken anyway. The Capitol building, with its gold pinnacle, loomed in the cloudless sky, right across the river. That building was as meaningless as these. The owner of the pizza place said so. Jesus said so.

I told the pizza owner that change was coming, but his brown face seemed unable to hope. "They say it time and time again. But still I live among drug-addict thieves." He was from North Africa. I brought Bill and Daniel back over with me. Walking deep in Anacostia at night, night-black Bill said, "Man I hope God is with us." Daniel was driven by the adventure, the sacrifice, and Swiss naivete.

We ordered the guy's biggest pizza. The guy was happy to see fresh faces but was determined to stay glum. He cautioned us to walk back carefully in the dark. Daniel invited him to church.

The SAIS Bible Group was lead by Professor Anne Dean, and she had a slender frame and brown hair and professor suits and possible sexual inexperience, and I bent my thoughts away from her. Each week in her cozy DC apartment one student presented a chapter.

Paul's opening to the Galatians warmed my heart and focused my mind. "Grace and peace to you from God our father and the Lord Jesus Christ, who gave himself for our sins to rescue us from the present evil age." I was grateful for this man who had walked across many deserts to teach and encourage the new fellowship of his day. Anne Dean's group, however, went too heavy on that grace. They wanted to be fine no matter what.

And they wanted the book to say so. Sure, they gave righteousness the old grad-school try. But why stress over it? This was how the first guy presented his chapter. The next week's presenter stayed right on message. "'We know that a man is not justified by observing the law but by faith in Jesus Christ.'" He proudly sing-sang the verse. The group nodded approvingly of Paul. "'I do not set aside the grace of God, for if righteousness could be gained through the law, Christ died for nothing.'"

So they were sure of their evidence—believing was enough, Christ's death was the end.

The next presenter was equally proud about her powerlessness, quoting chapter three, "'The scriptures declare that the whole world is a prisoner of sin, so that what was promised through faith in Jesus Christ might be given to those who believe.'" Their faces were confident.

But their hearts knew. So did the scriptures. "In chapter five Paul writes," I stated when it was my turn, "'The acts of the sinful nature are obvious: sexual immorality, impurity and debauchery; hatred, discord, jealousy, fits of rage; dissensions, factions and envy; drunkenness, orgies, and the like. I warn you, as I did before, that those who live like this will not inherit the kingdom of God.' No, righteousness could not be achieved through worldly power—but Paul was saying we now have a source for it. Next verse, 'The fruit of the Spirit is love, joy, peace, patience, kindness, goodness, faithfulness, gentleness and self-control. If you are led by the Spirit you are not under law.'"

Kelly nodded in agreement. She added gently in her own words, "Paul was reminding the Galatians that faith had freed them from Old Testament law. Never does he say that faith replaces righteousness. My childhood church taught that too. But I knew my life was wrong." She re-referenced chapter two, "'When Peter came to Antioch I opposed him to his face, because he was clearly in the wrong.'"

They hated us. I read verse five, "'But by faith we eagerly await through the Spirit the righteousness for which we hope.'" I re-read twenty-one, "'I warn you as I did before, those who live like this will not inherit the kingdom of God.'"

Their chorus was, "It depends how you define, 'Live like this.'"

They refused to meet and discuss their lives. It wasn't part of Professor Dean's process. At church, I told Daniel about my lustful thoughts for her. Daniel patted me on the shoulder. I never had them again. Daniel flew off to the Paris Conference, a meeting of the movement's French speakers.

"Reks," said Bill the black grad student at my first Leaders Meeting that afternoon. "How many visitors did you have at church today, how many studies did your Talk have this week?" He was holding a pad and pen.

"Really?" I asked. My heart and head might have twinged a bit. Bill might have seen it on my face. He said, "It's just for statistical purposes. Nothing more."

I told him about Ludmila, who had attended again, and our *Galatians* group, and Daniel's and my meeting with Philippe, plus Daniel and Olivier driving down to pick up the North African pizza-guy for service. Bill laughed. "I guess that one counts to your Talk even though I did brave Anacostia with you."

I went home and curled up in my reclining chair and watched the afternoon light move across the blinds, and I thought how God was truly right there, acting slowly. At the next service, John Goodman introduced new Brothers and Sisters—the church was growing—and he welcomed them to their new family. He also reported that John Causey, our sharp-suited energetic black preacher, had been promoted by Kip McKean to be a Regional Sector Leader.

John Causey pounced up to great applause. He quoted *Philemon*, "I pray that you may be active in sharing your faith, so that you will have a full understanding of every good thing we have in Christ." The *Post* article had lead to our losing the GW Center with its sunny windows. We were meeting in hotel conference halls. Afterwards I stayed in the hotel lobby with Olivier and Bill as Daniel told his incredible Paris story.

"I met so many fired-up Christians, from so many different nations. I thought this was blessing enough, but God decided it wasn't. I saw a young Polish woman who had once worked as a nanny in my home town. I have not seen her since those years and now she has repented and become a disciple, and I mean she totally loves

God, so committed, so pure. I always knew her as a beautiful young woman, but now, this is totally something else."

"Amen Bro'," hummed Olivier from Benin. Daniel continued, "So I plan to visit her in Paris again, after a long talk with John Goodman of course." Daniel laughed—we watched his giant smile. Before we left the lobby, John Goodman asked me to prepare a little sermon for next Sunday—we would be dividing up into House churches around DC and in fact around the world.

"Reks," said Tracy in Russian class, "if you're preaching—God what a weird concept—I guess I can't miss it. Or can I? Well, please no fire and brimstone." She had heard most of my pitch—she had wanted to continue calling herself Catholic but, after our talks, she gradually acknowledged discomfort with all the Jesus and Bible aspects that came with that title.

So she was searching. Another schoolmate agreed to be dragged along with her, and lo', French Philippe came too. I biked up on Sunday morning and John Goodman hurried out to me on his porch with a surprised and warm expression. "There's a great fellowship in there." He meant all the visitors, the SAIS students and the guests of our outspoken Daniel and Bill and Kelly and her sharing partner, Teresa from Cuba. Though John himself had been unable to bring anyone, he did bounce up and ignite the couch audience and introduce me. I called the sermonette, "Let go, and let's go."

The point was that we had so much we didn't want to give up in order to follow God through Christ. "But these are the things we truly don't want in our lives anyway. We just don't see this until we let go. That's when God reveals himself. When you get to the other side of the process, it feels great."

I ended, "Let's go improve the world through God's formula, which is to pair us up and put us on the street, purified of all those damaging things we used to do. But Jesus says that even if we keep quiet, the stones will cry out. So, since he doesn't really need us, there's no pressure, just fun getting it done. Let go, let's go."

Everyone stayed and chitchatted and we set up studies for the upcoming week and John Goodman jotted down the number of visitors and I biked home in the sunshine and did my Russian homework.

After Midweek, one of the new Brothers navigated the lobby crowd toward me. "I heard about you," announced big-faced jolly Tex-Mex Eduardo. "Wow I hope you don't mind me just coming up to you. This is so not me. I'm like blushing. But I heard from my new discipler"—he made quotation signs—"That you were good at reaching out. I want to learn how to share. I want to bring people into the family"—he again made quotes, mocking away any embarrassment.

"The family of God."

"Yeah, all that," he continued. "I want to get out of myself, I want to not be shy. So I guess, I guess"—he repeated with self-mockery—"I guess I'm asking for, quote, advice."

He paused. He said, "I'm totally serious."

"Where are you when I finish school at four by Dupont Circle?"

"Oh my gosh I work there, at Red Hot & Blue. I'm in management. Table management. Can I get you coleslaw with that?"

We smiled. He said, "I'll have a table awaiting you."

John Goodman called around on Saturday and soon the University Leaders were sitting on the grassy Georgetown quad. He wanted more outreach among students.

"It's time for you guys to take it to the next level and actually use the gifts God has given you, in order for the sheep to be led and the world to be saved, frankly. The book of *Matthew* says, 'To those whom much has been given, much will be expected.' We are the movement, there's really only us, that's it. I've spoken with Daniel about him leading a new ministry, with Reks assisting. The new International Ministry will comprise disciples like Teresa from Cuba, Olivier from Benin, Daniel of course, and Reks who just lived in Russia—and some of them will be leaving your ministries to join this. These are exciting times. This new ministry will reach out to the countless international people in this city. We live in a global capital, why are we not serving its needs? Well, I'm glad someone here is finally asking this." John laughed again.

I asked, "What about Eduardo?"

"I hadn't thought of him." John jotted something down. "Let's meet again Tuesday, so we can be prepared for Wednesday Midweek." He lowered his head for prayer. Soon I was walking with John, wheeling my bike. I figured we might as well take advantage of seeing some quality-looking guys. Such a guy might be walking confidently alone, a well-dressed student maybe, seemingly able to make a mature decision about his life. I didn't mind initiating for us. I said to one such guy, "If you have a sec, we're Christians and we believe in spreading the good news. John, would you hold my bike a sec?" I leaned the handlebars aside for John to hold—the fellow seemed to be listening.

Slam, my bike banged down on the sidewalk. I glanced at frozen John but continued the share. Three shares later I realized John was able to do nothing, and my bike was suffering. He mentioned, up the street, his wife's being pregnant again. "So you can expect I'll have even less time to get out there and share, instead I'll be relying on the Talk Leaders to get it done." He held my gaze, but he blushed.

At Red Hot & Blue, shy Eduardo was actually everyone's buddy and they even joked aloud—while punching in pulled-pork orders—about his conversion and Eduardo said, "I can hear you, I can hear you." In fact, he had met a SAIS guy and had scheduled a study for us right here in this booth. "I'm always meeting those types, business guys and students and everyone, but I really am shy, I am, I'm serious, I want you to know this about me. Ignore the grin, I can't help it. Deep down I'm like totally insecure."

I told him how my main motivation for that whole Russia quest might have been women, in addition to planting a new economic mind-frame, and getting some credit for it, and thus some women again. Now Eduardo's face was dead blank.

Then he grinned big. "No," he said, "it's everyone's motivation, it's in everyone's heart, if they admit it." In came the SAIS guy, actually an older professional. He had brown hair and he looked like he had simply lived twice the same life I had, including work at that same shelter, and including living in Russia, where he had had a girlfriend, whose photo he now showed us.

He was wrestling over whether to continue at SAIS, and what to do with his career, and which way to take his faith. He seemed to know everything, and yet he was lost. He told us so at our Red Hot & Blue booth, before I then biked home and did my Russian and squeezed in an hour of revising, and then sat in my lazy-boy recliner and read the Bible and fell asleep and in the middle of the night nestled into bed.

Steve Nelson of SAIS came to Sunday service with Eduardo and me. Preacher John Causey was passionate about our ridding whatever golden calves might be causing us complacency. "How is God going to grow us if we stay like this? The first-century disciples were totally committed! Look at *Philemon*, 'I pray that you may be active in sharing your faith, so that you will have a full understanding of every good thing we have in Christ.'" He called us to be, "Indignant against the complacency and mediocrity around us, and to give our best to God—our time and hearts and bodies and money. Yes, our money! We're not afraid to talk about money in this church. The Bible says don't let your left hand know what your right hand is giving. Special Contribution is coming up and every one of you needs to get your hearts right!" At times the preachers joked about this preaching style, for example John Goodman introducing us to the Leader from the Indonesia Church by saying, "And you in the front rows, you will get spit on."

Steve Nelson said at Red Hot & Blue, "Man, you guys can sing. In all my many years and miles, I've never seen singing as powerful as that. Everyone participates, everyone in unity, everyone clapping then snapping." But he wouldn't discuss the sermon. We studied a bit of scripture but he wasn't committing to us.

He wasn't committing to SAIS. Instead, his thoughts were focused on how he had done some years of work and had lived in some exotic places and didn't have much to show for it, and was unmarried, and certainly wasn't any younger. He shook his head, wearing a sad smile. After he left, Eduardo and I stayed at the booth. "He'll come around," said Eduardo. "It's about seeing the fellowship, the friendships. That's what influenced me to change."

Steve Nelson got a part-time job for National Geographic in Russia and he left in a hurry. Eduardo and I sat in the booth and Eduardo said, "There'll be others." I was nearly done with SAIS. I had analyzed the range of development and trade theory, plus Keynesian and Friedman, and I was ready to attack their chinks. And I was coming to the end of my Interwar reading.

> ***The German defeat at Stalingrad was the same old story. If properly led, men in distress will rise above themselves; if not, they will panic and cause others to do likewise.***

All SAIS knew about me now. Someone asked Tracy from Russian, "Why are you even friends with him?" She told me she had shrugged and answered, "He's not that bad actually." We still had our final Intensive, for which Ludmila passed us on to Natasha the Terrible, who criticized us, drilled us, and piled on intensive assignments. It was for our good, she said. At noon break we stood glumly around the hot courtyard, counting the remaining weeks of gulag. Tracy and Larry were there from SAIS, plus some Georgetown gal, and the token CIA guy. I got Natasha's worst glares. On Wednesdays I walked to the hotel for Midweek. Afterwards, I awaited my uptown subway.

While boarding, some tall Asian kid brushed past me. I nudged him in order to make room and to have a reason to talk. "Crowded."

"Sorry," he said, "I was just lost in thought." He kept his gaze away from mine. "Thinking about big stuff," he volunteered.

"Political stuff?"

He said, "Yeah I guess, but bigger, like about my parents because they're from China and now we're here and I was wondering why me, you know?" We set up a study. I didn't once consider what the others in the subway thought about our conversation. I was teaching people God's love, joy, peace, patience, kindness, goodness, faithfulness, gentleness, and self-control. Passionate John Causey had made us memorize the verse.

We gave Natasha politico-economic speeches prepared at length and she tore them to shreds. My themes included, "There is No Political Solution", in which I described my returning home a few years past burdened by political thought, having seen a people mistakenly sure they finally possessed their beloved free society. I'd then been unburdened by learning that only through spiritual change can people behave appropriately—myself included—and thus be free.

I recounted my trek to New York to recruit a group of activists into my political effort, and how they in fact recruited me into their non-political effort, showing me—I had already known it inside—that no social plan could work. Change came through obeying Christ. "Then the truth will set you free. Of course, the same words are written in the CIA lobby." I looked over at my pleasant classmate.

"End of the Intelligentsia" was my speech on the Russian thinking-class no longer possessing a Western utopia to dream about—that illusion had crumbled—and no longer did they have any socialist ideal, so they had essentially stopped thinking.

So they didn't exist anymore. And the current generation didn't even know there had been anything to stop believing in. They were too lost. But, there was no political solution anyway.

Tan Liu and I met in a sunny Bethesda park surrounded by small business buildings. One contained a Japanese restaurant, and its Korean cooks came out and sat in the park and Tan invited them to study the Bible too. They told him to go to hell, but Tan understood that the asking still had value. He understood ideas before I said them. "Of course the Word judges us, of course it's all God-breathed, of course you can't hide." He was a junior in high school.

Nor did I feel bad about possibly influencing him—I considered him as wise as the smug SAIS closed-heads, who were already trapped in their stubbornness and wanderlust. Tan asked, "Do you, like, go to one certain church?" I showed him. Then Eduardo joined us in that park. In a week we were walking down from John Goodman's house toward Rock Creek, to baptize Tan here among the summer trees and into the Father, Son, Holy Spirit, and a life of discipleship.

He came to the first ever International Ministry brunch. Members prepared dishes and Olivier wore full African robes and the fellowship was thriving. Elma from Nigeria converted her friend Pasquale that next week, and a Native American gal was converted too and she insisted that she be part of the International Ministry. Members from other sectors came to observe the brunch and ministry. Daniel and I hurried off to Leaders Meeting to report the good news—Daniel had also visited Paris again, and the Anya miracle uplifted the whole DC church, and perhaps Paris too. "Because," Daniel explained, here on John Goodman's couches, "Paris can use her for an upcoming planting to her very own Warsaw."

Daniel took off his glasses. "I'll tell you, I always thought that falling in love would be the end of impure thoughts. But I am so tempted now, it is incredible. The thought that my day might actually be arriving"—Daniel shook his head—"It is a battle."

Jake, an inner-city Leader, said, "You're an awesome Brother, Daniel."

III

But after Daniel's next trip, our Anya disappeared. Daniel received no letters, no answers to his calls. With chin up, he said, "I'm focusing on God. He has a mission for us and it isn't women." We stared at one another. I cared about him. He said, "I've heard preachers joke that Jesus comes back for us but some disciples complain they had yet to marry."

During our gulag breaks, the Georgetown gal said, "Homosexuality is banned by the Bible and that's intolerant so I cannot accept Christianity." I responded that there might be a case for it being not biological but environmental. I told my Prague story. I said, "I fled, but I think it was a place on the path of our lust and loneliness. Maybe some are more inclined to stay there. Didn't Freud say we're mapped out during our early years?" But she and Tracy were still affixed to the image of me in that BMW. "Ughh," moaned the Georgetown girl, "that's more information than I needed." I still thought she needed information.

In the library on a Saturday night, I took small breaks only for reminders from Jesus about the waste of time by worrying. When I stepped out to the lobby, a few other students were visible around the counter. I nodded hello to a tall, black fellow as he put on a dignified dress hat. Africans had a different manner than my black countrymen—I had uncountable of each as church brethren and I was glad. This guy was not brethren. He ignored my hello.

In fact, the same guy was at the pizza place where I then sat with Larry from Russian. Since I had pledged to say anything to anyone, I kindly greeted his mean face again. Again with morbid shock he disregarded me. Larry noticed none of it.

Larry wasn't one of these elitely together SAIS people. His handshake was weak and sweaty. Were I not a disciple I never would have spent more than minutes with him. I would've still wanted him to be happy somehow—I always felt sorry for crooked-faced guys like Larry or little old ladies on my downtown bus and so on—but I would have been friendly and moved on.

As an agreeable study though, Larry gave me a chance to serve him through Christ. I ate meals with him. I listened to him. Eduardo sat there too, nodding. With his father dead, Larry wanted to honor his infant baptism, but he knew fully nothing about the Bible. I asked, "Is there a Christianity outside of the Bible?" He stared, he squinted, he squirmed. Eduardo and I sat there with our Bibles open.

At the next study, Larry admitted to the porn. He admitted to the lies, hate, stealing, anger. His hardest thing to admit was that he had never had a girlfriend. A fellow walking by our table said, "What are you guys doing there?" He was wearing sunglasses indoors. I studied with him the next day. He was thin and tan and slightly effeminate in eyes and hands and tone. "I love God," he said. "And I don't love no one else. I have no relationship with no one else." I asked Eduardo that evening, "What is it with these Latins?"

Eduardo answered quite seriously, "It's a promiscuous culture, through and through."

"Is it the hot weather?"

"I think a lot of them were abused."

"What do you mean?"

He said, "As children. I don't know. It's like a cycle." With Larry and this Bolivian Brian coming regularly to church, a pleased John Goodman approached me to see how we could move them forward more quickly. I said it seemed largely out of our control. John paused and squinted. We agreed at least to ask more disciples to pray for them.

Natasha's final assignment concerned the 'Stalinsky Gypnosis', the Interwar trance similar to that which Hitler utilized to cause a citizenry to not even think, let alone speak, when insanely wrong things happened around them, and to them, daily. Evidently, Khrushchev's farewell-Stalin speech finally lifted the hypnosis—people looked around and could suddenly see again.

So my speech discussed how fear was no excuse, people had to somehow speak up. Natasha's scowl told me that once again I didn't know what I was talking about. But she did say, through the scowl, "You are a leader. Yes it's clear. You have potential to lead." I passed the course. Daniel and Olivier cajoled me to attend the final SAIS Happy Hour. There I toasted a beer with Tracy, who was now searching for work in Moscow. I had to meet Larry at the pizza place. Daniel and Olivier, bright-eyed about all the internationals, dipped into the bar room for one more reach-out.

I took Larry to the tall tower, *Luke* 14:28: "'Suppose one of you wants to build a tower. Will he not first sit down and estimate the cost to see if he has enough money to complete it? For if he lays the foundation and is not able to finish it, everyone who sees it will ridicule him, saying, "This fellow began to build and was not able to finish."'"

I concluded, "A convert needs to know exactly what he's getting into. Or don't start, says Jesus."

Larry said, "How could this obscure scripture mean so much?"

"Here's more, '"If anyone comes to me and does not hate his father and mother, his wife and children, his brothers and sisters—yes, even his own life—he cannot be my disciple. And anyone who does not carry his cross and follow me cannot be my disciple.'

"'Make every effort to enter through the narrow door, because many will try to enter and will not be able to. Unless you repent, you too will all perish.'"

Larry stood up from his couch. He began to tidy up his living room. He began to moan about schoolmates being too judgmental and about not having found a job and about wishing he had a girlfriend. I myself, sitting on this guy's couch, was wondering whether I was doing enough writing, whether I was using my time right. But I recalled my heavenly bike ride when I had promised God I would put discipleship first. Swiss Daniel joined us next. "Yes, Larry, perhaps you know that I fell in love with a Polish disciple. Then she had struggles, and she was silent, and next she was completely gone. But I had to focus on God regardless of all and anything else. Now I have news she is back with the church and she will be ready for me to propose. We will be together soon."

Larry laughed awkwardly and shook his head. I said, "There is indeed a right way, Larry. And it makes sense. Daniel has been a Brother for nearly five years." Daniel looked deeply at Larry and said, "How can you think you have ever made yourself right with God? Look at the scriptures, look at your life. *Isaiah* says our sin separates us from God. *Romans* says those controlled by the sinful nature cannot please God. You never practiced this because you were never taught it. You are blessed that God has sent Reks into your life. God is reaching out to you."

Larry said, "I just had no idea that's what this religion actually was. Yet, part of me still wants to think I've been a Christian my whole life." He laughed. Daniel told us, "You know, we got a study from that SAIS Happy Hour. He doesn't know you guys. He is moving along swiftly, I tell you." Larry was listening closely.

Daniel and I soon walked up the street. The miracle was back on. "It was a deep, deep trial, Reks. But faith held me up, every single day. What she did when she disappeared, I don't know, and I would be afraid to ask. That's between her and God. Finally, finally, she appeared at the Warsaw planting. She had searched them out, and now has joined them, and her Leader told me they feel very encouraged, very aided, to have such a Sister. Reks, it feels so good to trust God and then to see—when he's ready—his loving plan for us."

We arrived at Leaders Meeting. John Goodman said, "Boston has a new Sister from Russia. Her Leader called and said her former boyfriend is working down here. He's coming over tonight." Soon Daniel and I were in the midst of listening to Bob of the World Bank.

He had spied Luda at a post-Soviet flower shop and thought, "That's the girl I shall marry." Now, Luda's new conversion, though they had previously thought themselves Christians, had put a wall between them. On his own path, baby-baptized Bob had once tried an adult altar call too, then visited Pentecostals who told him if he had faith he could speak in tongues—when he then said something to Luda in Russian the Pentecostals were thrilled. "'He's doing it, he's doing it.'"

We laughed. Bob from the World Bank was thick-set, with fair and curly hair. He liked clause-filled sentences. "But you know," he started, "those guys were big on baptism too, just so you realize that others out there have some of the pieces that you guys feel so strongly about possessing solely, or I guess monopolizing, one might even say, though that can sound sarcastic. And of course sarcasm is called the lowest form of speech, though this hasn't prevented me from often being accused of using it, or abusing it. But I mean it sincerely and respectfully when I say that no matter what you call your group, such as 'the one true church', which actually, not sarcastically, the Catholics, and others, come to think of it, also label themselves—but what your movement has done, what has occurred coming out of Boston, has brought so many people to the faith, it can only be commended. Yet I'm just saying you can't think you're the only ones reading the scriptures properly? You couldn't think that. Could you?" Bob blinked.

"They don't teach repentance," said Daniel.

Bob agreed, and disagreed, at length. I was realizing the need to simplify the sentences in my book. I said, "Some teach that repentance means to be sorry, not to change." John Goodman presented scriptures to prove Bob's lack of status. Bob's arguing, over the course of a few days, slowed. It turned out he wasn't just struggling with words, but also chewing tobacco. "Ah, it's just for the stress," he said with a smile, but his eyes acknowledged the power it had over him. Daniel and I decided to fast for Bob the next day.

Late that afternoon, after biking downtown and lunching only on scripture, I called Daniel and told him I wanted to eat. He said, "Are you kidding me?" He actually thought I must have been kidding. He said, "Don't you realize, Bob's salvation is at stake. If you and I cannot use God's strength, how can we expect Bob to? How can we expect God to give him extra evidence? I ask you from love not to eat." I did not eat. But unlike Luda, our Boston Sister, skeptical Bob could not sign on to having never been a Christian—he had no scriptural stance but he still blinked and fidgeted and debated. We told him scriptures, he told us the names of some of his past ministers.

Then he admitted that he had chewed tobacco during a stressful stretch today. John Goodman closed his Bible. Bob, rising a bit in alarm, gave a defense. When he was done, John Goodman said calmly, "Bob, do you realize that Daniel and Reks have fasted all day today? They ate no food in order to move God's heart regarding you. They are sitting here this evening having not eaten since yesterday."

Bob's smile, scanning the room, now stretched wide. Something seemed to break in his golden-boy Harvard veneer. "Guys, guys, I have let you down, I have let God down. And I guess you all might say—you're certainly thinking it, and I don't judge you for it, because if the shoe were on the other foot I'd think it too—that I mostly let myself down. I appreciate you having done that for me. You are men of God, no doubt. You two." He pointed. He was baptized the next evening. He asked me to do it. Then we went to the diner.

"SAIS," said Larry at the next International Ministry brunch, "is a shadow of this. I've never seen this diversity, especially among people who care for each other." I looked at him closely, he seemed to be getting it. Olivier came up and put his arm around Larry—"How come this guy hasn't been dunked yet? Hard-hearted? We all were, don't you worry." Larry squirmed a bit under the attention. Bolivian Brian was listening. Olivier said, "You guys know about Danny's and my SAIS guy? French speaker. The dude is cruising through the studies." Nigerian Elma approached me and said, "Reks, I'd like you to come to a Georgetown seminar this week and meet the speaker. He'd really like what we have going on here."

Bolivian Brian decided to be baptized. "God is moving," said John Goodman at the next Leaders Meeting. "In fact, we've been thinking about creating a Latin Ministry under Daniel's and your International." Here on John Goodman's crowded couches, Daniel and Olivier closed the meeting by again reporting about their repenting SAIS guy, and then praying.

That week we gathered for the SAIS guy's baptism. I said, "This guy?" Everyone stared at me. I said, "You're kidding, right? This guy?" It was the tall, well-dressed African. I said, "He's the least open guy at the school."

The guy said, "I'm Joseph Kira, your Brother." He gave me a big hug. He added, "They said I certainly must have met you, that it was impossible I hadn't. Finally I guessed who. I love you, Bro'."

"I love you too."

Joseph Kira and I sat on the SAIS bench, and even though school was winding down for us, and Joseph would be joining the Montreal Church, I had my SAIS Brother. It felt good.

Bolivian Brian missed Midweek sometimes. He still seemed effeminate in his walk and talk. John Goodman said, "His repentance actually has to go further. You're his discipler."

"I'll take care of it," I vowed. I biked home, showered, revised, got in that lazy-boy chair, and read the Bible. The warmth of these New Testament passages—I consumed them very slowly—including Jesus's teachings and Paul's adventures re-converted me every night. While Jesus strained under the knowledge that his life was concluding, he washed the feet of his disciples, in a dark ancient night of real characters who didn't even understand what was occurring around them. The writing just didn't seem divined by man. "'Trust in God, trust also in me. In my Father's house are many rooms. If it were not so, I would've told you.'"

The next time I sat on Larry's couch, he said, "I just want you to know that, well, I believe I'm suffering from an inferiority complex." He walked in and out of his living room, cleaning and fidgeting. He said, "Sometimes I feel very alone, very."

I said, "We've shown you how and why to become a Christian, to get your confidence from the right source, and to have the fellowship and support and peace."

Larry said, "Look, I became a Christian twenty-five years ago."

I threw my hands up. I was due at Brian's. I continued down the sidewalk wondering whether I would lose this guy too. I stopped in his building's stairwell and went down on my knees. "Please, God, hold this guy up, keep him in, don't let him fall." I exhaled. This was all I could do, other than continue upstairs and knock on his door. Brian greeted me with a smile. "I'm fine," he said. "You worry so much. I will be at the next meeting and the next. I love God. I am skinny, I am not gay. I love the church and I try to come to all the meetings, but sometimes I just cannot. But I am a completely honest person. My mother teach me this, and then God teach me this, and you too, you teach me this. You, you are very honest. I know it for sure. But so I must tell you, because you are my brother and I love you like a brother, that, though I am not gay, sometimes I go to certain bars, just to see, just to see people I know, but I am not interested in men—nobody touch my body ever, it is pure for God. But I tell you that sometimes now I see your visitor Larry at these bars."

Jubilee Jobs was around the corner from the shelter, and at my second interview, the director said, "I get plenty of mail for Mr. Terry Flood. I guess it's a way to screen whether they're really writing to me. So, how tough would it be for you to work for a woman?" We were smiling. We were on couches two creaky flights up in their city rowhouse. I answered, "I don't think I noticed, I mean, thought about it." Now we were laughing.

Terry Flood might have been nicely pretty one day, her eyes still bright beneath her silvery hair. She asked, "How hard would it be to work here knowing that your fellow SAIS grads are earning ten times more at various world banks?"

I answered, "Never thought about it." The room's table didn't match the desk. She wanted to meet for a third time. First I attended their 'Jobs' dinner. The handful of speakers were success cases who had raised themselves to a certain wage level. And the rest of the black faces at the dozen tables were our chronically unemployed, and Terry's gentle, suburban voice called them all to introduce themselves. Each added, after their name, "Unemployed."

Mixed in were the Jubilee staff, whom I watched intently, because they were the insiders, they knew this deep world and its people and problems and the why. Big Ethel wore Caribbean hats but said in street tone—when prompted by Terry—"What attitude do I try to bring to work? Well from nine to five I just want to treat people like they was walking into my own home. No it ain't easy. But you don't come to work thinking it's gonna be easy." When I introduced myself I added, "Unemployed." I got strange eyes from the other white guy there, who was wearing a suit and may have been one of the corporate funders and may have been trying to figure out how I fit in. Terry and I soon sat again at the unmatching table above the floors of the counselors and unemployed.

"So are you going to offer me a job?"

"So do you really want to work here?"

"Why do I keep coming back?"

"I understand," she said. "But this is a life decision, in that you will be giving something up. Myself, I've been a Christian for some twenty years—God might see it differently—and this has undoubtedly been the workplace where I belong. But people should be here only if they feel deeply called."

I said, "I will do what I'm supposed to do in this life."

"Well, okay, fine," said Ms. Terry Flood. "I believe we would be blessed if you worked here."

I biked off to Georgetown. Nigerian Elma's friend was a little white guy with thick glasses and a big passion for telling his audience what could be done better in Africa. "Misguided," Elma said to me, "but the passion could be great if applied to the kingdom." Now that Daniel was married in Geneva, Bob of the World Bank joined me in commencing studies with eager Sean.

Soon we were spread around John Goodman's couches. Sean knew about development economics and he knew about Christian-Left movements that fought poverty, like Terry Flood's Jubilee, and he knew for sure he was a Christian, like Terry Flood knew. And he knew nothing about the scriptures.

But he was agreeable, touching his glasses and thinking as he stared down at a given verse, then saying, "I can accept that."

On Sunday he asked me whether we were really saying that all those other people were going to burn in hell for eternity. I said, "Sean, I know what you mean. I'm not saying that. I'm not the judge."

"Right," said glad but still-worried Sean, "God is."

"Right," I said, "but Christianity says he judges through the Word. That's the manual. We just have to choose whether we follow it." Later he said, "But this church isn't helping the poor. They're collecting money for something, but there are efforts out there which directly aid so many with much less money. You know this." I was now leading the International Ministry. And Eduardo's Latin Ministry was set to launch. He would be aided by devoted Sisters, Teresa and Paula and Michelle, and his blank face looked like he would need it.

On Sunday the whole region nearly filled Constitution Hall. John Causey, in introducing today's preacher, let us know that, "We have got to end our complacency and mediocrity. Some of you are just sitting at home, some of you haven't had visitors all summer. And we have got to end our lust. Some of you haven't left all your worldly habits. You're in *this* church? God's church?" It was British Fred Scott whom he was introducing and I was glad.

Fred said, "Yes, I'm here at your pulpit again to say I have fully recovered from being labeled an evil cult leader. It was truly a severe struggle for me, so severe that at one point I had planned to resign. Yes, quit, can you believe it? I even flew in here to tell your Mike Fontenot about it one day." The crowd applauded. "Yes, Mike, your prematurely white-haired Virginia elder who planted the London church himself. And I didn't care that he would likely tell me I was going straight to hell. The pressure of it all was too much. But of course when I told him, Mike responded quietly, 'Gosh Fred, I didn't realize you were feeling this way.'"

And Fred looked up at us. "Oh no, I never expected Mike to take the humble, understanding route. My sinful mind had expected him to be aggressive. But we talked it through. I cried. We resolved things. A month passed and Mike asked me whether I had repented. I told him, 'Thank you, Mike, yes I've repented.' And he said, 'You're welcome, Fred, but no you've not repented. I know so because you're not happy yet.'"

And Fred did seem to have lost some shine. "And Mike was right, I had to do more to get my heart right. Well, finally I'm back in London again and I'm happy again and the church is growing, amen. DC, thank you for my year here." We cheered.

"Upon returning home," Fred continued, "I looked some people up. I suppose time compelled me to do a sort of inventory. Well, one old bloke from my football team who had always had a temper, now it had got the best of him. He apparently took on a whole other team in a fight—this is not funny—and his teammates didn't help him, and he was beaten to the point of brain damage. He damaged himself for life. Another mate graduated into a very high-paid computer job up in Liverpool. He became financially very successful. On Friday evenings he takes the train to London and spends the weekends with expensive prostitutes. That's what he does with his time and money and self. A third fellow killed himself entirely. He did it, apparently, out of sheer aloneness. A fourth friend is a minister. He is teaching people that they're just fine, that their lives of sin are simply forgiven, not to worry. He is misleading people. And he knows it. Brothers and Sisters, people in London are lost. They can call me 'dangerous leader' if they want. But the kingdom is fighting for purity. Jesus says, 'Blessed are the pure in heart for they will see God.' Do you see it? The Bible says you can see God. Enjoy the rest of your Sunday."

I had seen it. And I reflected on it every night in my recliner. Seeing did come through purity. Impurity clouded it. "Hold to my teachings and you will see the truth." I saw God in what the world would never accomplish. It would never right itself. That was why I belonged now at Jubilee, simply serving.

I shared office space with the bookkeeper. Kelly from Wisconsin biked over. "Teresa disappeared," she told me.

I shrugged. "She simply didn't call you for a day."

"No," said Kelly, "when you have a partnership like that, you know when it's amiss. I'm really worried about her." Three days and three Jubilee visits later, Kelly hadn't found her.

Disciple Michelle stopped by Jubilee and said that her psychiatrist had just told her to stop being a disciple. Instead, free time and reduced stress and sexual freedom were recommended. On Saturday morning, Elma, Sean, and Pasquale knocked on my door.

I stepped outside and raised my brow. A white-haired man sat in the front of the car. The back door of the car opened. Out stepped Teresa. She walked, smiling, up the driveway.

Next came her father. We sat in my basement den. They played an MTV video criticizing the New York City Church. Elma said, "It's a cult, Reks. You know it is." Sean smirked. Teresa's father described how he had flown her down to Key West for a holiday—waiting there was a couple who had once led in the church and now offered to de-program members. "Reks," said Teresa, "it took about three days. I was fighting it, I didn't want to face it. It was so hard."

I said I would watch the video again sometime. "What else do you want me to say?"

Teresa's father asked, "Isn't it true they don't let you hear criticism? But the Bible says, 'Test everything.'" Now he was a Bible scholar, after a week in Key West.

They handed me the video on the way out the door. Elma said, "We just wanted to say goodbye, because, we respect you, and we know they won't let you talk to us again." Pasquale hugged me. How was I going to explain this to Bob of the World Bank?

The video showed a former Sister from the Arts Ministry who said she had been pressured into contributing a large portion of her father's bequeathal and now it was gone. They interviewed parents of a former Hawaiian Brother who felt their son took his life because of the church. It interviewed a cult psychologist who said actually there was no such thing as brainwashing, the truth could not be washed from people's minds. "They can still choose." The video tried to interview leader Kip McKean but he and his wife declined to comment to the camera, while awaiting their hotel elevator to slowly, finally close away. It ended with the New York congregation singing, everyone standing and snapping and singing in rhythm, the lyrics fading out slowly into blackness, "C'mon, won't you join us today? C'mon, c'mon, won't you join us today?"

Bob blinked, outside Leaders Meeting, and he watched my face to see whether I was serious. We went inside and learned that Tan Liu had left the church too, and also Paula, the third and final of Eduardo's would-be Latina leaders, accompanied by her church boyfriend, suddenly now her worldly boyfriend. Bob whispered, "Is this a normal week in the kingdom?"

I tried to cheer him up with Eduardo—we had lunch and Eduardo used a Bobism, "Hey pass the sauce, buddy, uh, I mean, Bob." And when Bob allowed a smile, Eduardo laughed his big laugh, which could shake the rafters. So we all laughed. Plus, Luda was moving down from Boston to retry the relationship.

After work, Eduardo was sometimes waiting on Jubilee's front steps. To get here he walked the bridge that crossed over from the subway station. Here at this edge of the expansive Capital slum lived ethnic mixes and young professionals and local-bar goers and some artists and even embassy people.

"Okay Eddie, here's the plan," I said. "We just take the Bible to the people. We don't belt anyone with it but we don't hide it. We're straightforward, showing people the open book, its pages and words, whoever'll listen." Eduardo nodded. He wanted to break out. He said, "That's perfect."

I said, "We'll take it to that bridge with those rush-hour walkers. No more sharing just to waiters. No asking for the time so we can start up a conversation. No handing out the occasional Sunday invitation—we're not satisfied with that. That's not what they did in *Acts*, that's not using the sword."

Eduardo said, "Or those other churches handing out pamphlets."

"They're handing out litter. They're not opening their mouths. Not to mention they have the wrong doctrine. Even the occasional freak who speaks through the megaphone on some busy corner, he's not talking to anyone. You and I are going directly to the people, politely and honestly, book open. We will literally reach out to them."

Eduardo said, "If we're going to be disciples we should do it right." I locked up the Jubilee door. The late afternoon sun hung high. We read Jesus's final prayer-in-the-garden, and then we prayed.

"Rise, let us go." We walked the street toward the bridge. My fingers already marked certain pages. Eduardo was right in step. I remembered a pre-bullfight quote from Hemingway.

> ***It was like certain dinners I remember from the war. There was much wine, an ignored tension, and a feeling of things coming that you could not prevent happening.***

IV

The bridge had wide sidewalks. No one needed to feel trapped. Our worst response was, "Are you really doing this? Are you really this type of terrible, invasive person?" No one stoned us. We were ignored plenty. We often got, "No, thank you." We got, "No, I've read it."

On future outings we saw the same people. A blond guy patted my shoulder in order to put himself past me. On another occasion he stopped. "You guys are kidding, right?"

We met the next day up in a plain Chinese restaurant on the subway side of the bridge. "I thought this was some fraternity prank or something." We studied all week. The blond guy worked in his congressman's office. His five-o'clock shadow thickened each day. Eduardo said, "You're so open, it's obvious you care what it says."

The blond guy said, "I guess my mother used to read a bit to me. Otherwise I don't know why I'm sitting here."

I read aloud, "'If anyone comes to me and does not hate his father and mother, his wife and children, his brothers and sisters—yes even his own life—he cannot be my disciple. Anyone who does not give up everything he has cannot be my disciple.'"

The blond guy looked down at these words for a long time. He said, "She didn't read this one." I said, "Without it, a disciple couldn't survive. Too many loving hands would pull him out." He was still staring downward.

"He's the perfect white guy," said Eduardo when we were alone eating our hot-and-sour soup. "Smart, friendly, confident. He's the guy the fellowship needs." But with the blond guy we were back to just hello on the bridge. The next guy we plucked up was a skinny young photographer for the *City Paper*. After several sessions at empty Bruce Lee's Chinese restaurant, he revealed he was drowning in lustful thoughts.

"You guys have made me think, that's about all I'll give you right now, but it's something. And what I do want to tell you—and it's not a confession—is that I've now been to a psychiatrist, just this week, in search of therapy. I haven't found it yet, because they're just giving out pills. Anyway, I'll be looking for you guys out there. I just don't have more to give right now."

"I've always wanted to be an artist," said Eduardo when we were alone again.

I said, "New York has a whole Arts Ministry."

"Listen," Eduardo said. "This bridge thing is right. People see we're real, we're living it, we're trying."

I said, "Through us they might get a glimpse." The late afternoon sun glared down again the next day we meandered across, stopping when we wanted to speak to an approaching walker. If they planted their feet and gave that extra second I calmly hurried to a verse which might meet their needs.

"Dear friends, let us love one another, for love comes from God. If we love one another, God lives in us and his love is made complete in us."

One guy in a suit lingered, subtly smirking as I read. He said, "You have books missing."

"You're Catholic. You have Jesus missing."

"No, we simply acknowledge he had a mother, that's all."

I said, "And many Fathers." We were standing in the middle of the bridge's wide sidewalk. The guy asked, "How do I know you even believe this? You're influencing people but maybe you don't believe what you're saying." I looked him long in the eye—it was the smirk that concerned me. Eduardo said, "But we do believe it. Don't be upset at each other." Mark Ham agreed to meet at Bruce Lee's.

He brought his rotund friend Frank, who knew even more about Catholicism being the true church. I used scripture, Frank used logic. "Wouldn't the virgin mother of the Lord be worthy of reverence?"

I had to quote the, "'Hate your mother,'" and also Jesus addressing this very mother of his, "'Who is my mother?'" She had been standing outside wanting to talk to him—she wouldn't even come in where he was doing whatever he did. So he pointed to his disciples and said, "'Here are my mother and brothers. For whoever does the will of my father in heaven is my brother, sister, mother.'"

Frank popped large pills to enable his General Tso's Chicken—he already had a shoulder twitch going—and these scriptures weren't helping. In response to their priest power being stronger than scripture, I showed Apostle Paul instructing us each to put on the full armor at all times—including the Word—and Jesus calling us all a royal priesthood, saying about leaders, "'You know that the rulers of the Gentiles lord it over them, and their high officials exercise authority over them. Not so with you. Instead, whoever wants to become great among you must be your servant, and whoever wants to be first must be your slave.'"

John Goodman asked me, "Leadership wants more baptisms this month, so can you be accountable to make that Mark guy happen by the end of the month?" I said I couldn't know, but let's try.

In a church office where Mark Ham did volunteer accounting, John Goodman related his own Catholic background. Mark smirked. John recounted learning the wrong doctrine and thus living the wrong life, until he "got it right with the God of the Bible".

"Show me verbatim," said Mark Ham, "where the Bible says, 'Do not masturbate.'"

John paused. But he liked a fight—he quickly adopted a combative tone. "It means nothing to you that Jesus says cut off your hands or eyes if they're causing you to sin? Or that Paul goes to the effort of specifically ruling out sexual immorality, impurity, *and* lust? How explicit does it have to be for you to remove that smile? *Ephesians* says not even a hint of sexual immorality."

Mark Ham's expression was unchanged. He said his eyes and hands weren't necessarily a problem, nor were lustful looks at women. "Sometimes I've masturbated over the Bible, looking at the verses and thinking about our Lord."

We left. Eduardo and I met a Saudi guy on the bridge. He had a bright, constant smile and he nodded agreeably to most everything we read, and then he hurried off to his pizza delivery job. The next time we met he showed no sign of having heard a word we'd said. He nodded and nodded. Then he called us late at night and wanted to sleep at our houses or wanted us to drive him to different neighborhoods. We visited his pizza place and his bright smile widened and he expressed honor at length about our visiting. We stopped by again and he was gone, the owners knowing no whereabouts. We met a soft-spoken Turkish guy and I biked to his grad-school apartment and we peacefully studied the scriptures. At the end of the week, John Goodman joined me there.

When we came to the chapter in Antioch where the disciples won many converts while others stoned Paul and left him for dead, John said, "What do you think about these responses?" Our mustached study said calmly, "Yes, this is very near my home." We stared. Suddenly Paul's ancient adventures were on this same earth as ours—John said he would squeeze this into his next sermon. But we couldn't make Abdul follow along. I shook hands goodbye with him.

Eduardo and I met a British guy on the bridge. He was young and tall and balding and dignified. He wanted to meet with us. We upgraded slightly from Bruce Lee's. At Pizzeria Uno's we ordered drinks and we gently probed to no avail for his Bible outlook. He wasn't biting.

When dinner arrived he said, "Doesn't the Bible say to keep one's acts of righteousness unseen, and that those who announce it in the street actually have no reward?—is it appropriate for you to pray aloud like that for the food?"

Eduardo closed his whispering mouth, then opened it again but nothing came out. Our Brit ate. Maybe he had simply been looking for friendship, even Christian friendship. But not the type that talks about it.

Jorge just appeared in our daily routine. Eduardo and I sat around trying to figure out whether we had found him on the bridge or whether some Sister had handed him off to us. But because he wanted to meet every day, and was deadly serious about this, he emerged above the many and became our top priority. The little Chilean, within his quiet humming and his long glares at the verses and then us, was determined to come fully clean before his God. "You can," said Eduardo. I said, "People grabbed Jesus in the street, even when his disciples blocked them."

Jorge said, "Though I am young, I was a judge in my Chile. I put people in prison whom I knew were innocent. They were standing there in front of me and I did this."

"Okay," I nodded. Big Eduardo was listening carefully. Jorge said, "I struggle daily with sexual thoughts." We nodded. He wore little suits. His stubbly face showed that more cleansing was coming. "And impurity." We met again.

Jorge said, "I have continued to have impure thoughts and acts. Sometimes regarding you," he said to my eyes. Though we were supportive this young little man refused to smile. "But I know that God is calling me. I know it. I want to arrive there, with your help. It is all I want. I want to get up to the top of that pure tower you mentioned." He was taking us there with him.

"My heart is so refreshed," said Eduardo on the phone. "Oh my goodness, this study is so powerful."

I said from my Jubilee desk, "I'm converted all over again. This is food. This keeps us alive." I called him again at noon—I shared a verse—and I called again at day's end. Eduardo said, "I know, I know. Man cannot live on bread alone."

I said, "Man cannot live on scripture alone, let's meet for dinner before Jorge arrives." On Sunday, after knotting Eduardo's tie, we drove down to Catholic Law to pick up Jorge. He quietly hummed in the back seat, his new Bible on his lap, no smile. For another week of evenings we sat together, Jorge looking long at the verses, his hand on his stubbly chin. "My grandmother was sick and dying. I was asked to care for her. I beat her. Many days, I just beat her."

We nodded. He admitted he was still struggling with impure thoughts and acts. "That's bad," I said. Disappointed Eduardo stared into Jorge's eyes—Jorge didn't flinch. We had all hoped he was making divine progress. We had hoped to see the power. I said, "If your hand causes you to sin…" We sat there sharing gazes. I leaned toward my satchel and removed my Swiss Army knife. I unfolded the blade.

Jorge slowly extended his arm, exposing the wrist. I put the blade on the wrist.

"Wait," exclaimed Eduardo. "You don't have to, you can change. God can change anything, if you want it." Jorge wanted it. In another week he became our Brother. After the baptism, Eduardo, Bob, Luda, and I sat around the late-night diner.

Bob seemed to have recovered from those fall-aways. Luda said, "I read Elma's negative article in the Georgetown paper. She criticized Leadership and also what she called our unnatural openness with one another."

Bob said, "She's living with Sean."

I said, "What I miss is that Eddie was supposed to be leading a new Latin Ministry with those three Sisters."

"Oh my goodness," said Eduardo, "I prayed and prayed." He laughed so loud and long that we were beginning other conversations when he re-emerged and said, "I prayed so hard for God to get me out of that, for him to kill it."

Luda said, "And so three Sisters fell away." Bob said, "Three strong Sisters." I said, "All into sexual sin." Eduardo filled the diner with his laughter.

"I'm so sorry," he said, "I had no idea I was that powerful." That week, I got a call from a Sister I didn't know—she was asking whether I would go out after the Singles Sermon and have coffee with another Sister I didn't know. I thought, Dang, I wasn't planning to go to that mandatory event, since I had Leaders Meeting on Tuesday and Midweek on Wednesday and International on Saturday and then Leaders again after church on Sunday. I'd been silently considering skipping Friday.

But I agreed to this coffee arrangement. This Sister was apparently an artist. If she was black, fine—many in the church were smart and pretty. I made Eduardo cancel his work shift—this could otherwise get him out of a meeting or two.

A new guy was giving the sermon, some tall muscular single Brother transferred in from the Dallas Church. Afterward, I glimpsed, from the back a new white Sister. She was in the lobby, talking with another Brother. Dang, she was wearing a dark top and from behind I could still see the edge of the outcroppings on her front. I looked away. In the parking lot she came right at me.

So it was her. "I've never seen you before," she said with outright interest. She was wearing jeans and nice sandals. Her dark hair was cut as short bangs, though her eyes were not Debbie's green but a sky blue. I really hadn't seen a Sister anywhere near to my tastes before, I now realized.

At our group coffee she shone a big white smile at me. She had a friend with the same artsy black hair, though without the comely structure in face and body. This other watched me sternly from the end of the table. Eduardo got her laughing, and in fact she and this mysterious Catherine had both been Maryland disciples for over a year. They were still laughing about non-disciple subjects, such as old relationships and potential new relationships. Then Catherine, back in the parking lot, said, "I'll definitely call," which was unsisterlike, but I sensed that it was from maturity. I went home and curled up in bed and begged God not to play with my heart. I felt intoxicated with hope and desire, and I told him that I was entrusting it all to him.

I was downstairs at my counseling desk when she did call me. Her friend was celebrating a birthday—would I bring some Brothers out on Saturday? I wanted to make it special. Olivier from Benin said, "My man, after a nice dinner, we take them to the roof of the Kennedy Center for cake."

First I would meet Catherine at her mall—she managed an art store or something. She wasn't wearing that dark top tonight but a pale-green dress and I almost walked by without noticing her awaiting me on a mall bench.

She too wanted to make the date special—on the Kennedy Center roof she had a cake not just for Jenny's birthday but also for me. "We have many births," she explained.

Later at the diner she said, "No, I wasn't happy after baptism! I cried. I was wondering how I was going to do this. And how I could bring anyone into this impossible thing. Plus, no sex? It could be years." I gulped. Her sister had met disciples but Catherine ended up converted. When I dropped Eduardo off, he said, "I want to be an artist."

I asked, "What about that little camera that guy gave you before disappearing from Bruce Lee's, can't you use that?" But Eduardo was off in some daydream.

We walked the bridge and talked with hundreds. We ate alone at Bruce Lee's. I biked home and sat in my chair and read Paul's *Corinthians*. "While we are in this tent, we groan to be clothed with our heavenly dwelling." I finished up the last Tolkien book. It ended with farewells among the longtime adventurers. The author had brought us to the very end of his deep wide epic.

> ***At last the three remaining companions turned away, and never again looking back they rode slowly homewards; and they spoke no word to one another until they came back to the Shire, but each had great comfort in his friends on the long grey road.***

At Jubilee my desk phone rang and it was a literary agent. My heart sped—it was the voice of an industry guy who had actually read my chapters. I didn't know how many precious seconds I had. But he did the talking, while I did the agreeing and thanking.

Jeff Kleinman's point was that he felt both intrigued and confused. "Normally if I'm reading a submission and it describes a character watching what's outside his train instead of showing us what's seen, I'll pass. But yours almost works. Still there's some intrinsic problem there."

"You're right."

"But I read on."

"Thank you."

"The problem is subtle but it's in every sentence, such as subjects put at the end like, 'Out the window passed a shrill whistle,' or, 'On the table sat a book of poems.' How to explain the awkward syntax?"

"Slavic languages and Victorian novels."

"If you fixed it, I might look again."

"Thank you."

Bob said with his stressed, humorous cadence, "Imagine if they told James Joyce, 'Ah, James, we've now read your manuscript, uh, *Ulysses*, and, well, the language and style don't completely work and, uh, the syntax is confused, entirely, and oh, by the way, it's going to be the greatest novel of all time." I smiled. He was on the phone with me from his World Bank office.

I was glad to have him beside me at Leaders Meeting. But while Leadership outlined our goals, including heart changes among all our members, and growing each of our Talks this year by twenty, and four to six more dating couples in each, plus more monthly baptisms, Bob began wiping his brow—church Sunday had now gone into Sunday evening. We headed out but John Goodman took me aside and said, "Annapolis Leadership says Catherine has the most potential to lead out there, bar none."

I nodded. There was some thrust in the statement. I felt it in my chest as I looked in his eyes. John knew best how I could lead and follow. Did they know I had questions about the statistics measuring and sometimes even the loudness of sermons and also the over-mentioning of sharing faith? I was looking forward to the opportunity to discuss these.

Bob and I took the subway home—I had convinced him not to drive—and we waited twenty long minutes for a train and the same again at our transfer, and Bob's face looked irritated, worried, tired.

I sat down in the dark, fragrant interior of Catherine's car and realized I was sitting on a disc case. It contained both the Smiths and Everything But The Girl, precisely what I would have wanted her to have. The case actually didn't belong to either disc and she couldn't locate their cases but we did find many other empty cases. She said, "Oh well."

On the way home I did the driving and we caught glances while chatting. Each time I looked over at her she had that big white smile. She was wearing glasses. Their silver frames nicely emphasized her eyes and cheek bones. Instead of phoning her that week, I decided to write a letter. I wrote that maybe we should keep our focus on God, and not see each other until the upcoming Regional.

At Jubilee Jobs staff meeting, Director Ms. Terry Flood calmly jotted notes while letting the Reverend Bobby Barnes lead. Terry was a reverend too, though in an entirely different church than Reverend Bobby Barnes. Gloria the bookkeeper called him the Rev.

The Rev was a roly-poly black walrus, I thought while watching him joke with George our custodian, whom Terry also invited to present a staff-meeting update. The Rev said to me, "But we don't joke when it comes to the Applicants. You see, Reks, you can't baby them. They need to *work* their way out of their troubles, their addictions, their unemployments. Work is their way out. Ask George, he'll tell you."

"I'll tell you," said George, "I been there. You can't baby 'em. The Rev ain't lying."

"No, I ain't lying," said Reverend Barnes. "If you baby them, they act like babies. Some of them's older than me. But they still need to be pushed out, pushed forward—they still need the tough love. Sometimes you need to cut the unbiblical cord. Just cut it." The job counselors quietly listened, including strawberry-blond Annie who was eating it up and night-black Tracie who rolled her eyes. Terry calmly took notes.

She asked for the weekly statistics and we reported the number of job interviews and job placements. I said, "Maybe more Applicants will keep their placements if we strengthen our structures." Terry asked, "Reks, can you say more about that?"

"You go, Reks," said both George and Gloria.

I said, "Maybe we need to mimic a job right here for a week, with them showing up on time each day."

Tracie said quickly, "He's right."

Annie said, "We could teach some workshops."

George and Gloria said, "You go, everyone."

Terry asked, "Ethel, what do you think?"

Big, blank-faced Ethel the receptionist raised her gaze from the floor and again betrayed that she did have opinions. "I think they need more practice here before they keep going out there and quitting or getting fired or not even showing up at all."

George said, when he and I were alone in the office during lunch, "Yeah, Mr. Reks, I'm blessed to be here right now, pulling trash. You know I jumped out a third-story window, don't you?"

I asked, "You didn't want to live?" He laughed, "Shoot, that was the point—I wanted to live. There was a gun pointed at me. I ran through someone's bedroom and went right through the glass. I broke my leg. I ended up at the shelter. That's when I started going to the Program."

"Whose gun?"

George laughed again, showing his gold teeth. "Shoot, I don't know, I was just drugging. I used to live on a bench in Lafayette Park."

"That's opposite the White House."

"Maybe so. My sister used to come down there each day and scream at me to get up and fix my life. I just wanted her to go away—I was just trying to sleep. I was drugging, that's all."

Why did I almost feel like crying for this unknown sister who wanted her brother just to get up from the bench? I said, "Maybe the problem wasn't the drugs but the homelessness, and you just needed help out of that." George responded, "Man, one night it was raining and I was with a buddy on those benches and some Chinese guy in a suit came up with his two fists closed. He didn't say nothing but just handed us each a big wad of money. Man, we was each holding eight hundred bucks. That guy just walked off into the fog."

"That's three months rent."

"That money was gone by Monday. We had the biggest party. We was drugging, Reks, that's what I'm trying to tell you. First I needed the Program. That's how I got off that bench. I've been clean five years."

When I stepped out for lunch, Counselor Tracie was coming back up the sidewalk. "Reverend Tracie," I joked. She scoffed. I asked, "You go to any church?" She groaned, "Ah, man," as if she had stubbed her toe, "I stopped going two years ago. I think about it every day."

I asked, "What kind of church?" But I had a feeling. She said, "Ah, man, it was the best church, everyone committed, everyone living it. I just got tired or something, and my husband had stopped going and all. He fell away. Man I miss it, I need it."

"I go to that church."

"Get out, no you don't!"

"I'm a disciple."

"Oh my goodness." Counselor Annie ran up to us. She took both our arms and tried to walk us back the way I'd come. I left them and crossed the street to Jubilee Housing. I wanted to get to know a fellow there—he was bright and he had said he might visit the church.

Disciples were abuzz about the upcoming Regional—we would see Brothers and Sisters from other Sectors, we would hear a sermon from one of the top guys, and we might finally fill every seat in Constitution Hall. We would be seeing God's movement with our own eyes. This Jubilee Housing fellow came down with me and Eduardo, and we linked up with Bob and approached one of the many doorways. It happened to be where Catherine was ushering.

She wore a blouse and skirt and heels. She was surprised by us suddenly standing over her and my introducing big Bob and tall Jubilee John Hildebrand.

Afterward, Bob said, "She was very poised." Of course he couldn't have said she was very hot, even if he thought so. But I was curious. Meanwhile I still worried about him—he looked a little strained as we navigated the crowded Hall.

John Causey was on fire. That was how he described it himself, and the crowd cheered. He said, "No more complacency, no more mediocrity, out of your comfort zone. Now! I'm not here to wear a white hat, just like you're not in the kingdom to be happy—you're here to do God's work. Jesus says deny yourself. He didn't complain about being tired!"

Causey continued with a tale, "There were two rooms, each with a giant pot of stew and a giant spoon and a group of hungry people. A visitor entered one room and saw that the people were starving. There was food right there! But the spoon, it was too long to use. The visitor went to the other room and the people there looked nourished. But their spoon was too long too. They were feeding each other! Disciples, how do I know we're not feeding each other? Because I hear about your sin! If you were feeding each other's hearts, you wouldn't be in sin! How do I know you're not feeding each other? Because you're not sharing your faith, not bringing visitors for God. How do I know you're not feeding each other? Because you're not giving. Average contribution is going down. It should be going up, every single month. How do I know you're not getting fed? Because you're criticizing the church. You're being negative and critical about the Leaders. Younger disciples are hearing your criticisms. You're killing their faith!" Big-bicep Anton, Singles Ministry Leader, gave the close. "I am so convicted! I need to start taking better care of my Brothers and Sisters. Amen? Amen!"

"I thought it was powerful," said Catherine, as we gathered in the lobby throng. John Hildebrand said, "Wow, the passion here. That's one of the problems in the global church today, young people aren't active."

Bob wiped his brow and said, "It could really seem like there's a mold for these sermons, no?" He spoke cautiously but seemed unable to resist. His Bible was tucked under his suit sleeve. He continued, "I think the mold includes making the disciples—the members—take home a certain stress, no?" I wasn't happy about him asking this in front of John Hildebrand, but Bob then kindly volunteered to take him out for a bite with Eduardo so I could have my coffee-talk with Catherine. Catherine and I walked to a café and sat caddy corner at our table. We had the green light to start deeper dialogue. First we prayed, during which we took each other's hands and fingers.

I said, "I think that having been born again makes this a first for me, so I don't exactly how to say this." She said, "Reks, this is new territory for me too." I thanked her. She was awaiting me. I said, "I like you."

She said, "I like you too." She gave me a little bag of gummy bears. I gave her my best Bible, blue and bendable—I had been buying dozens for $9.99 to give to studies. This one I had seasoned the best, with passages underlined in a range of colors. I gave her a hug."

At Jubilee, Terry Flood told the dozen faces at our first-ever workshop, "We have increased our structure a bit. It means that, for those of you who choose to continue coming here on-time this week, there might be a job for you next week. And it might be in fast food or cleaning or dishwashing or a nursing home or some form of labor. The pay, meanwhile, will be near to minimum wage, or likely, minimum itself." The Applicants jostled and murmured—based on Terry's demeanor they sensed they could even complain aloud. "Okay," said Terry. "But how much are you earning now?"

They were silent, they had to think about it. I thought with them. Terry said, "Zero."

"Yeah," they all agreed. "That's right, she's right." They nodded with understanding. Terry said, "So, as low as the minimum sounds, it's actually a step upward. Then what's the next step?" She was drawing stairs on the board. One fellow, wearing his Sunday suit, answered, "To show up and work hard until you get a promotion or a better job."

The group said, "Yeah, that's right, he's right." Terry said, "Good, but what happens on this first job when you get sick and still have to work, or when the supervisor yells at you unfairly, or maybe he's the wrong color, or maybe it's a woman, or your old friends don't like that you now go to sleep early, or you realize the paycheck doesn't cover your bills and so working simply doesn't seem worth it, or they cancel the bus line and now it takes three, not two, transfers to get there? Some of this will happen. What do you do when continuing to work seems impossible? Do you quit?"

Heads cocked in thinking. Terry finished drawing her stairs. She said, "There are no broken lines. If you quit, you start again at the very bottom, unpaid, older, even further from your top step. To that second step they take people from the first step, not from unemployment, not from this room."

I said, "You can't get there from here." They laughed, saying, "He said you can't get there from here." I was wearing a floral tie. Terry said, "I'm sure that each of you already has interesting experiences to share, so Reks would like to sit down and listen and discuss." She gave me the chalk and said, "Thank you, Reks." They said, "Thank you, Reks."

When I was back upstairs, I began crafting a new fundraising path for the agency, while listening to Gloria on her adding machine at the other desk. We were bracing for welfare closing down. More and more Applicants were coming through our door—they sat in chairs facing Ethel's counter. Clearly, the corporate world would need to get deeply involved. I planned to spread this little proposal among them, and we would also invite them to help serve dinners and conduct mock interviews.

Terry hired Mary de Marcellus, a young Princeton graduate with a French mother but who jived right into the mission. She was coming from Catholic Relief, having tracked down Terry in order to be closer to the grassroots, closer to the need, closer to inner-city Black America. She was tall like Annie, though brunette. Annie came upstairs to visit me. Her strawberry hair bounced on her fair shoulders. She sat in my guest chair. I walked her right back downstairs, and I began interviewing the next dinner speaker—we were making a booklet of success stories. Tonishia wore a brown suit. She was a clerk at Perry's Lumber. She had health and dental. "For both me and my babies."

She said, "Ms. Terry was my counselor. I had just come out of the Program, so she got me the therapeutic job. I was making nothing and saving every penny of it. Ms. Terry is a smart woman, we all know. Problem is, so am I, and I let her believe I was ready to move to the next step. Child, I was not ready. But she got me to CVS and it was a raise and I was doing a register. Now, an alcoholic ain't supposed to be around money. No, no. I stole. Yeah, I stole money from the register. Their money, from their register. You think they didn't notice?

"So I didn't deny nothing, and they didn't press. But I was back at the beginning. Minimum. Night cleaning. Grandma having to watch my babies. This time I didn't even mention to Terry about next steps, I waited until she felt I was ready. In a year, a whole year, she got me the Perry's interview. And here I am, a speaker. You all serving that pasta stuff or you gonna get some meat this time? Nah, I'm just playing." She squeezed my arm. I explained, "A local church donates the meal—I'll check their budget."

"Now don't be starting trouble," said Tonishia. I went off to lunch with Jubilee John Hildebrand, who hailed from North Dakota, and who said, "Springtime is dangerous because women begin to wear less clothing." So he was indeed fighting the fight.

"More leg," I said.

"True," he said. "But that's not the part I struggle with." His journey had included helping numerous churches throughout the Midwest and inner-cities and South America. He was committed and he seemed deeply peaceful.

He wasn't a Christian, that was crystal clear. It was clear to one who read the Bible five times daily to himself and maybe five more to strangers and so knew precisely what it said a Christian was—as clear as the scriptures allowed, and they allowed a lot, the clearer the more I read.

When I opened the scriptures with John Hildebrand he did know all the books, but none of the answers. Who's a Christian? How do you become a Christian? What does repenting mean? What's the line on sex? What's it say about attending church? What's it say about attending multiple churches? Whom have you taught, how, whom are they teaching?

He frowned at me. But still he spoke peacefully. "Believers have been wrestling with this since the beginning." When I showed him how *Hebrews* says that the Word judges, he didn't like my judging. He said he didn't find this approach healthy.

But on his face I saw the common dismay of being suddenly trumped, of knowing that he should have learned his own book better, and wondering how he hadn't. Anton joined us at our next lunch. He was tall and experienced, and I was glad to see him up in our neighborhood—we could partner in a lot of studies here. "John," said Anton. "Just ask some people at your church, or churches, some of these questions we've been asking. See if they have answers, consistent answers, consistent with the Bible. See if they even bring you to the Bible." I liked John and didn't enjoy seeing him feel low. Anton patted him on the shoulder. "I've been here, man."

John and this world of the Christian Left didn't want repentance, they wanted tolerance. Terry Flood described another Jubilee minister's feeling wronged by her. Terry told me, "I apologized and she and everyone accepted it, but here this grown woman still needs to keep making soft little mentions of it, and no one knows what to do."

I said, "She hasn't forgiven." Terry said, "I think you're right—that's simply what it is." I flipped open the Bible, "'If you do not forgive men their sins, your Father will not forgive your sins.'" At last I was reading and communing with Terry.

She said, "No, I don't believe that." I said, as if she had simply forgotten today's date, "No, yeah, *Matthew* 6:14, right after the beatitudes."

Terry said, with eyes thinking, even glancing across at the words on my page, "No, I believe you just won't *feel* his forgiveness."

I said, "But it's right here."
She said, "Yes, but that's what I believe."

Catherine's and my next date was a picnic with Annapolis Brothers and Sisters. "Can you imagine," said a black Sister, "Solomon was the wisest ever, though David did write *Proverbs* and was the big king, or the little big king, but Solomon came next and wrote *Psalms.* David also did what he wasn't supposed to do, looking at that Bathsheba. And then he went there too, yes he did."

A Brother said, "If a guy looks, he's gonna go there." This Brother was thinking of becoming a police officer, though the Sister was encouraging him to start community college. She was a hair stylist. She earned quite well, said customer Catherine. Indeed when I heard the figure it revealed what little we at Jubilee earned. This Annapolis group praised me for my work. They praised the stylist's work on Catherine—Catherine disagreed, "I don't look good with short hair." I liked the blue eyes under the dark bangs. I told her so.

The Sisters had prepared fruit salad and Popeye's chicken. The Sister said, "He also wrote *Song of Solomon* but of course us single Sis's and Bro's don't turn there. Yet." Everyone laughed.

I said, "Some scholars say it's describing Solomon's love with God."

The Sister responded, "They had some serious intimacy, my goodness." Catherine said, "It says that a cord between three is stronger than two." The Sister said, "That's why non-disciples have so much divorce."

Catherine asked me in a letter that week, "Did you know that the New Testament says, 'Expel the immoral brother'? It's so much more hardcore than anyone realizes, until they finally get humble and study. Jenny and I studied with a waitress from Pizza Hut and it allowed her to release and confess and break from her flakiness. It was a transformation in front of my eyes. When she saw this scripture she said half her current church should get expelled. How can she go back, now that's she's seen the standard?"

I penned her back, "There's so much I want to say and know. I know it's not the right time. That time may never come. But maybe some day we'll be advising young couples about godly discipline." Then I checked in with Eduardo, as I did regularly with quick shouts, "Stay focused." "Man it's tough." "Bro' you're awesome." "Make that follow-up call yet?" In the background I would hear him peeling tape and sealing packages at one of his jobs.

I called Bob at his World Bank office and he said, "I was just reading—you'd be proud. In fact, I see more of what you're getting at with your tall tower, how a person is supposed to sit down and measure out the life before deciding whether to even start building. Of course you're going to say it's not your tower but Christ's, and you're right, Bro', it's in there. But it's just amazing how nobody else seems to even know about Peter's required repent-baptism formula, or what repent apparently means. And I know you're going to cite John the Baptist's quite clear definition in *Luke* 3, as I'm sure you've already cited once or twice to someone in the last hour. But you know, sometimes at those Leaders Meetings I just get a bit tempted—when John Goodman is pointing around the room to collect and judge our weekly stats—I get tempted to say, 'Oh John, my man, how about your group, your stats, how many visitors and studies you have this week, this year, John old boy? Not zero? Say it isn't so.'" I listened without interruption, hoping it might keep Bob encouraged. He went on, "And c'mon, that advice thing? The seeking of advice which they preach on once a week, at one of the many meetings—and yes they quote the one or two proverbs that mention advice—but c'mon, to them it means permission, not advice. Permission? We need permission?"

I said, "I think you should talk to John Goodman about it. Get his advice. No seriously, John's on our team. You should ask John, we should talk to John."

Eduardo called back—he had made the follow-up call. He said, "Oh my goodness, remember how open that visitor was? Even now on the phone he was saying how great we were, the best Bible Talk he'd ever seen, a total blessing from God. He was saying all this stuff so I asked, 'But how can you call yourself a Christian if you're living with your girlfriend?' And, Reks, oh my goodness, he started cussing me out in the worst way, saying he was going to rip my throat out and all, and he would not stop." I said, "Eddie, I'm so sorry you had to go through that. It's part of the job. And you're a true disciple." And Gloria heard it all, sitting up in our office, she punching into her adding machine, I maybe with my feet on my desk.

Anton the Singles Leader came to Midweek with Jubilee John Hildebrand in tow—our suited ushers approached and hugged him in the hotel lobby. John Causey, however, took the sermon off-course a bit, too fiery about some tree with roots two feet wide, in a long critique of our lack of roots.

He wasn't applying it to practical life, nor to scripture, as done by British Fred Scott and that Sam Powell from Colin's Harlem theater. Causey then ripped into us because too few members had pre-registered for the upcoming conference. He blasted our mediocrity and complacency—the conference was mandatory for members anyway, regardless of pre-registering. I made a mumbling joke that it wasn't preaching but screeching. And John Hildebrand, well it seemed that he was actually feeling sorry for me, so showed his face. It seemed that he wouldn't be coming to that conference. As we walked out, we saw a newcomer still dazed and praising the preacher's passion. He was the other white visitor this evening.

John Hildebrand did still want to come serve at the shelter—Eduardo and I had committed to a monthly slot. Bob regretted not being able to make it up in time from the World Bank. I invited Catherine to put next month's dinner on her calendar and, since the timing now seemed proper, to consider walking the bridge with me.

The next day I received her latest letter. "Dear Reks, I needed to go talk to Jenny about the church, me, us. I had developed some attitudes towards the conference. But I guess if ever I'm going to complain about not having time, I need to look at where I used to come from. And so what, we have to pay for hotels in DC, and for the conference, and for the books, we should be grateful, it's going to be great. Especially the other Christians. I spoke with Eduardo this weekend (you urged him to call, I think). He is a very positive and energetic person. He loves you very much. So, lots of stuff floating in my mind but not going anywhere. See you there."

I put the letter down and I considered that Eduardo hadn't called me today. When by the next afternoon I couldn't get him on the phone, I dropped to my knees, then took the bus to his Georgetown store.

His dark expression, when he stepped out from the shipping room and looked over at me standing amid his oblivious co-workers, betrayed that today something was very different about this man. We walked outside and around a quiet corner and sat on a brick curb.

"There's this house," Eduardo started. I adjusted my sitting. "No one talks, you don't look in the eyes, you can pay something at the door if you want. Everyone has sex."

I nodded supportively. I said, "It's only men." He said, "No one even talks and you can leave like ten dollars in the basket if you want."

"Suggested contribution."

"There's some movie theaters too where stuff happens. It's dark. Once I saw a Virginia Brother there."

I blinked. He said, "I think I don't want to go to these places anymore and so I don't know why I do. Doesn't the Bible talk about this?"

"Does the Bible talk about this," I mused slowly. Eduardo's face was still darkly serious, nearly unrecognizable.

He said, "So I couldn't do our phone calls anymore. We've been saying that if we're gonna do this walk thing then we're gonna do it right. And we need to do it. So."

I said, "I'll help you." He said, "Thanks."

To the conference I brought a positive attitude and a smile and a Bible and a notebook and hugs. I came seeking wisdom and nourishment and fellowship, and I took my seat. White-haired Mike Fontenot said, while preparing at the podium, "Do you know what it means when a preacher takes off his watch like this and sets it up right here where he can see it closely?" We considered.

He said, "Absolutely nothing." We roared. He said, "I do actually have a lot of important things to say today." During his hour, Mike addressed the beginning of the movement and the thirty would-be disciples who met in that Boston basement. "What a would-be disciple is I can't quite say, but the feeling was very intense. We felt that something meaningful was going on."

He reiterated the high standard that they felt the scriptures were now revealing. "But today, you know what is Kip's toughest temptation? He says it's to live a normal life, that's it, that's his toughest temptation. He worries constantly about our lives normalizing." Mike read about the crucifixion, "'Those who passed by hurled insults at him, saying, "Come down from the cross and save yourself!" In the same way the chief priests and the teachers of the law mocked him, "He saved others, but can't save himself. Let this Christ, this King, come down now from the cross, that we may see and believe."'"

Mike looked up at us and said, "Disciples, don't come down from the cross. Don't come down. I know this life isn't easy, but the Bible says we've been crucified with Christ. Be glad it's only symbolic. Don't come down from the cross." When the cheering subsided, Mike said, "We're going to do another Special Contribution next month, we have to get our hearts right. This money supports foreign missions, the very thing we live for, creating Brothers and Sisters in distant places, many of whom are much poorer than our fortunate selves. Some of them walk to church, no joke. Now, I know that we suggest a contribution amount. But it's just a goal, it's just advice, something for you and your groups to aim at. But amen, we hit our goals don't we, church? Do not come down from the cross." After the cheer, he said, "Special Contribution is awesome! Let's get our hearts right." He lowered his head for prayer.

John Causey closed the conference with his fiery talk about our lack of fire. "I'm not here to wear a white hat." He said he was here to cut us, convict us, challenge us. He related again about that room of starving people sitting around a pot of stew, looking to get fed. "They fed each other!" It was now late Sunday and I went home and prepared for Jubilee.

"Mary De Marcellus," I said, and she turned her tall frame from her counseling desk. "Our Terry Flood has asked us to collect computer equipment from a contributing corporation downtown."

Mary said, "You've chosen me simply for my automobile. Or perhaps you and your Terry see me not only as a taxi but also a heavy lifter of corporate-contributed equipment."

I said, "Heavy lifter, unlikely. Not that I've looked." Tracie said, "Y'all are crazy." Annie said, "So intellectual." Mary said, "I'll have you know that my roommate and I jogged yesterday and I exercised thereafter with a barbell." The three of them had placed a dozen Applicants into jobs today, plus the Rev's two, and Terry's one. While driving, Mary said, "Did you hear that Terry wants to hire even another counselor? She really wants to grow this thing, huh? Tell me, tell me. You two have your secret talks upstairs."

"She wants to fire you."

"You're not funny, she loves me. Doesn't she?" We loaded up her car with the donated monitors and computers and keyboards.

But it was all old and obsolete. Mary said, "They gave us their junk—basically they got us to haul off their trash." She reversed down their alley and we hurled it all up into their dumpster and sped away. I said, "I guess I'll have to actually fundraise for this expansion."

"You're doing great."

"Oh Mary, there's still a fax machine behind your seat."

"Oh I hate when that happens."

Upstairs, Terry said to me, in her nurturing tone, "Reks, we are experiencing a sort of golden era here at JJ, and now we are being asked to expand with a satellite office, deeper in our inner city. I do think it is our calling but because of the funding I want you to reflect upon the potential and to find your peace." I nodded. She continued, "I would like you as both manager and lead-counselor there at the satellite, while continuing the fundraising."

We sat through a pause. Terry's voice then rose with some excitement. "Oh, I got a response to our job ad. A hundred responses actually. But one fellow truly seems to have the right heart and calling. And you'll never believe his name." She squeezed my hand. "Mike Bliss. Bliss. Do you think that's a sign? What do you think? At least you'd probably like another white male around here."

She laughed. "Though, they do sometimes think they control everything. I was married to one. My father was one. But don't you think we should call in Mike Bliss?"

Divorce in the Jubilee community wasn't rare. Terry was a single mother by definition though her children were grown and she lived in a large Georgetown house. She differed in other ways too from the single mother whom I had placed as a receptionist with one of our contributing corporations that had wanted to do even more.

But now this single mother's previous employer discovered her having written a check to herself from their ledger. She was begging me not to tell the new employer.

"No," Terry said stiffly when I approached her on this. She took me out to our front steps. "C'mon, you know you must call Calvert Funds and tell them what Angela has done. You know this. If something were to happen at their company and we had known in advance—c'mon Reks." I told her she was right. I told her that Angela seemed sorry and the previous employer had been weeks delinquent in paying her and she had acted out of desperation and she admitted it was no excuse. I told her that Angela had a little baby. None of this uncrossed Terry's arms. She asked, "How is Angela going to learn? How is she going to know that her own decisions caused this? You cannot enable her. You have to make that phone call."

It was two phone calls, because after speaking to Calvert's human resource office, they had me call Angela myself. She picked up on the first ring. I told her the bad news and she stayed silent, until saying a final okay, and still she stayed on the phone, but said no more. This was easier with Tim, an ex-offender with computer skills whom Calvert also hired—on his third day he used his key to enter the office at midnight, on camera, and Calvert asked us to release him.

Calvert now said they would take a small break. Terry still counted this as two Placements, for the funders. At each Staff Meeting we reported our statistics.

Eduardo and I were back to our encouragement calls. "We're given thorns, Eddie, because, well I don't know why exactly. But this isn't heaven yet, maybe we're supposed to learn some things first. Let's keep fighting. We'll go Pizzeria Uno's tonight, where we dined with that British guy who didn't enjoy our gratitude for the food."

Eduardo yelled in laughter, "Oh my goodness I saw him on the subway, him and his accent. He asked me, 'Are you still trying to convert the converted?' But he wouldn't talk with us about anything, he wouldn't let us share about our lives, he wouldn't even let us pray—the guy would not even let us pray." Eduardo faded out in laughing disbelief. I was smiling wide.

"Okay," said Eduardo. "Let's stay open. I know you have your own struggles. Struggles with John Goodman. I know about that." He peeled off a loud piece of tape at the store. When we met up, he said he had a secret.

"Again?"

One ear was bigger than the other, that was what he said. He was sure everyone was staring at it at all times. He was sure too that people could see on him that he'd been abused as a child. "Oh, I was abused."

"When?"

"Always."

"By whom?"

"Everyone," he said.

We laughed. "No," he said, "I'm serious. Stuff was happening to me before I can even remember. I'm sort of remembering now. My brothers. My sisters. They told me not to tell my father. Oh my gosh, my neighbor, he promised it wouldn't hurt. It hurt so much. I bled for a week. I didn't tell anyone. But I was sure everyone knew. I think it was happening all over town. Crazy stuff. I mean, in our two-room house there were twelve of us, each trying to hide their porn and all. Plus my father, I'm remembering something there maybe too."

Bob flew to Boston to propose. First he stopped for advice from Luda's Leader, who said, "Nah, I don't think you're ready." Bob was asked to get back on an airplane. When John Goodman later called up to that Leader and pushed for permission, that Leader explained, "It was probably better to err on the side of caution." Bob thanked John.

Yet in his eyes I sensed he wasn't at peace, not with the "rules made by men" as he called them when he lead our next Bible Talk—we wanted our Talk to examine all sides. Bob looked around our little audience and said, "Jesus called the leaders of his time 'blind guides', and then a bit later, five chapters actually, but we don't know the actual duration, which isn't a reason to doubt the gospels, it's more a sign that time isn't what needs to be analyzed—though does anyone know?"

Kelly from Wisconsin raised her hand. "Yes, but I think you were trying to discuss another point?" Bob read, """You know that the rulers of the Gentiles lord it over them, and their high officials exercise authority over them. Not so with you. Instead, whoever wants to become great among you must be your servant, and whoever wants to be first must be your slave—just as the Son did not come to be served, but to give his life as a ransom for many."""

Eduardo took me to Parents & Friends of Ex-Gays, a religious group helping to enact that change that they attested could indeed occur. One guy in a suit stood up and he didn't look unlike a smaller John Causey. And though he didn't aim for quite the fierceness, he did occasionally lick his thin black mustache.

"Sure I played Little League. No my batting average wasn't the world's best. I was just nine or something but once when I struck out my father said, 'You're no son of mine. You're no son at all.' And I believed him. I stopped playing ball. In high school I found myself going to clubs and thinking unusual things—it was no longer about being a perfect son, a perfect guy, instead my mind began entertaining other thoughts and I found people who said, 'You should listen to that. That's you.'

"So I bought into the lie. Next I'm changing my behavior, the way I talk, the way I walk. I mean, dang, I rebuilt everything around attracting not women but men. I went years and miles down that path. And you can be sure of this, I never would have told you I thought I would come back.

"But somewhere in me there was a voice, man, something from somewhere, and finally one day I listened to it. Finally I met the right people and I admitted I was meant for something else. We are meant for something else. PFox saved my life. I'll be getting married later this autumn. You can see other photographed couples on the wall. People are changing through God and the gospel of his son Jesus Christ who laid down his life for our sins."

Though not living or teaching discipleship they certainly were attempting some change. And wow was it required. So the leader told Eduardo in their private meeting. "You're gay, accept it." I was seated out among the assorted mothers and friends. Eduardo said, when he and I were again walking through the evening city, that he didn't like the guy's oversimplification. So we went to Sexaholics.

More anonymous and less religious, its members could choose their own behavior bottom-line. Eduardo also sought advice from John Goodman. Wide-eyed John said he himself would get advice and get back to Eduardo. Colin gave me perspective on it from his days in the Arts Ministry.

"I was discipling a Brother who used to go to public bathrooms and, wearing a diaper, masturbate and crap at the same time, there in the stall. Imagine him having to confess that to me."

"Geez."

"Your DC Brother, he actually does need to accept who he is. The truth is he's a disciple of Christ. But I'll tell you what, since DC Leaders might not be so used to this, I'll call my guy in the City, Steve Johnson."

"Kingdom Global Sector Leader."

Colin laughed. He said, "Do you know I once sent a letter to Kip humbly expressing that I thought these titles were getting a bit Trekie, and perhaps not quite biblical. I never heard back. I think I sent it. I think I wrote it." He sighed. "Oh, did I tell you I started seeing a psychiatrist? A shrink, Bro'. You are my true brother for life, I'm baring my soul to you. Do you know what Prosac is? The guy on the phone with you right now is on Prosac. And I'm telling this shrink things I hadn't realized I felt. But my Regional Sector Leader approves—therapy isn't the most common thing for a disciple but he's not the most common Leader. He's actually cool. He gets how this can actually help my commitment."

"And Jesus probably doesn't mind either," I ventured. Colin chuckled.

I wrote a letter to Regional Leader John Causey. "I want to thank you for the conference. I was excited to meet my Brothers and Sisters from the other cities. Bringing large groups together is so encouraging. And you pulled it off with polish. I also wanted to ask your input on another item. Seeing the ferocious lions on the conference banners, I wondered about the message. Jesus said we are lambs (*John* 20). He did say he's coming back like a lion, but for now he is sending us as sheep among wolves (*Matthew* 10). It's the devil which roams around like a lion (*Peter* 5). As you know, God's Spirit is love, joy, peace, patience, kindness, gentleness, faithfulness, goodness, and self-control (*Galatians* 5). I've had visitors say it's missing from our preaching, that's all. I understand you must inspire us to be bold and courageous and to bring more visitors. I just worry that we emphasize growth disproportionately to actual scripture, and thus to the detriment of growth itself. What is your insight on this?"

I mailed it. At Midweek, John Goodman introduced another new Brother. I was sitting some rows back from him, and from my assigned group too, as I'd begun moving away from the loudness of the speakers. Martin Blackman—his father was Ambassador from Barbados and Martin had played pro tennis and roomed with Andre Agassi—said when I introduced myself, "Yeah, I might not have gotten maximum use from my tennis tools. I might have even squandered them. But hey," he looked around and he looked at me, "here we are, God gives us better tools." He smiled freshly.

"I've heard about you," he continued. "You seem to be known as a fired-up Brother." He laughed with poise. He said, "I probably shouldn't be using kingdom-speak too much. I wouldn't be surprised if it starts losing some meaning. Am I right? Right? But I'm sure it serves a good purpose too. Anyway, we should read together. And I hear you share a lot, huh? We should meet up. But I hear the schedule fills up, am I right?"

On Saturday, I stood at the altar while John Goodman united Bob and Luda as one. Bob's family was here from upstate New York. They then wrote a letter to Bob, expressing their delight in hearing such a nice young passionate preacher.

What I had heard—I couldn't help it—was John Goodman criticizing Bob. John had seemed to aim his sermon at Bob's skepticism and questioning. To outsiders it was rib poking. I struggled—I tried—to not see it as an attempt to alter Bob's thinking, and speaking.

John Goodman read that delightful letter to the congregation. John Causey charged up and said, "Anyone still prefer to be in a lukewarm church, a dim light that outsiders can't see? That was a letter from God. And it's calling you to repent and imitate your Leaders like John Goodman!" I again saw visitors wowed by this man's passion.

After Leaders Meeting, I picked Catherine up at her and Jenny's little apartment, and Jenny was sniggering and Catherine begged me not to walk into her room. I walked in.

Was it that the bed and floor were covered with crumpled papers and crumpled clothing—I flicked on the light switch—or was it that the overhead bulb didn't work? She said cutely, "You think I'm a total loser." I said, "Let's just turn on a lamp." But these also had no bulbs. She said, "I didn't want you to see this."

"I can't see anything."

"Don't ask how long it's been like this, because I'm a disciple, which means I can't lie."

"It means you have the discipline to buy a light bulb."

She said, "I just want to quit my mall job." Jenny said, "They sell light bulbs at the mall." Catherine said, "Be nice. Or Catcat's gonna scratch you."

"I thought you were an artist," I said.

"I did some modeling, but that wasn't healthy. I think I like photography."

I said, "That's great, you should get a project." She said, "Whatever. Take a chill pill, big boy." I looked at the photos on the fridge and asked, "Is this your Ohio sister?" The photographed girl had a wide forehead and long hair splayed to each side.

But I hadn't recognized bang-less Catherine, and I now paid with pinches. I reassured her how stunning she looked now with short hair. She said she wanted to grow it out again. We decided to make a plan for finding her new work. "Write down ten contacts who might lead you to your right spot."

"Oh, it's so hard."

I said, "You mentioned photography." She said, "I guess I know a guy who shoots weddings."

"Make a list. Call."

She moaned. I said, "If you want I'll call the first person."

At night I wrote her, "We just parted from our date, and all I can think of is how determined I am not to kiss you yet. Purity is important, and has great rewards. I'm focusing on how comfortably you sit in the car with your socked feet on the dash as we drive in the dark. Meanwhile, you listen to my skiing stories and Stalingrad stories. Thank you." I was determined to do this right. I wanted spiritual discipline. I didn't want to be controlled by feelings.

Meanwhile the kingdom didn't take long to discover Martin Blackman. No less than Kip McKean wanted him out in L.A. to run a kingdom tennis program—Kip's children had made their high-school team and Kip then converted the coach. John Causey asked us, "Don't you want to follow your Leader's example?" I saw Bob cringe in the row ahead of me. Colin called me that evening and invited me out to Aspen. Cool young Princeton Leader Dave Mitchell would be coming too.

I started packing well in advance. I still had my square, durable LL Bean bag from my Debbie trip that matched my black-and-green fleece from the Steph days. The bag had efficient inner pockets for sunscreen and other important items. I picked up *Into Thin Air* and settled into the recliner.

Dang, this Jon Krakauer had lucked upon a story. He took me up his mountain. There was even an Aspen couple on one of the ascent teams. On the descent, they all got clobbered. While the teams were inching blindly down the south face, a north face pair of Japanese climbers was ascending past a dying Indian.

He was hypoxic, his brain fogging—the Japanese guys touched the top and stepped back over him on the way down. They said later, "Twenty-eight thousand feet is no place for morality."

Martin wanted to write about his tennis days—he told me over sushi—and each anecdote would begin with a relevant scripture. "So many characters on tour." He laughed his meaningful tatter. "Reaching out to these guys will be interesting. Most are still their own god. Andre, he's getting divorced, so that's sort of an issue between us, even though he has a rep for having faith. Jim Courier, no such rep. I saw him in Manhattan last month. He said he just wanted to smoke weed and date models."

Martin continued, "The world, it offers something that is missing only one part." He was considering each word. "But that one part counts for everything. And it's that it can't last. Think about those perfect days you had, the weather was nice, the day unfolded just right, maybe there was a good-looking woman involved. And what do you have to show for it?" He laughed. "Huh? What do we have? It's the emptiness that exposes it, and the world was made that way on purpose. Once, there was a French gal on tour who was ranked way above me and I just dug the way she carried herself. One year I made it a few rounds into the French so I was invited to the Players' Party. I got to meet her and we decided to hang out. And suddenly a longtime crush is being lived out. She thinks I'm great. I think I'm great.

"We spend that whole two weeks together in Paris, having fun, obviously being together, sleeping together. The Majors are the only time that the men and women are in the same city, but she wanted to keep it going—Wimbledon was only two weeks away—and so I agreed. But actually, I had already tapped out. I saw that I wasn't going to marry her and that's what it always comes down to. So now I want out of this relationship I used to dream about. We meet up in London and I get brave. She's dropping me off at my hotel and I break it nice and clean and honest. I go up to my room and I look out my window. And she's there below in her car, crying, absolutely weeping. And she was a nice person, a very sincere person.

"So that was a terrible moment. It was one of those moments when you see what's really going on, you see the trap."

I said, "So Jesus is the answer?" Martin considered with his fingers on his jaw. He said, "Jesus lasts. Nothing else seduces me now because I know it won't last. I possess the one thing that lasts. Converting people lasts. Serving the poor and doing things for the body of believers, these last forever. I believe in Jesus and heaven because the Bible describes the world's futility so well."

He was quicker than others to find the church rules about counting visitors and even pre-counting visitors and donating pre-determined amounts and donating again at Special. He said, "I'm sure they have their reasons. These guys have been studying and praying and submitting to God for years now. Trying to run this whole thing is probably not too easy, you know?"

I wanted to sit next to him at church but I was expected to sit with my Talk—anyway I slipped away from the speakers to a back row. Bob found me afterward and said, "Leaders Meeting again." He wiped his brow. He said, "I confess I'm still tempted to ask, 'Goodman, why aren't you telling us your own stats? Why don't you have to call *us* every Thursday to say how many you yourself are bringing?'

I just nodded. I got home in the late evening and rocked in my chair and read, "'Come to me, all you who are weary and burdened, and I will give you rest. Take my yoke upon you and learn from me, for I am gentle and humble in heart, and you will find rest for your souls. For my yoke is easy and my burden is light.'" I reflected on it for a long time. I breathed. I switched over to the thin air on Everest, where the author was still struggling down toward the highest tents.

> ***It was much easier to remain at rest than to summon the initiative to tackle the dangerous ice slope; so I just sat there as the storm roared around me, letting my mind drift, doing nothing for perhaps forty-five minutes.***

But alas, he made it down and made it safely home.

> ***The ordinary pleasures of life—eating breakfast with my wife, watching the sun go down, being able to get up in the middle of the night and walk barefoot to a warm bathroom—generated flashes of joy that bordered on rapture.***

I reflected on this. I acknowledged I was not quite experiencing the rapture of those peaceful nights and warm bathroom floors.

Martin said no to Kip McKean. He wanted to finish grad school and to honor his family here and to grow in the DC fellowship. I said over sushi, "Tough phone call probably." Martin laughed. "You think? You think Kip minded applying some pressure? 'We need you here, Bro', God needs you here.' Tough phone call indeed. But mainly it was a tough decision. Because, I do want to be sacrificial."

Sexaholics Anonymous indeed gave more space. Participants could stare blankly forward while sharing whatever they wanted without response. One sharer stated, "I was reading a running magazine and saw an article on this female athlete who was blond and beautiful and a Rhodes Scholar and I thought, I could have a girlfriend like that—I run, I'm successful. So what to do? I could go out and sleep with a prostitute who looks like her, or I could act out at home alone, or I could play the club-and-bar game. All of it seems so worthless, so I drag myself to a meeting and endure for one more day. Thanks for letting me share."

Another guy, who had a handsome happy face, shared about his growing depression. He had left his kids for a gay relationship and needed to keep his employment in order to pay child support even though he felt he currently wasn't mentally healthy enough to work.

And as always I stepped out from these meetings and felt addiction in the air—it was in every molecule—and I was so glad and amazed I'd been given a way out, free of this thing that controlled so many. Eduardo and I chased down that despairing guy and caught him on a Dupont Circle corner and he turned around, pleased. "Hi," he said, curious why we had pursued him.

"We were worried about you."

He shook his head to say that all would be fine. I said, "Maybe we can help you feel less low. Jesus says, 'My yoke is easy, my burden is light.'"

The man's face darkened. The three of us stood there in pause. "Are you proselytizing?"

Eduardo asked, "What is that terrible word?"

"I can't even believe it, proselytizers." He huffed off to whatever life. Eduardo was done with this group anyway. "I wanted a sponsor and not one person even approached me."

"They're not disciples," I explained. "Listen, we have mountain-moving power." We took out our notebooks. I said, "We're making a pact. Two weeks. You don't go to the House. I don't masturbate. Our own bottom lines, baby. Sign here."

Eduardo said, "It's not just the House. It's parks. Cars. Hotel bathrooms. Some are as busy as bus stations."

"That's crazy."

"It's everywhere, everyone. Guys that could be your father, men in suits, men from banks, the World Bank, married men, teens." He said that the bathroom at the GW Campus Center was popular. We had studied with so many guys in that eatery. At times I had read the whole school paper in a stall, or at least the pages that had been on the floor. I had never sensed anything going on around me. Were they waiting for me to leave? They must have been hating me. Eduardo said, "Twenty minutes and something will happen with someone, guaranteed. It's quick and silent. No one speaks."

"Two weeks, you don't go." I signed his notebook, he signed mine.

Meanwhile, I was preparing the Jubilee satellite office at the refurbished old Perry School amid another broken-down community. Up at main Jubilee, Mike Bliss would take over the workshops, helped by George the custodian. Mike was soft-spoken but confident. When I mentioned church to him, he calmly shook his head, and looked away.

Mary de Marcellus also wouldn't hear of visiting but her reason was her devotion to her own group. "Cult," I said. She said, "There reigns Mary the Virgin Mother of our Lord." We were able to joke about it. We joked about her French Catholic boyfriend. They were observing certain tenets. So she let me call her Mary Dee. She knew my situation too.

Gloria the bookkeeper had a cavity. "Root canal?" I asked.

Tracie the counselor walked up to our floor and said, "Black people pull teeth. We can't afford no root canal."

I said, "The periodontist who did my root canal was black."

Tracie said, "Well he ain't from our neighborhood. And if he is, he's done good and got out and shouldn't come back here. Find me one guy walking around with full teeth."

Gloria said, "That's from drinking."

Tracie said, "You're right. They's poor and drinking, and that ain't changing. Not since slavery."

Gloria said, "None of them was slaves."

Tracie said, "You ain't lying. But I guess they're still feeling something. Ax 'em."

"Shoo'," said Gloria, "I ain't no counselor."

Tracie said, "Damn straight you ain't."

"Tracie," I said, "you're a former disciple, you know you shouldn't be talking like that."

Gloria said, "Oh I heard that." Tracie said, "And you heard right. He's right. I gotta be getting back there. I was so good then." The Workshops ended and Mary Dee came upstairs. She and Tracie hugged. Mary Dee said, "Oh Reks, we're going to miss you." Mike Bliss and Annie came upstairs. Annie said, "Oh, he's so cool with his new little satellite office." She cocked her neck with attitude.

Mary Dee said, "I mean Reks is going on vacation. Wait, didn't you say you won't take vacations until your book is finished?"

Mike Bliss said, "So it's a book, I knew there was something."

Mary Dee said, "He's got lots of secrets."

"Funny," I said, "I don't believe I have any."

Annie said, "He has them, he just tells them to everyone." She and Tracie hugged. I said, "Actually, when I'm done with this final revision, I'm going to take a long nap."

I came home late that evening and Martin Blackman was sitting in my reclining chair. I said, "Bro'." He said, "It's your writing hour, I'm sorry." I said, "You wouldn't be here unless it was important."

He said, "How about my having just spent three hours with Rick Bauer?" I said, "That's important."

Much like Rick Bauer and wife had been awaiting Teresa in Key West, today they'd been waiting in Martin's home. The Barbados Ambassador had hired them to deprogram his son. "Reks, I hope you don't mind what you're about to hear. I wouldn't want, as some Leaders say, to shipwreck your faith."

"Martin, I'm open. That's how I became a disciple."

"That's why I came here tonight. You can imagine I needed to speak with someone."

"Brain a little rattled?"

"Just a little," he said. We laughed lightly. We held gazes. I prepared to think clearly. Martin added, "Not just the brain, it rattles everything, heart, body, soul." He sighed. "Here's the point. Leadership doesn't want to listen. They don't want to listen to God. Also, the idea of being the one and only true church, that never felt right to me."

"I understand," I said. "But I can believe that we have something special. I read it clearly every day and I find no one else on the street possessing it, regardless of their credentials. I can't explain that away too quickly."

Martin scanned his thoughts. "Possessing a powerful insight into the scriptures does not give license to treat rules and people how you'd like."

"Agreed."

"It's abuse of leadership."

"And I'm sure that's what Rick Bauer says."

"He's not alone. We just don't hear about it in the ICC. Insiders who speak up are flushed out." Martin handed me a thick booklet. He said, "Indianapolis." The word had meaning bigger than the place—though I'd only heard rumors—in that our Leader there had tried to reroute his branch and then Kip had flown in to stop him.

"Judge for yourself," said Martin. "We might never know the true events. But the authors of this version seem to be in touch with their hearts. You're the first person I've told." We hugged goodbye for the night. I continued packing my square, efficient Aspen bag—I put my goggles and gloves inside my boots, an old trick.

The next day, I visited Bob unannounced at the Bank. I told him. He stared at me and smiled. "Reks, you? Let's step out for a beer immediately." He said at the bar, "You? I never imagined it."

"I'm just saying that this Brother is making me realize we all share concerns that need to be addressed to Leadership. I didn't always tell you when I agreed with you because I didn't want to discourage you."

"No," said Bob, "you didn't want me to be negative and critical, negative and critical, negative and critical, about which they regularly criticize us in sermons." He shook his head. "Wow, listen, I respect your desire to approach them. Just be careful. I wouldn't want you to get discouraged. Not you."

I got on an airplane. The flight attendant didn't know what I was reading, that I was actually being transported to Indianapolis two years past. She didn't know that Indianapolis Leader Ed Powers had thrown out his back and while hospitalized had thought through some things. His staff wrote out what then transpired. I was slowly turning the pages of their document.

V

They had written sparely, much like scripture, letting the reader complete the images. They noted when Indy had been told to report more statistical categories up to Chicago, including weekly attendance, weekly visitors, weekly growth, and monthly expectations for the same. They noted when the Special Contribution multiplier was upped again, now to fourteen times the weekly tithe—while I was reading on this airplane the multiplier was twenty. If a member failed to pay it, Talks were still responsible for the sum, they noted. They noted that their leading couples had returned from a mandatory L.A. Conference troubled by Kip saying, "I am God's man, leading God's movement." Injured Ed Powers was then separate from all this for two weeks.

When he came out of the hospital he gathered his staff. They agreed together that the statistics were "choking love of ministry from the heart." The second-in-command asked where Ed was heading with this. Ed answered that he didn't know where, but he had to begin teaching what was right. On a Sunday when "the congregation met in house churches throughout central Indiana," Ed asked all to convene again that evening.

"He stated repeatedly that the church was committed to remaining in the ICC but would simply ask for freedom from the compulsory reporting and compulsory giving." They wanted some freedom in thought. If the congregation voted against it, Ed would step down.

One member voted "No". Six abstained. The text added dryly that precise attendance was in fact not taken, nor reported, that evening, but the crowd was estimated at 600 adults. Staff then returned to Ed's for the call upward to Chicago. Midnight Indianapolis was resembling some dim-lit Soviet spy drama—I thought about Khrushchev's speech purportedly lifting the 'Stalinsky Gypnosis'. I shook my head lightly at something the flight attendant was saying.

At three a.m., Indy members began receiving calls from ICCers around the country, hundreds of calls by morning. "We heard that Ed is trying to lead the congregation away." Rumors sprouted that Global Sector Leaders were flying in to meet with members directly. They were circumventing Ed.

His staff stuck by their new principles and they found themselves not invited to this upcoming gathering. The big guns had come, the giants of the movement, spearheading with *Proverbs* 18:17, "The first to present his case seems right, until another comes forward to question him."

They preached about Ed Powers' emotional instability. "One member of the crowd, Roger Croswell, spoke up to state that he did not believe they should talk about Ed, but the issues." Ed meanwhile was trying to schedule an issue discussion with the Leaders—his staff had been pleading with them not to start a new congregation. When Leaders did finally see Ed, "It is important to note that Bob and Marty did not open their Bibles during the three-and-a-half hour meeting." It was a done deal, they were starting anew in Indianapolis, gathering as many as would come. "Communication between the two groups was decreasing dramatically." Kip warned his crowd that, "If they had any contact with anyone who remained with Ed, they would be marked as divisive." Ed urged his own group, "'Love the person who has set themselves up against you.'" He was quoting *Proverbs* 12.

Colin and Sue met me with hugs at the airport. I was wondering how to broach it. We drove up into the mountains. Dave Mitchell, the young Princeton Leader, had yet to arrive. I wouldn't have minded meeting that Ed Powers for lunch sometime, somehow.

That evening, Colin came into my room. He leaned his back against the wall and slid down to the floor. He sat there and sighed. "Sue and I," he said, "we were looking forward to seeing you. When I think about the people in my life, you're about the only one with a real job. But it's funny, we worry that you think too intensively about things. God knows though—and I do talk with him about it—that I myself face a long drawn-out struggle now to have a spiritual marriage. Plus I'm probably depressed. Plus I'm on medication. And my best friend lives with his parents." I knew now that I had to take it easy on him. Colin was wrestling with the basics, for whatever reason, not this plane of kingdom and celestial politics.

But after a morning of skiing we sat in the lodge and I just broached it. "Colin, Indianapolis." I tried to play down the meaning. He blinked for a second but nodded that he knew what I meant. He said, "I heard their Leader had previously been unstable, even suicidal." I could see the quick struggle in Colin's mind—should he avoid discouraging me or should he tell me what he felt? He said with a huff, "The guy was probably just depressed." The official position was that Kip had saved the Movement there and that Apostle Paul had warned us about being pulled away by wolves. Colin said, "My advice would be to humbly mention it to Dave here when you get the chance."

The next day, back up in the mountain lodge, I saw my chance with Leader Dave. He sat there amid the tables. His wife kissed him goodbye as I approached. The voices around us were fresh and high while Dave and I kept ours level.

"At times, I'm just not getting nourishment from Leadership, and my real worry is that this is intentional, that they think the sheep, if fed, will get lazy. Is it possible that our practice is a bit askew?"

Dave sat poised and attentive. He said, "It's unfortunate that you feel discouraged, Bro'. And we need to work on fixing that. But for you to say our practice is a bit askew, that is extremely dangerous. You need to check your heart, see what's going on there. This is very serious."

I was back skiing soon. Then we three guys hot-tubbed and talked about the great snow this week. I returned to DC on a misty night and got an immediate call from Bob. He asked me to visit him and Luda.

Martin Blackman was there, sitting at the table, along with a spectacled Virginia Brother who was one of our proud scientist conversions. Bob looked at me with a warm, wide smile. Luda offered me tea. Bob said, "You were right, your boy Martin here has good insights. And he discovered Steve here, who has some of the same questions, as you call them, Reks."

I sat down. Bob said, "All I can say—and I'm curious as to your response though I unfortunately have a prediction—but we've found additional ex-member accounts and they are right on. Listen to a Leader from Nairobi, 'As I was originally so impressed by their apparent commitment to the scriptures, this is what made it so difficult to finally see the truth.'"

Luda said, in her Russian accent, "ICC is so dishonest, so not what they pretend." I had never seen her so animated. I guess she had withheld her thoughts before, perhaps even from herself. Scientist Steve said calmly, "I just don't believe the doctrine anymore." They were watching me. I looked at Martin, who allowed a poised, meaningful chuckle.

"After that night in your basement," he explained, "I went home thinking I could still be part of the body—Paul said the body has different parts but stays together—and so I would stay unified while still doing what I myself discerned was right. But after looking deep inside myself, I asked whether I could really convert someone to this group, could I with a clear conscience bring someone into this church knowing how that person's spirit would eventually get ruined, and knowing that they'd be brought in unaware of what really happens inside. I considered how unhappy I had truly become during my year. So many hopeful, faithful people just worn down. So I had no choice but to finally fully leave, even though in doing so I've felt extremely lonely and isolated."

Bob said, "It's not easy to leave the one true church, choosing hell instead, and taking your friends there with you." Again they all looked at me.

I said, "I've been organizing scriptures that show our points. We'll take it to Leadership. I know what you're going to say"—Luda was about to burst—"but it's the only way. They have to be shown the Word. They have the right. I'll bring it here tomorrow."

In the morning I phoned Singles Ministry Leader Anton. "Anton, I need your advice." He came over to Jubilee. I gave him a copy of my new document, "Stand Firm". He said, "Wow, it's even formatted and double-sided." He thanked me. I was glad he was taking it seriously. At lunch I took a bus down to Bob's—they had all taken the day off and were again sitting around the table. I handed out my five-pager.

"The point," I summarized, "within the twelve scriptures and my own text, is that the church has chosen to use legislated pressures instead of spiritual motivations, and so they're burdening the disciples, tiring their hearts, when otherwise we could all be doing more good."

"No, Reks," said Bob, "I mean no I haven't read it yet—and I'm looking forward to it and can tell it's a thoughtful piece—but Bro' get real. Do you know that Kip McKean demanded to be labeled a modern-day Apostle at a leaders conference some years back? The Indy guy was sitting right there. Rick Bauer, now a deprogrammer, was sitting right there. Kip thinks he's an Apostle, Reks. And let's be honest with ourselves, those are prideful guys, Causey, Goodman, Mike Fontenot. They're not trained to listen to this stuff, they're trained for something else. I just wouldn't want you to get caught up in a struggle that's going to hurt your faith."

Luda said, "They'll simply cite, 'Obey your leaders.'" I said, "I address that." Bob said, "And what a cheap shortcut, abusing that singular and contextual verse—just ask patrons of certain horny Catholic priests. Anyway Reks, while you were gone—and we've been slow to tell you this—we visited another church. Rick Bauer suggested the place. He thought they had a certain awareness. And it's not even his group." We sat there in a quiet pause. Bob massaged his brow. "And I told John Goodman."

The people at this table were on the other side already. I was expected at Bible Talk tonight yet it was with them that I wanted to spend my time. They were open and discerning and trying to get their lights back ashine. Martin said, "Let's look at his scriptures."

Soon I hurried back up to Jubilee and turned past Ethel's counter and there in the chairs sat John Goodman. He had a copy of "Stand Firm" in his hands. I looked into his eyes. He said, "When Bob first came to me, I wondered what was really going on. But I had a hunch."

"That's not right."

"Let me just ask one question. Have you left yet?"

"No."

"Daniel Bertholet is flying in tonight. I have Bob coming back over too."

Regional Sector Leader John Causey was also there. Daniel and I hugged for an extra moment. John Causey stood and we hugged. Martin and Bob and I joined them on John Goodman's couches but it felt different than our past studies here.

John Causey began belittling Martin's spiritual and scriptural tenure, and his pride for not having moved in with Brothers and for not taking advice. John Goodman added, "And saying no to Kip McKean." Bob stood up in protest, his Bible and notes gripped in hand, his eyes and words darting around—how could we allow this? I was sharing a stare with Daniel across the room.

Martin said only, "I can see why you might think some of those things." The night was already fizzling out. I said, "We should talk about the scriptures."

At breakfast, Daniel said, "Okay, you are correct, what you have written, much has some truth. But leave the kingdom? Leave God's kingdom for that?" He was headed back to Geneva for Sunday service. I had secretly agreed to go to Bob and Luda's new church just once.

They picked me up at the subway. It meant I was away without leave. Martin was in the car. Catherine knew none of this. She also didn't know that I, this evening, was scheduled to meet alone with John Goodman, John Causey, and the regional Elders.

"It's going to be great," said Bob. We drove out to another corner of this concrete expanse in which we existed and survived. Where had my cottage dreams gone? I had given them up for God, and for my writing. Martin said, "Let's keep it sober—this place isn't perfect, but it is the rare place where disciples can make a spiritual home."

"No," said Luda, "it is perfect, the people are sincere, they are not overburdened, nor are they asked to lie. Sure, not everyone hugs maybe. But they don't get in trouble if they don't hug." Bob said, "That's my wife."

Martin chuckled. The Lord's Church of Greenbelt was a group of forty, none of whom sat in the front row, to which I now led the four of us. "Uh oh," said the preacher. "He must be new."

He had a warm smile. His brown beard had tints of orange. His parents and siblings were ICC. He did preach from the Bible, using a good Jesus-walking-and-talking passage, and he brought it to life, and with a bedside manner too. It made me want to do right. If this group, including the preacher, simply lacked someone to pound the pavement and show others how, I could humbly and happily lead that.

Bob and Luda wrote out a large check to the Lord's Church of Greenbelt. That afternoon Martin and I walked the DC sidewalks. I was now delinquent from Leaders Meeting too. I showed Martin some of Eduardo's and my techniques, the open Bible and the politely direct approach and the verses ready for any ensuing discussion, so that people were making decisions based on Christ, not on us or pamphlets or church itself.

"Very first-century," said Martin. So in theory I had a Greenbelt partner too. We stopped by the house of a young professional guy whom I had already led through some studies. Martin dialogued with him while I excused myself and stood in the bathroom and looked in the mirror and shook my head.

How could we teach a guy when we didn't even attend the same church, when our minds were embattled with the struggle over kingdom or cult?

I looked at my watch—I was due up at John Goodman's. Martin walked with me up to that door.

John Causey answered it. He said to Martin, "We have nothing to say to you, you're not wanted here." Causey barred the doorway with his arm. He was dark and strong-voiced. Poised Martin nodded but looked stunned as well. He told me he'd wait outside. Causey walked me upstairs.

We joined the couch sitters, DC Elder Randy Jordan, who was an attorney, Virginia Elder Mike Fontenot, the white-haired planter of the London Church, and John Goodman. I looked around at them. Causey said, "Reks, we've all read your document. You have written some very serious criticisms. You have distributed it to other disciples, newer disciples, and now they've left God's kingdom, now they are out alone in the world, on the path most likely to hell. Yes, that's right. And do I understand that you, with this heart, actually have a girlfriend in the kingdom? You're leading a godly relationship? And you're leading a Bible Talk?"

"A ministry," said John Goodman. Causey said, "A whole ministry looking to you for leadership? Well, tonight these devoted men have sacrificed time with their families to come out here because we cannot delay in addressing this." He looked over at Elders Randy Jordan and Mike Fontenot.

Randy said, "This really is very serious, and as your Elder I want to say that one of the reasons why we are here, as John Causey knows well and feels in his heart, is because we care about you and your salvation." John Causey nodded. Randy continued, "And admittedly you did come to me last month and maybe also last year with some scriptural concerns and I didn't respond as I should have. I regret that. But from what I have now heard, the International Ministry has truly suffered since the departure of Daniel Bertholet. There have been many fall-aways. I knew Elma and Teresa quite well over the years. I think what concerns us here is that many of these fall-aways somehow pass through you on their way out."

"Most," said John Goodman. Randy said, "And I don't know what you tell them but it isn't that they should stay in the kingdom. It doesn't quite make sense that they would decide to depart the church for good and yet come see you." I said, "I think they respected the way I had treated them." Randy said, "But you don't do much to keep them faithful." I began to respond but John Causey exclaimed,

"Fall-aways are knocking on your door with smiles. How is that? Worse, you let them walk off into a life of sin and destruction. And now you have printed and distributed your criticisms. There is an independence and pride here which I don't know how we missed all this time."

Elder Mike Fontenot calmed the room with a smile and nod. He said to me, "I've read through your points, and much of it is well considered. Yet, be sober about yourself. For example, you mention Christ saying that the yoke he gives is light and easy, but he's also saying he *is* applying a yoke." I was sitting before the Elders and Leaders and I wanted to show no bad attitude and I wanted to give them a chance—I bit my tongue. John Goodman also seemed respectfully reserved.

White-haired Mike Fontenot continued, "You quote Paul that 'we should not use deception nor distort the word of God, but set forth the truth plainly.' Well, those are strikingly strong words. You do know that church sermons can't always be peace and love and everyone's okay—that's why the denominational world is lukewarm and lost and not growing. These denominations also lack accountability, which the Bible clearly prescribes. No, it doesn't say to use statistics or not to use statistics, but we just try to come up with good methods. You cite Leaders lording over the people. But you should have seen the church before, when we just got started. If you just have a little patience, God's kingdom can mature and make its improvements. I minister to Virginia parents and they ask my advice why their kids are unhappy in the church. And I tell them, 'Because you're unhappy.' And it's like a revelation, they never saw the connection."

The others in the room all laughed. Mike said, "They walk around the church with heavy frowns and then they wonder why their kids wear frowns. That's what you're doing to your ministry. That's what you did, Rice Rekstein. And listen, it has to stop immediately. And fully. I am dead serious. You need to understand this at this very instant. It stops. Right now." And Mike Fontenot's face turned meaner than I would have thought possible. He was filled with some severe feeling.

John Causey said, "With all due respect, Mike, I'm not sure it's so simple. I don't think, Reks, that you do understand. You've been aggressive even from the moment you walked up the sidewalk. You bring Martin Blackman here? He is in the hands of Satan. These Elders might be humble in saying you're simply not doing enough to stop these people from dropping like flies around you, but I'm not going to be humble. I'm not a Regional Sector Leader in order to wear a white hat, I'm a Regional Sector Leader in order to speak God's truth. Am I really holding a negative document that you just distributed to attack the church and its members? We are God's army, trying to spread righteousness around the world, as God has called us to do, but instead we are sitting around this room with *you*. And I hear you're writing a book? You've just published attacks on the church and now you're writing a book? You've caused fall-aways, attacked the church, shown endless pride, been endlessly negative and critical. And you even said things about my wife, my own wife."

"I've never said a single word about your wife."

"Well, you can say you don't remember but my wife sure does. A Sister had to approach me in humility and respect one evening to say that you made comments against my wife's preaching, her leading, and even her character. My wife." I shook my head, no. He shook my document. He said, "The Bible says Leaders are appointed by God. By God." He went on about his wife and I shook my head. John Goodman seemed willing to slightly step in, saying, "Yeah, it's the unknowns which are the danger. We don't really know how much you have said or written. We don't know the full damage. And these men are paid to be careful, to protect their flock."

There was a knock at the door. Causey went downstairs. I heard Martin's voice. Causey said to him, "We are not finished here." Martin responded, "It's just that I'm Reks's ride and it has been two hours." Causey said, "What do you want?" Martin said, "I just want to make sure he's okay." I looked around at the faces and then I said toward the stairs, "Martin, I'm okay. I can get home."

He responded, "I'll wait."

When I sat down again, John Goodman said, "Eduardo is another concern. We have no idea about that Brother. He attends all the services but no one has any idea what he's thinking. He's in your complete control."

I looked deeply into John Goodman's eyes a moment. I said, "Eduardo is close with Brothers and Sisters all over the region." John Goodman said, "But Leadership is responsible for him, do you understand? I have no idea what's influencing Eduardo, and who he might be influencing."

I opened my hands for a moment, but John Causey jumped back in. "You're not getting it. *Exodus* tells us how some disciples got negative and critical to the point that they held secret meetings against Moses. That's you. You lead secret meetings, you hurt other disciples, you insulted my wife, and you are a best friend to fall-aways."

"I don't believe that I ever said a word against your wife in my life." Two hours later, John Goodman presented the final recommendations.

"While letting Leadership worry about solving any problems in Leadership, thank you, I'm recommending that we dissolve the International Ministry. It's just not right anymore. And we'll put you under Jake Scott, who is leading a DC Talk not far from your employment. Maybe eventually, Catherine could join you there." He looked at Causey and blushed and laughed. But they let John Goodman lead a hand-holding prayer, after which I walked down his stairs, feeling that my concerns had been heard, my words read. I felt the peace of having dialogued, finally. I opened the door to the night and found Martin up the sidewalk.

My mood dropped back to the ground—gone were the possibilities for me to join Martin and Bob where they were going. Instead I was still in that old heavy routine. Martin and I drove in silence. Then we stood outside my house while the bugs buzzed and the ducks quacked.

"Greenbelt," I said. "It isn't really disciples."

"We could behave as disciples."

"I liked that preacher," I admitted. "Yet, why are they still that size after five years? We might have to start a completely new church."

"If that's God's call, we'll do it."

"But we would need to build from scratch, a whole new structure, everything, usher teams, communion trays, church plantings, everything."

Martin was smiling. "So we would need to buy some communion trays."

"Just so you realize, we're talking here about starting up a whole new global movement."

"Why does it have to be a movement?"

I was surprised. "I believe this is what the Bible calls for. Jesus told fishermen to leave their fishing nets. Forget normal life."

We decided to let it rest tonight. Martin and I shook hands and then pulled in for a hug goodbye. I went inside and realized that I would not sleep this night. My brain was spinning. I lay in bed and stared upward. In the morning I took the bus to Jubilee and finished my grant requests and planned the satellite move and then called Catherine.

Everything was going to be okay, I assured her. She said the Annapolis Leaders had warned her to guard her heart—her voice rose in an unnecessary panic here on the phone. I had to breathe for a moment before calmly repeating that everything was going to be okay. As requested, I ate lunch with Jake of the Inner-city Ministry. His expression was darker than usual—of course he had been speaking with someone. "I have to know you'll take advice. And that the other members won't get discouraged by you."

"Jake, you know me."

He said calmly, sternly, "Sure, we have history. But these disciples are my responsibility. God holds me accountable for their salvation." I met with Eduardo after work. We sat in the afternoon sunlight and watched the bridge and its flow of walkers.

Eduardo said, "C'mon, Bro', don't worry. We have a good thing going here." After a long moment, he said, "What about Bob?"

After another moment, I said, "They didn't make it, Eddie." Eduardo chortled small and quick. We sat quietly again.

We walked the bridge without speaking. We ate our dinner. The next day we met up with John Hildebrand of Jubilee Housing and served dinner at the shelter. Catherine brought a co-worker. She had found a new job at an auction house here in DC. I stirred the green beans while Eduardo flipped burgers. Catherine, while serving, asked each resident about his health. Her co-worker giggled. The residents weren't much for chatter—most had a Program meeting to get to. Later I thanked Catherine for trying to encourage them.

John Causey was removed from Leadership. Curiosity buzzed across the fellowship, but we stifled any gossip. Leadership divulged no reason.

Bob called instantly. He'd been calling often now, sharing his freshest insight and checking on how I was doing in his former church. He said Greenbelt was great, the preacher and the other leaders were humble, and the racial mix was right-on.

Sometimes I had to hold the phone away. Bob said, "The Causey thing could be just a power move, so that Kip isn't threatened by anyone growing too strong. The more I reflect on it, the more Soviet it all seems, with the systematic quelling of independent thought. If you try to speak up, they silence you, for crimes against the people. It's a totalitarian personality cult, complete with purges and reporting and information control, all behind a wall—or fence—of fear. Fear that they might break you up with your girlfriend, or not allow you to marry, or demote you down the ladder, or just slander you. Fear that if you don't say the right thing—c'mon Reks, people are afraid to say the wrong thing or speak the wrong way or not sing loudly enough—fear that someone might report you to your discipler. Oh, and fear that you might go straight to hell in a bucket. Bro', Brother, if I can still call you that—and in my heart of hearts I know I can—I don't want you to have false hope that any of those Pharisees might change. They are straight out of *Matthew*, the exact leaders who resisted Christ, resisted changing. Reks, do you know about the suicides? There've been more than a handful, and it can't all just be members who had depression or whatever. There are testimonials on the internet now—I don't know why you won't look at the internet. Of course, not every church out here is the right home, but many ex-members have moved ahead as Christians. Try Greenbelt again. Hear me." I watched Gloria counting away on her little machine. I only sat at this desk on some fundraising afternoons now, otherwise I was at our satellite office. When I put the phone back to my ear, Bob said he had a headhunter looking to place him in Moscow.

The rehabbed Perry Center was occupied by eager agencies including day care and computer learning and Tracie and me. I was the only white guy on the bus. I bussed from the suburbs to our main office and I transferred to go deeper into the ghetto projects. When we opened our new office doors, Applicant flow was so large that Terry asked Mary Dee to join us. So, sometimes Mary gave me a morning ride.

Mary said from her desk, "The bus makes me nervous because Terry calls me sharply at nine to check my punctuality. The other day I was yelling evilly in my head for the bus not to kneel for some old lady. She can get up those stairs herself!" Tracie was laughing. We each interviewed a dozen new Applicants and told them the workshop schedule. Then we picked up the phone and called around town on their behalf.

"Dang, Reks," said Tracie. "You getting all the toughies."

"What?"

It was true I had been last to realize that Erica, my six-foot-three Applicant who already struggled because of enormous dresses and lengthy unemployment, was a man named Eric. Mary Dee moaned, "Bad enough he-she was born a man, why did he-she have to be the size of a professional football player?"

"Shoo'," said Tracie, "I was talking about the other Eric, Eric Hunt. I saw what happened, Reks." Mary asked, "What happened, what happened?"

I said, "You saw that? That wasn't normal?" So I told Mary Dee, "Eric Hunt's been coming in for several weeks. He has a slight limp, and a missing tooth, and nary a day's work. He does the phones at his shelter sometimes, so they've let him stay longer than the limit, while he looks for the job.

"Yet he has trouble finding interview locations. Au Bon Pain was hiring if he went downtown right away, yet Eric didn't make it in time to meet the manager, who later complained to me and hired Tracie's Applicant." Mary high-fived Tracie. I continued, "So I sent him up to that Silver Spring cafeteria."

Mary said, "You mean where they hire everyone?"

"But he couldn't find it. They've hired dozens yet Eric Hunt said it wasn't there. The next day I gave him even clearer directions and sent him back, yet he still couldn't find it. I told him he was going back again anyway, that this employer was waiting to start him right away. And then—Tracie saw it too—some tears welled up in the guy's eyes." I looked at Tracie, I looked at Mary.

I said, "The guy was crying. Right here." Driving back that afternoon, Mary discussed her French Catholic fiancé. Marriage was imminent but she said, "I consider married people dead. Their lives are over."

"Even for Mary Dee?"

"Yeah," she said, "I worry about my personal needs, my future needs. I need someone cool and cute and funny." We were stopped outside the main Jubilee. I was looking out the windshield.

"Reks," said Mary, "you're funny." I continued looking out the windshield.

"Well," I said, "what's-his-name seemed like a nice guy. And couples grow together." We opened our doors and exited her car.

Eduardo and I walked the bridge. Someone waved hello, recognizing us. We had read to hundreds of people here. Thousands had refused. I slapped Eduardo on the shoulder. "Jesus sent 'em out two by two for a reason. You're the best." We got several phone numbers and we set up a study for tomorrow at Bruce Lee's, and then we sat down renewed our two-week purity pacts.

Joseph Kira came back to town. I gave him a big hug. He said, "The Montreal Church is awesome. It's smaller than DC but everyone is fired up and committed. We're like family, with everything visible, no one independent." It didn't matter what he said, every word from his African ex-SAIS face was gold. We dropped his bags at my house and lunched with Olivier.

In the morning, I rode the bus to work. The Jubilee steps, where Eduardo and I sometimes sat after work, had begun to crumble. George came upstairs and asked me, "How do you spell 'Cautions', like 'Be Cautions'?"

I pretended to think about it. I didn't want to be right, not while George was leaning studiously over his new sign. Maybe there was no right. I suggested, "Please Use Caution or Please Be Cautious."

George stared skeptically. Soon there was a cardboard sign taped on the steps, "Please Be Cautions." I watched other faces read it while obediently stepping over it. No one tripped. George had a high-school diploma, like many of our Applicants, one of whom I asked, "You wrote, 'Antionette'. Did you mean 'Antoinette'?" She shrugged, "Yes, but we spelled it wrong. Too late."

Maybe there was no right. I wondered the same with our many Isaihs and Antwans. They were unemployed. So was Dwonn. Mary Dee introduced me to Janine spelled Jeanne. According to her application, Jeanne lived in Vagina. Mary Dee stared at me for a moment, then picked up the phone to seek out job interviews for her. Tracie said, "We had one named Anita Job."

She added, "Psyche."

In the morning, I met Joseph at the breakfast table. He said, with his big smile, "Gosh, I got so much rest." And I actually got irritated because I had awoken tired and tense. I handed him a can of tuna for mixing while I prepared sandwiches. When I came back he had immersed it in mayonnaise. "What the heck, Joseph? It's swimming." He laughed even though I was truly inflamed—I was trying to fight it—with my skin and eyes prickled by my premature waking. I apologized. We rode the subway to the airport, and I hugged him for long and told him I missed him here. I returned to work.

Mary said, "Annie says Terry is driving her crazy to meet the daily quotas, and that Terry has been even harder on Mike Bliss, and that Tracie went to the doctor and has ulcers and it's because she has worked here too long and Terry only cares about the number of Placements and not even who's still on the jobs! Is she trying to please the board or something? Can I even say this to you?"

I said, "She seems like a good leader. Maybe she just needs to spend more time at the office, instead of using those statistics as her way of leading. Maybe I'll say something to her." She was driving us back to the office for staff meeting.

Mary was pulled from the satellite. Terry said it was necessary.

I asked, "Why?" Terry answered, "Reks, I fully trust you to lead down there, but in the end it's my responsibility that certain people get enough supervision." I nodded. Terry continued, "It's not just Mary. I've realized that Mike Bliss needs more accountability than anyone. But that's only one reason why we report our monthly stats."

"Weekly and daily too."

"Of course. Everyone has accountability in their lives, Reks."

"Of course," I said. "Some people are also driven by mission."

"They are. And one doesn't replace the other."

"Good. But I think Mike's a good worker. And he cares."

"That's fine, Reks. I have doubts, but he'll get a fair chance like all." She knew I looked up to her. She sat there a moment longer in case I had anything else on my mind. Then we closed up the office together. Eduardo was sitting on the steps. Terry gave him a warm hello and walked on. I sat down and we enjoyed the quiet for a moment.

"Yeah," said Eduardo, "I've been thinking. I guess, I'm gay. I guess, I'm accepting it. That's who I am." He sat there big and contrite. He said, "I still want to marry a Sister and all that. But that's who I am, I see."

"Well," I said, "you say this is who you are, and I have many arguments against it, including those of Apostle Paul and Sigmund Freud and Charles Darwin and the PFoX guys and your abusers and maybe your own words. But who am I to argue? Well, I'm a disciple of Christ, that's who. But what do I really know? I know that I desire women and it's not a decision but such a force that I actually have to war against it. And Christ gives me the power to do so, and marriage will help too if I choose it, which seems wise. But if you feel something different than what I feel, can I tell you not to feel it? Anyway, so you're getting married you say?" He was staring heavily. The Jubilee office was dark and closed behind us.

"Anyway, Eddie, my main man, my Brother, we gotta do what we think is right."

He said, "Bob really disappoints me. I'm not sure he was ever real with us. Maybe he came just to get Luda out. And that Martin, oh my goodness, who does he think he is, coming in here and ruining a good thing? We had a good group. I don't even want to hear his name. Ever." I stared ahead at the street. He said, "And your Greenbelt thing, c'mon Reks, that's no church. Who are those people? C'mon, get real. Not going there."

Catherine finally walked the bridge. "This is not natural for me." She gave it her all. She spoke to strangers, she showed her open Bible, she didn't deny Christ.

Afterward she smiled and hugged me a bunch. She clung to my neck. She even stuck out her tongue in jest that we might kiss. I told her to not even consider it—we wanted to be pure examples. She said, "My disciplined guy, my righteous guy, my guy." Catherine, with her blue eyes and cropped bangs, was also a gal who could wear a skirt. And she had that size up top, too. I had actually stolen some glances in recent months, and I wasn't sure what exactly could be awaiting there, and I wasn't sure whether it was supposed to matter. Tracie called in sick the next morning so I ran the satellite workshops alone. "Where do you want to be in a couple years?"

One guy responded, "I don't care what I'll be doing, I just know I'll be earning more than that sorry minimum. And I'm gonna have me benefits too." The group applauded and asked for more details, and he said, "I don't know exactly but they'll be the best benefits, French benefits, that I know." This struck me because in this expressive group another fellow had just criticized our politicians who hadn't raised that sorry minimum. "While they're sittin' up there in their Eiffel towers."

Soon I stood at the Perry Center bus stop, many layers within the ghetto. No one bothered me. No one looked. The passing black faces didn't know my work. They didn't care. In fact faces were few in this cityscape, where, waiting for a bus that just would not arrive already, a certain human might think himself alone and isolated.

But no, the corner was jammed with loud car traffic, the converging of New Jersey and New York Avenues, the drivers diverse, all windows up, strangers seated and separated. Standing here, I was worried whether the next fundraising check would arrive. I thought about it in my recliner that night. I prayed and read away the worry, while awaiting sleep.

The next evening I was at Jake's Bible Talk. Jake was a high-school teacher and coach. Leo the new convert from Mexico was the only other non-black member, and he seemed to fit well with the group's culture and dialect. I called him Leo Lionheart, from Ted Woods's old Jean Claude-Damme videos. I invited Leo out to lunch in the Jubilee neighborhood.

His response was silence and hesitation, perhaps not knowing that disciples needed to bond across boundaries. I said with a smile, "It's important for spiritual health." He didn't smile but we did lunch later in the week.

I asked non-smiling Leo Lionheart how he was doing, and he said, "What do you mean?" I said, "How are you doing in the church, are you happy, is your faith growing, are you encouraged? It can be tough sometimes." He didn't seem to like the question. I worried about his humility and discernment, but I had confidence in Jake as his discipler.

Preacher Daryl Reed of Detroit was brought in to lead the DC Church. At the pulpit, Daryl was very serious, even indignant, about something somewhere, he apparently not here to take anything easy and light about Christianity. When I approached him for insight he cut me off there in the hotel conference room, saying, "Actually, you were once a fall-away and now you're out operating on your own."

His scowl surprised me. To have labeled me a former fall-away, when I had missed nary a stride, this was a stab. At the pulpit meanwhile he blasted on about our negativity and complacency. "Get something done for God already!" Preaching style was evidently not the reason that Causey was removed. Daryl introduced a faith-sharing campaign during which each Talk was required to meet designated baptism goals. It was being called a blitzkrieg. Again I wondered, when we were able to stand and step out of the aisles, what was the audience reaction? It was like coming out of foxholes, assessing the damage.

People were hugging. They were praising the blitz. They were dispersing the blitz invitations among their Talks. Catherine said, "That was so convicting." Here in the aisles, someone brought me their visitor, a Muslim fellow. The member must have thought I could help explain it all. I said to the guy, "The creeds may all seem similar. But if we look closer we see they are plenty different, even mutually exclusive. The New Testament is living and active with a man carrying a pure message and proving it with his life and death. Christ freed us from the dark rule of the Old Testament, and Islam seems to try to bring us back there, no offense."

"So where did the book come from?"

"Well, where did the Mormon book come from?" This guy was open enough to be showing doubt approaching anguish. I added, "Someone even gave me a Third Testament once, no joke, I have it at home. A thickly bound Third Testament, there on the sidewalk. But it wasn't living and active." He wouldn't agree to study. I needed a partner like Daniel Bertholet who could listen discerningly and then speak strongly from the soul. Singles Leader Anton tried with his Texas smile but the guy didn't buy it. So it was one less shot at a baptism during blitz month. Anton went off to the Leaders Meeting for another Daryl Reed sermon. I was no longer a Leader.

Daryl's Midweek sermon was about our need to get committed. Daryl at the pulpit with his big wingspan and ever-frown said, "Break from your complacency, break from your comfort zone, the disciples must repent. During singing, some of you weren't even clapping and cheering—I was standing in the back, I was watching. And you call yourself disciples? In this church? I was watching!" A big crowd lined up to greet and thank him.

Eduardo and I pulled another study off the bridge, and though staff knew we were out here, some of our stats weren't getting up through Jake anymore. God was my shepherd and I spent late evenings with him, and with my revising, ideally then reading myself to sleep in the reclining chair.

> ***After the attempt on his life, Hitler called his leaders together and leapt up in a fit of frenzy, with foam on his lips, and shouted that Providence had just shown him once again he had been chosen to make world history; and he ranted wildly about terrible punishments for all. The court fell silent as the Fuehrer raged for a full half-hour; the visitors thought he must be mad; "I don't know," said one, "why I didn't go over to the Allies there and then."***

But that guy didn't go, according to this Interwar reading. Neither did others, named Shellenberg and Schwerin.

> ***They were longstanding members of the Nazi administration. Their belief that they could preserve their independence within it, could influence it for good, and could be accepted themselves as anti-Nazi or at least non-Nazi, only showed the extent of their blindness.***

At Bruce Lee's, handsome-faced Lance said, "Do you know how many converts a Mormon missionary averages in his two years? Eight. Know how many I converted in Italy? Fifty-five. People just liked me."

I asked, "But didn't they see signs during their studies?"

Mormon Lance thought for an instant and said, "You hoped so. That always helped." I was trying to be a good listener, like my Christian-Left John Hildebrand. At our most recent lunch, John had said very kindly, "You seem to have a lot on your heart. But they say a healthy faith has a healthy doubt. Don't worry."

At the next study with Lance I read from *Hebrews*, "Faith is being sure of what we hope for."

Lance responded, "I like your guys' style, out there with the book. But I saw internet reports on you. Mandatory numbers of visitors? Pressured conversions? The goal to convert someone can infect your every action, every sentence. Even your agreeing with me now is a manipulation. When you simply pour all this attention on someone new, it's called love bombing. I might have been guilty of it."

In the morning I was picking up breakfast, across from our Perry Center, for Tracie and me. Fearful Asians were operating the grill behind bulletproof glass. Food and money were transferred through a small bulletproof revolving window.

No one said a thing about it. At midday I left Tracie and stood at the bus stop. I stood there for one hour. Again, there was no one who looked like me, no one looking at me, no one to talk to. I was the invisible man.

Jubilee was on track for an unprecedented seven hundred Placements this year. I found a cleaning job for a male Applicant named Terry, but two bus transfers only put him in cab-ride distance to the place of employment, so I lent him twenty dollars. Tracie laughed at me.

I didn't really expect to get it back, and I was happy that Terry Smith was getting to work. I was striving not to be motivated by being able to report a Placement. One afternoon, Mary Dee came to me upstairs and said, "Reks, I just have to tell you—please let me—that before we opened up this morning, I joined the Terry Flood prayer huddle in our front lobby, with George and Ethel and Gloria and Mike and the Rev, and with Annie opting out as usual. But the point is it was pouring cold rain and Terry stood with us next to all the empty chairs while at least twenty Applicants stood outside, faces pressed to the glass, in the rain. And Terry so calmly led our prayer.

"No one else seemed to notice. So I questioned Terry and she said, 'No Mary, they know we don't open until nine. And they can bring an umbrella. They can learn.' So I realized what it is, her mission is more important than people. It's so messed. At least I've realized."

"We should get an awning."

"Reks!" Mary yelled.

I said, "She should've let them sit inside, you're right, she should've made an exception. I'm proud of you for speaking up."

Back on the bus, I heard a black guy saying, "They keeping us down, there ain't nothing a black man can do to rise himself up." Another black guy responded, "There are so many opportunities here, I can't even believe it, I can hardly choose."

"Where you from?" asked the first. The answer was Haiti. The black Haitian began to explain to his fellow rider the concept of American community college. Late in the rainy afternoon, I walked out of Perry back toward my bus.

Terry Smith came running out after me. "Ms. Tracie said you just left. I need another twenty to get to work." I gave it to him. When we learned he had already quit, Tracie laughed. And she sighed. I was tired that morning, not groggy tired but tensely exhausted again. I felt it while dialoguing with each Applicant and counting the others still awaiting me. I let Tracie go uptown early so I could just recline in my work chair.

But our New York Avenue had trucks with screeching brakes. Why couldn't I have gotten lucky with a backside office? I walked down to my bus and eventually arrived at our uptown office. For the second time this year, Jeff Kleinman called me in response to receiving a manuscript. Apparently my syntax was now crisper, but Mr. Jeff Kleinman said, "I can't put my finger on it, there still might be a systemic flaw. It's a beautiful book, it'll never get published."

I thanked him. This was goodbye to *Both Sides of Winter*. I did indeed feel closure. I had done all I could. I would put my pencil down.

That night I got on my computer and typed up a little "Encouragement" study to carry around just in case. *Acts* 14: "Paul and Barnabas preached the good news, strengthening the disciples and encouraging them to remain true to the faith." *Acts* 15: "The people read the Apostles' letter and were glad for its encouraging message. And Judas and Silas said much to encourage and strengthen the brothers." *Acts* 16: "After Paul and Silas came out of the prison, they went to Lydia's house, where they met with the brothers and encouraged them." *Acts* 20: "Paul sent for the disciples, and after encouraging them, set off for Macedonia. He traveled through that area, speaking many words of encouragement to the people." It was everywhere.

Thessalonians 2: "For you know that we dealt with each of you as a father deals with his own children, encouraging, comforting, and urging you to live lives worthy of God, who calls you into his kingdom and glory." *Thessalonians* 5: "Therefore encourage one another and build each other up, just as in fact you are doing." I knew well that I was starving.

Of course I did appreciate Jesus's harangues. "Repent or perish; I came to divide; I came to bring fire; stick to the narrow path, few will find it; attempt the narrow door, few will be let in; deny yourself; lose your life; carry your cross; count the costs or don't even start." I utilized them all the time, in tandem with the joy and light, the good news, and Christ's thrice questioning of Peter, "Do you truly love me? Then feed my sheep.'"

VI

I arrived at work to learn that Terry Flood had fired Mike Bliss. The counselors sat subdued at their desks, telephoning potential employers. Upstairs, Terry told me that Mike had been struggling to make Placements. I said, "He wanted them prepared to last. He spent time on securing their housing, clothing." Terry said even when Placements didn't retain their jobs, many lessons were learned. I walked off to meet Eduardo and another study.

He was a GW grad student. I considered how GW had been the location of my first DC service, in the sunny Campus Center, before we had been kicked out, and before Eduardo divulged what was occurring in its bathroom stalls. Our GW Study volunteered to attend Midweek, where Daryl then screeched about the many verses showing Jesus surrounded by a crowd. "Yet you in the DC Church are trying to stay at home, trying to live alone! You're living independent and complacent! *Acts* says, 'All the believers continued to meet together. They broke bread in their homes and ate together with glad and sincere hearts, enjoying the favor of all the people. And the Lord added to their number daily!' See, they were growing, because they brought visitors! Yet some of you don't even want to come to our meetings anymore. Here's ten scriptures with Jesus in the middle of a crowd." And while Daryl Reed screeched on, our GW visitor whispered, "He could have easily shown ten with Jesus spending time completely alone."

Daryl said, "Some of you are endlessly negative and critical about Leadership! You think this is easy? You think you can lead better? If you want to lead, if you think you can do better, come down here right now. Right now." He licked his little mustache and stepped back. The crowd cawed in support of him. Daryl repeated, "Come down right now if you think you can lead better. Here's the podium. Come down."

I had the Encouragement Study right here in my Bible. I would stand up and walk down and just put my Bible on the podium and lead them gently through the verses, saying nothing else. I would have to scoot past my visitor—such disunity in front of a visitor!—but eventually they would all hear why. Yet they were still yelling in support of Daryl, who was still yelling the challenge.

And their misplaced loyalty might rain down on me. They might see Daryl as the victim. Most everyone was black—they might see it as racial. They were disciples, but did I really know their hearts? Then again, maybe encouragement was exactly what they needed and they just didn't know it. Yet maybe it was me who didn't have the right heart here—I racked my brain to understand. I had hesitated, the window closed. Maybe a better chance would come. The next day, I again sat unrested in front of my Applicants.

Daryl Reed never called as promised. Bob called, to say he and Luda were moving to Moscow. "Brother, we love you, we care about you, take care of Eduardo.

Maybe we'll see you over there one day. Oh, Luda and I watched the wedding video again. Geez did Goodman get his barbs in. Now I see it. It's so odd. Now I can see it. Anyway, you and I, we were in the trenches together. Front lines."

"Fine," said Eduardo at dinner, "I'm willing to go once. But then I don't want to hear about Greenbelt anymore at all ever again."

"Oh, thank goodness," I thought. I called Martin.

That Sunday, Eduardo and I traveled the other way on the subway and then we punched the machine to get bus transfers and the transfers read, 'Greenbelt Station, September 29th, 1998'. I was finally making it back to that little fellowship.

The preacher again was the orange-bearded knowing son of Boston ICC disciples. Once again his smiley sermon was positive and biblical. Martin was sitting with his new girlfriend. Other members remembered and greeted me. What to do about Catherine? Such treason would never cross her mind. No, I needed to remain part of the one true body. Martin gave me long, knowing, patient looks. He felt the Eduardo tension. He dropped us back at the subway. I saved my bus transfer, slipping it in my favorite Bible.

At times, a dozen Jubilee Applicants sat waiting in Ethel's lobby chairs. They sat with their fists to their chins. I had never seen one read a book or a magazine or newspaper, not once, zero times. Today when Tracie and I walked in, there sat Perry Morgan. "Remember me? You gave me five bucks for a hammer a few years ago."

"I'll never forget it." We paused. I said, "You're unemployed."

He said, "Yeah, no that job didn't last, I mean I couldn't keep it, the supervisor was all bossy. And it was way out there and our guy with the car got all arrested. Since then, man I ain't had much. But catch this, one of them SAIS guys at the subway told me you worked up here. I was like, man, that is my man. He can help me out. So I came up." We had him book with Ethel for next week's workshops. He didn't attend. I said, "Oh, Tracie, why, why, why?"

She answered, "Because they don't wanna work."

"What?"

"They don't wanna work."

"What are you talking about?"

"They don't wanna work."

"But what do you mean?"

"What do you mean, 'What do I mean?' They don't want to work. Do I have to draw you a pitcher?"

Gloria the bookkeeper jumped up. "I'll draw you a pitcher. They come in here all pimpin'." And she imitated the guys who walked with one dangling, swinging arm and some weird cool unnecessary limp. "And the girls come in here all switchin'." She did their walk, shaking and showcasing the rump as they slowly paraded through. I looked past Gloria's shoulder out our window, where I could see DC rooftops on their way downtown and then finally the tip of the Washington Monument. I stared for a long time. Gloria left for the day and I sat a bit longer.

I biked home. It was early but I laid down to sleep. And still then, at my Perry morning, on brake-screeching New York Avenue, I felt that prickly unrest, wherein sleep hadn't really come. I sat with my Applicants and wondered how, feeling like this, I could be of much help. My brain and eyes were straining, less focused than theirs for sure.

I called Jake and told him that I just couldn't phone in the Expected Visitors stat this week unless I was allowed to tell the visitors I was doing so—could we be open about this? Jake said he would get advice. The next day, I called up Colin and told him I was getting engaged, and he again left the phone swinging while rushing down with Sue for congratulations.

I caught Catherine jogging and she stared at the ring wide-eyed and stunned and messy-haired, and she stared the same at Colin and Sue arriving to join us. They were treating us to a nice dinner and Catherine remained uncharacteristically quiet. "Rekstein," asked Colin, "you got advice from your Leader, right?"

Now I did get a call from Daryl Reed. "Mike Fontenot regrets that we didn't deal with this long before." Catherine and I were invited over to the Reeds but it wasn't engaged-couple's counseling. I watched Catherine's nervous face. Daryl said, "We're not sure we want Reks in this church anymore, in God's kingdom anymore."

Catherine said, "Oh my gosh."

Daryl said, "Unless something intervenes sort of miraculously, it's probably a done deal. He is disfellowshipped."

Catherine repeated, "Oh my gosh."

Daryl said, "Reks, you have nothing to say?" Catherine said, "Yeah Reks, I mean my goodness."

I said, "Is there a specific charge?" Daryl said, "Yes, the charge is that of being independent and critical. Not necessarily spoken, but silently critical." His wife said nothing. Eyes were on me. I said, "We're in a spiritual battle, as you know.

So I want to be humble and patient about this." Daryl interrupted, "Enough leaders, high in the kingdom, have already supported this." This week was my fifth anniversary as Christ's disciple—I felt the floor dropping out. What Catherine was feeling I could tell by her ghost-white face. When we were back outside she wanted to hug but then didn't want to. I had a call set up with Daryl for tomorrow. Maybe I could get others to lobby before the door sealed shut.

Singles Leader Anton didn't pick up, so I left him a message and another in an hour. I called John Goodman and left a message. I was blind to what discussions had already occurred. I read, "If you have faith as small as a mustard seed, you can say to this mountain, 'Move from here to there,' and it will move. Nothing will be impossible for you." I called Colin.

"No," he said, "it isn't supposed to happen this way—I think the Bible calls for a dialogue and defense. Let me call Steve Johnson, Global Sector Leader. Pray, Rekstein, pray. Get on your knees, get in the scripture. You do have your pride and arrogance you know? Of course you know. God's in control so it's okay, but crucify your pride. I'll get back to you."

On the phone with Daryl Reed, I politely defended my case—my disunity might have come from the encouragement lack and the yelling excess. He seemed to be listening a bit. It was me and this Regional Sector Leader deciding my fate on the phone.

"It's true," said Daryl, "Kip McKean requires voice raising, or yelling as you choose to call it, in each sermon." At least Daryl could admit it. He made no ruling. Colin called again—Global Sector Leader Steve Johnson had responded positively. "He says Mike Fontenot is a meat-and-potatoes guy who isn't used to eccentric types. Luckily, Steve is the one who started the Arts Ministry here, and he planted the DC Church. He said he would call Mike and then you're to call Mike later. How's the humility?"

"I'm trying. I feel hollow." I breathed nervously when I finally picked up the phone to call Mike. His personal assistant answered and I knew her from over the years and her voice held worry for me and she said, "Mike's not here but he'll call right away. Don't worry." I thanked her. I re-read the move-mountains scripture. Nothing was impossible.

Jordan McCloud called. I hadn't seen him since Popeye's in Harlem. He was calling from Israel. He and his dream wife were leading the Jerusalem planting, the return of first-century disciples. "Dude," he said, "what is this madness?" I tried to explain.

Jordan said, "All I can say is pray. Pray for God to forgive you, to save you. Do anything to get back in the kingdom." Catherine called. I began to quote my mountain scripture to her but she said with alarm, "They must've not expected me at Midweek tonight, Reks, I mean Daryl even saw me and said, 'Oh you're here?' Because then they read out a letter against you—it was written by some private lawyer, like to protect them or something. I was sitting right there. They marked you. No one is allowed to have contact with you. They said you had distributed negative documents about the church, and that you were writing a book against it, and that you made websites against it."

We both held the phone in pause. I said, "Are you waiting for me to confess to that?" She cried, "Reks, Jenny says they read the same letter in Annapolis. They said you're a wolf. What am I supposed to do?!"

I was holding the phone and staring into the distance. I quoted, "'If you have faith as small as a mustard seed, you can say to this mountain, "Move from here to there" and it will move.'" I called Jake. I could picture his unsmiling face. Jake said, "They consulted me on the decision, yes. I responded simply that I couldn't think of a reason for you to be in the church, in the movement. That's all."

"That's incredible."

"I prayed about it. But Brothers had even reported to me that you asked them at lunch or something how could they be happy in this church."

"Now that is incredible."

Mike Fontenot's assistant called me. She said, again with emotion, "I swear he's going to call soon. He is. Hang in there." I stopped leaving messages with Anton. Meanwhile, Eduardo had stopped attending. I visited him at his Georgetown store and there in the shipping room we called up Catherine and arranged for Eduardo to take her to church. I wanted him to support her. Plus, the more bodies involved in the fellowship and righteousness the better, no matter.

Big Daryl Reed took Eduardo out of that chair beside Catherine. And there by the door on the edge of the audience Daryl asked him, "Why are you here? You are yeast. We don't want you here. You are yeast, you are yeast."

Silent, open-mouthed Eduardo was thrown out. At the Leaders Meeting that night, Jenny asked Mike Fontenot's assistant when the Elder would be calling Catherine back. The assistant answered, "He called her back. I know so because he told us he called her back."

Jenny said, "I live in the same room with the girl and know for a fact that he hasn't called." They put Jenny and her boyfriend on open warning.

Catherine quit the church, as they had in fact assumed she would weeks earlier, they misjudging her level of devotion and trust, and how far she first had to plunge.

She wasn't warm to the Greenbelt idea. She was sure, despite the presence of Martin, that it was lukewarm non-disciples. Eduardo just laughed and started scheduling other things on Sunday mornings. I asked, "But who's gonna tie your tie?" He laughed again. He said, "Trust me, for this I won't need a tie. No, it's not what you think."

Seated in my rocking recliner, I gazed over at my desk and lamp and computer. And though the book was closed and the urgent message gone—what had the message been, that post-communist Czechs had briefly lived happily and sustainably?—my hand evidently still yearned to form sentences and images. I considered the collection of characters around me, peers with their very different paths, Martin Blackman and Ted Woods and George the Custodian. I took Eduardo and a tape recorder to Bruce Lee's. I asked him everything.

He answered. Then I biked home and jotted it down and crafted it up, listening to his voice within the Chinese music. He told me how his father had put their whole family in a truck every summer and driven to Michigan to pick peaches. I typed up a ten-page Eduardo portrait and then I called up Ted.

> ***"Actually I wonder what my dad did with all the money," says Eduardo. "There were about twenty of us earning cash every day yet we were always poor. I wonder what was actually going on." After high school, Eduardo packs up a box and makes some sandwiches and reserves a bus seat for DC. He has two hundred dollars saved. His father drives him to the station. His father asks to borrow some of the money.***
>
> ***Instead he gets some of the sandwiches. Now, Eduardo wears his classy Polo Store brand. "It's the image, the message." He smiles big and sheepish. He's the shipping clerk. He waits tables too. "The money's too good to quit. It's World Bankers and those other people in suits, I act friendly and they give me big tips." I smile, listening to Eduardo, my friend and peer with a big laugh, big heart, big secret.***

Ted Woods asked to meet at a fancy Bethesda restaurant where the manager then gave us a prime table and the waiter asked Ted for stock tips and they had our food on the table in five minutes. They must have stopped the whole kitchen for Ted. I guess he'd been working hard since Greensboro. I had brought the tape recorder.

According to Ted, he was the only one in high school who could get a zero on a ten question true-false exam. One teacher told me that Ted would grow up to be a door-to-door insurance salesman. Later he indeed goes door to door to ask people whether they have any labor for him, anything he might paint. He finds a few things, a room and then a house and then a building. He hires a couple of Mexicans and buys an old van. He ties his ladders on the van, about 15 ladders on the one long van, some tied with shoelaces. His Mexicans drive it around corners. The ladders stay on.

Ted watches movies as a quick break. He sits with his big tub of popcorn and wastes no time philosophizing, politicizing, sentimentalizing. He says, while munching, "Guns and martial arts, why not? I'm not here to think, unless it's about work." To consider the movie's morality would be a pointless distraction. Ted isn't even tempted. To discuss the movie afterward, pointless distraction. Ted has moved on. The Treasury Department needs its asbestos removed. Ted sends his workers. He expands to DC. He drives a big new pick-up truck between cities. He buys a Mercedes convertible. He buys a home in Bethesda, refurbishes it, sells it. He buys five more.

I said, "You got ten wrong on that true-false test but some might say you've have good luck." He sat thinking at this upscale restaurant, his forearms tan, he like some handsome Dean Moriarty, a character he'll never know. "No, I've slaved for it, the whole last decade I gave all my time and commitment. I remember trying to figure out whether to buy a table to eat on or whether to pay rent. Now I'm spending thousands on toys. I currently own seven million in real estate. I'll grind it out and buy another ten, and sell it all for about double next year."

"That's grinding it out?"

He explained, "The whole market could crash on me. You have to take risks, it's all about risk. Maybe you consider writing to have been a risk." He stared over at me. "But if you had gotten a real job when you came out, you could be worth a lot. If I were educated like you, I'd like to do something good for the world, like help with this internet boom. But listen, if you see life as a big painting with every color in it, you're wrong. At the end of the day it's black and white. This determines what you should be doing with your time. Life is tough. Be tougher." He had pegged my new insecurity. I was poor and stagnant, suddenly.

"Look, Reks, just be happy. It's simple. Be happy." He said it about ten times. Later that night I finally heard. He was telling me to worry about my happiness, do what I needed to be happy, let that be the priority.

At the Lord's Church of Greenbelt, Martin married Sennait. As far as this little mainstream church growing, Martin was ready and able to be my Eduardo. God could work through us. And Catherine had a partner in Sennait. The pieces were there.

Except that, even though I was sitting and listening with a smile, I was filled with that racing fatigue from another night of bad sleep. I told Martin about Ted racing out of the gate after high school. "He has more than a decade jump on me." Martin thought for only a short moment. He said, "Where is Ted spiritually? You have the jump on him."

> ***Ted is risking more inner-city hires for the asbestos. He wants to help. "But contractors don't want any attitude. None." He has been burned before — one black American fellow, when told he couldn't wear his doo rag, cussed out a contractor and lost Ted the job. That very night, someone broke into that contractor's office and stole the computers and, "Guess what's left on the window sill," Ted asks me. "A doo rag." The guy is in jail. Another disappeared with Ted's van, which Ted had to rescue deep in the ghetto one night. Yet Ted has me send him a hundred JJ Applicants. It costs him $250 per trainee — he will allow them to gradually repay him from their paychecks.***
>
> ***But there are no paychecks. Ted sends a crew up to a Connecticut job and upon arrival a tall black kid shows tall attitude by saying, "@!*%$# if I'm wearing that protective suit." The contractor fires the whole crew. Ted eats the job, plus the travel and hotel. Ted says, "The kid was probably just scared." In a week, only one of the hundred is still with him. Ted moves on, experiment over.***
>
> ***The fellow who does hang on is soon given the keys to Ted's cars and houses. At each dawn, Ted calls him and says, "Meet me in thirty and bring the big van," and they work until midnight. Ted reminds the fellow, "My grandmother can out work you." The guy tells me he has never seen anyone work like Ted.***

Eduardo, I gathered, was decompressing in other ways. He said, "Yeah I did hear all those screaming sermons, all those years. I just thought, why is this guy saying all this when he's just gonna be at home all week or in his car or at the gym?"

Eduardo and I stroll down the evening street. He says, "There is probably so much sex going on in there." I ask, "Where?" He says, "In the locker room of that health club." I say, "That's crazy." He likes the silence of the stalls, the lack of eye contact. "Anyway," he says, "you kept saying get a project, get a project, so I put an ad in the classifieds to photograph males nude. Six hundred guys called me that first week."

"What'd they want?"

"They want to be photoed. They want to be naked. They want to overcome. I got calls in the middle of the night. I got calls from California and Florida. You'd be surprised." Eduardo was shooting them there in his one room, curtains closed. "A guy from Denmark or somewhere. Straight men, married men, men in suits. You'd be surprised. They put the suit back on and slip back into the world." He stencils words on the bodies. "Meaningful ones." He wants me to provide some. He says, "I want to provoke people to think why society is the way it is, why everyone is addicted."

I caution him, "Don't go overboard." He jots it down." I say, "You're not listening." He jots it down.

For me, Jubilee's walls and rooms and people no longer shone when I walked up the front steps or lead a workshop or sat with my feet on my upstairs desk. It no longer emitted the aura of being the exact place for me, the only place.

Terry Flood changed none of her methods. She was absent each afternoon. Tracie's ulcers remained. Myself, I probably couldn't have just called up the World Bank anymore and simply joined my countless classmates there. The other half had gone to Goldman—and I had had youngest partner Mike Vonn—but their interests hadn't been mine. I hadn't even glanced that way.

Fair-skinned and strawberry-haired Annie has a figure. Her shirts grip her. They slope out with her and then tuck tightly beneath. That's how she wears them. Or is it just how they wear her? It's hard not to glance. We walk down the street toward a dinner we host for our inner-city unemployed and Annie puts her arm in mine. She is wearing a black-lace skirt. Heads stick out from passing cars.

At the dinner, Annie hugs her clients. She holds a client's little child in her arms. The child is wrapped around her, cozy and happy, not wanting to move. Annie gives a shoulder massage to a male client. Don't tell her she can't be friendly, don't tell her that men get the wrong impression. "That's their problem," she sasses, "I love people." Her voice is alive and intelligent. It is producing a longing in me. Should I feel guilty? The attendees stand and say their names and occupations. "Fulltime father of Annie, that's plenty," says her father, a US Congressman.

I consider asking him for a job. The next day, I teach a workshop to twelve former addicts. Later, a joke goes around our counseling desks, "Flirters Anonymous, are you joining?" We all admit we probably need some healing. Annie's not here and we say, "She's in denial anyway, she's not ready for recovery, she hasn't hit bottom."

The next week was our annual fundraiser. Annie came in a black dress, cut low beneath her shoulders. When we ran out of name tags, Annie pointed and said, "I don't have a name. I don't have a name for my chest." She had the corporate sponsors looking and laughing. "I don't have a name for my breasts."

"How about One and Two?"

"You know you love me, Reks."

"I like you, Annie, I do."

"Oh, Reks, you love me." She was smiling, laughing, holding me. She was glowing. She looked around at the gazing group and said loudly, "Oh, you guys are exactly like me."

I biked home and the Annie spell had subsided and so I had nothing to confess to Martin. I saw Annie the next day and she was a presence walking into the computer room, with her figure swaying and her hair shifting on her shoulders and her eyes on me. But I knew where it all led. I knew what happened when a man pursued his desire and then by chance fulfilled it, emptied it out, the desire suddenly gone, forgotten. I saw it clearly and I was glad I had the power to look away.

The day before the wedding, we treated each other to pedicures and manicures. Catherine wore a jeans-skirt outfit and I again saw those thin fit legs. She cut her bangs short and straight like the day I had met her. I had awoken with that strain in brain and heart, and now Catherine unexpectedly snapped and frowned at me. I asked, "Is this a sign?" She said, "Look, if you don't want to do this we don't have to." We were standing on the sidewalk.

I calmly tried to fix it. I stated how we already were a devoted couple, serving God by serving one another, and that this was our purpose and was in fact the only way marriage worked. I booked a posh hotel suite and Eduardo came up and we dined at the Cheesecake Factory. I joked, "I guess this is my bachelor party."

In the morning I woke up and felt again as if I had barely slept. My eyes ached like sores. I felt like I had just run up a staircase. I was confronted with a very long day. I put on my tuxedo and looked in the mirror and said, "I can't think straight right now. If need be, I'll just get out of this later."

I went off to the little Greenbelt church. And Catherine walked down, thin and fair and chesty with beautiful bare shoulders and big happy blue eyes under her bangs. I was in physical pain, I was focused on getting through the day.

Finally we walked along our hotel hallway, holding hands, passing another hotel guest who smiled and expressed congratulations—what a sharp happy pair. I could not wait to lay my body down to rest. Also, I would have sex for the first time in my new life. We got to the room and we lit candles and she asked me to remove her dress. I couldn't focus on the moment—I wasn't quite here. Touching her felt good. And soon I would safely sleep. Catherine said, "We're seeing each other for the first time." Her wide eyes expressed significance. She said, "More than seeing." Somewhere in my head I knew it meant something.

We had breakfast and went to the airport. On the plane to Denver, Catherine was smiling. We swam in a hotel pool beneath the big lonely western sky, and Catherine wore a purple one-piece and looked like a gem of a girl to have. We hugged in the corner of the pool and chatted calmly. Tomorrow we would drive up to Aspen. She said, "I've heard about married couples who did it non-stop on their honeymoon."

That sounded nice, but how did I get on a honeymoon? I couldn't possibly have been on one of those. Maybe this was just my odd sleep talking. I had laid there for the same hours as she but I had awoken several times and stirred without waking her. Now, with my neck and shoulders stiff, and my heart and mind weak, I felt absent again.

Catherine seemed serene and that was good and she was eager to investigate the Rockies for possible living—she might find her place finally, with employment in a resort hotel or something. She said with an excited clap, "We'll just tow out our bed and chairs and furniture and other thingies." I burned inside and said calmly, "You don't bring your bed to the Rockies. It's an outdoor adventure. You bring just what you need. A neck gator, sun cream." I thought about my efficient black-and-green boot bag. I still kept things in its pockets.

We drove up into the high, green slopes. Here was that magical terrain, the endless folds and yellow fauna and western trees. We unpacked at a wooden walled hostel. I asked some housekeeping kids about the job scene. "Dunno," they said. "We're doing this for a free bed tonight." For them this was adventure.

At night, Catherine and I again snuggled comfortably, I looking into her blue eyes and pink lips, she wrapping her arms around me and falling peacefully asleep. I listened, through the thin walls, to a neighbor snoring. I was facing a day of job hunting and interviewing.

At the first hotel, we got hired. "You're an attractive couple," said the manager. "I can put you both upfront. My wife and I came out for a year and have stayed twenty." I asked, "When do you need to know?"

He shrugged—he was relaxed and flexible. Catherine and I drove back to the hostel and hiked the grassy slope and gazed up at the dormant lifts and then down at the valley. I would have to teach her to ski and board, just as I had launched Steph and Deb. Even here on Aspen Mountain I could hear the flow of cars leaving and approaching the resort. Catherine didn't notice. Nighttime was coming to the hostel again.

"I want you to desire me," she said in our room. "It's very important to me. I want to be loved unconditionally." Her mouth was straight and serious, her voice high with emotion. The breasts that I had previously tried to assess through my guilt-laden peeks, here they now were, all mine.

But didn't the nipple point a bit downward, in some sag I supposed? It hurt to think so. Maybe we could get some fix job sometime, some year, in the future, the long future. Or maybe I would wake up from this. Or maybe I would finally sleep right. Or maybe God would help me. Catherine and I flew back.

And because I had tried sleeping in two different spec houses of Ted's, and from both I had heard the roar of cars and even airplanes, I was now moving back into my parents' house, and now with Catherine, my wife. And she was fine with this, thankfully. I crawled into the far corner of the bed. She said, "It's all okay,

Snuggle Bunny." And she fell asleep in my arms. In the morning I watched her hurry down the street toward the bus. I worried she might miss it. Her figure shrunk in the distance. Awaiting her at work was some phone answering and some assembling of catalogues, or something. I walked the opposite direction to my bus. The autumn leaves were now out, their faint scents finding me through the air. It made me think of Prague 1990.

Mary left Jubilee. Her reason, she said, was to get married. She was quickly gone to Arizona. "Tell her I miss her," I joked to Annie, when I gave up my computer seat so she could send an email letter to Mary. Oops, I glimpsed Annie signing in to the site, and she had typed almost entirely with her left hand. Possible letters jumped unsolicited to my mind.

At the first chance, I tried it. I knew her middle name was Therese. Good, it didn't work. I sat there for a moment. I put an A in front of it.

And lo, I was in Annie's email account. I paused to consider the significance. But my head was tired today, I couldn't think it through, so I just stared afar for another long moment.

Then I searched through her account. Here was her new boyfriend. I could identify when he entered her life. Oh, Annie was having a work crisis, she was completely burned out. Her friends were telling her how talented she was, how she simply needed to make a change. Anyway, with the boyfriend, a mutual friend had introduced them. It hadn't taken long before they started using the word love. She told him when she was sad. "I emailed like a hundred friends and no one's responding. I'm lonely! Oh yeah, I had this weird dream last night. I was in California, which was really Florida, and then I went to Nevada, which was really Texas. Am I crazy? And then you called and woke me up, in my dream. Oh my God, that's you on the phone right now!"

He responded, "Can we have sex tonight? A lot of it?" She responded, "You are so whipped! It might be messy." He wrote, "We'll do it in the dark, and use old t-shirts." Annie wrote, "You are so horny, it's usually me."

Well, Annie was on a new path. And apparently I had some issues now too. I planned to confess to Martin.

I figured out how to make an email account and through it I arranged to meet with Dr. Grace Goodell, still Director of Change Economics. I sat down in the chair opposite her and she said, "I am very happy to meet with you, don't be silly—to hit a wall in local NGO management is common. Alumni who reach that grassroots dead-end often leverage the experience for a national position, even international. Everyone was so proud how determined you were to help that community, and to write that exciting book." Grace had a pony-tail bun and she was unmarried for whatever reason, and she did have faith and wasn't completely silent about it, and she was hip, and she was encouraging, and so she had her little flock. I thanked her. I didn't tell her how I had been kicked out of a cult. I did tell her that *Both Sides of Winter* was now history, and that I no longer lived and labored in that dim-lit world.

It hadn't deserved to be published—I could see so now. It was a heavy sculpture that I had hammered out incorrectly and then could not fix. Maybe I had learned something about syntax. I still had a box of notes that I had never gotten to. They were written by different pens in different directions on every-shaped scrap paper. I glanced through while tossing them. Still my mind edited. My mind reflected on those days when there'd been so much more noticing of nature, sky, land. "There was meaning in the trees," read one scrap.

Catherine's boss called her in and said, "You don't seem to really find things to do. I don't think it's the right fit. Sorry." That night I hugged her for a long time and stroked her hair and nestled her nose into my shoulder. I said, "It's surely a blessing in disguise." We were back to asking what she wanted to do, what she could do. She said, "I could do admin I guess." I got a patch of sleep, then I lay in the dark for some hours before car noise would get me. School buses would also roar past, but for now I had some quiet. Yet, what had just awakened me?

Was it needing to urinate, needing to think? But there'd been something else, I sensed it. The bed had shaken—it did so several times per night, per hour, yes, she was shaking in her sleep, thick violent shudders. It didn't disturb *her*, in fact she was probably descending deeper into rest.

So I had this added problem. She said, "Oh Snuggle Bunny, I'm so sorry. You should try some meditation or something." We kissed. I left for the bus. I hadn't felt like tying a tie today, even though I had Applicants awaiting me with expectation. And I had the fundraising tasks. I wished Mary Dee still worked here and Annie wasn't burnt out. I typed up a little email to Mary, saying I missed her.

I said to Catherine that night, "Seeing as that you do this weird shake thing though I'm the weirdo for letting it bother me, and seeing as that I am going to so supportively assist you through another job search and soul search, maybe you should let me go out to meet Colin and Sue in Aspen for a restful week."

She nodded. "I love you. I'll miss you." She added with her cute little jump and her rise in voice, "Send me a postcard or you're in big trouble."

Aspen would be different this year because Mike Vonn and his third wife would be there. Also different was that Colin, after driving Sue and me up from Denver, halted in the snowy driveway and said to me, "I just wanted to say that Sue and I have strived for a decade to show Mike and Deb the legitimacy of the church, so we ask you to respect that and try not to pull it down."

"I have no reason to start negative conversations about it."

Sue said, "But they have questions—they heard what happened. They're like vultures."

But Mike and Deb were out to dinner and we retired early. Colin and Sue took the morning off, and since my heart was racing and eyes aching—though I said nothing about it—I eagerly laid down while they watched TV silently. And I actually napped. Suddenly then I could move without pain and could articulate. Soon I was on the lifts with Mike and Deb. Deb asked, "How's marriage?"

I said, "Great, of course." Mike asked, "How's the church? We heard you weren't a good sheep."

"Well," I answered, "the sheep metaphor does have some value—we do need to be fed and protected in this world." After a pause I said, "But I turned out to be a wolf."

"Wolf?"

I said, "The charge was silent criticism." They chewed on this. They shook their heads. And later when they were dressing in the lodge and Sue was here to pick us up I asked her, "So how are you guys really?"

"Oh great," quipped Sue, "Colin told me last night he's miserable with me." She spoke rather calmly—she was showing me openness while also venting. She stayed indoors the next day too and Colin and I went out alone. Here we were, enjoying a day on our mountain once again. Of course, I was unrested, and even afraid of some sort of cardiac event here in the thinner air. Feeling this bad-sleep pain, however, would help me remember how true were my upcoming words.

"Colin," I began, when we reclined outside the lodge. I sighed. "Colin, I may have made a mistake. I might not have been thinking."

Colin nodded. "I hear you. I can't support it, but I have to admit it rings a bell." He related his version of last night's telling Sue how miserable he was. "Here's an example. When Sue and I were dating, she told me she was really into skiing. But in truth she's overweight and inactive. So what do I do in response? I sit at home and eat, miserably." We sat there nodding in the mountain air. I looked up the white slopes. My words to Colin had felt good. At the end of the week, I dropped them all off at Mike's jet in the Aspen Airport and then I was to take Sue's father's SUV down to a Denver hotel where he kept a space. I had a long peaceful drive ahead of me.

The springtime snow faded behind me. Interstate Seventy descended down to Denver. In the line of airport hotels, I navigated the Red Roof parking lot, and I left the SUV in a remote space, and I unscrewed the back plate as directed and planted the key there and walked away. I hopped a shuttle to the airport.

As I approached my gate, I was picturing going back to that SUV and its hidden key. I could just drive back up into the mountains, alone.

My Jubilee days were empty and low. I was winded. I was the weakest in the room at all times. My mind had to labor up from the floor, just to meet the duties facing me. I was hypoxic, like the Everest climbers. Terry Flood seemed to see right through my situation. She might have even known more about it than I. She pulled away from me. Maybe she already considered me a victim, too far gone.

While Gloria added away on her machine, I checked my new email account. Mark Quinn had gotten my address from SAIS and informed me that DC had hosted a Bologna reunion. "Where you been, man?" I asked by phone. He didn't laugh. With a few half-grunted statements he signaled that, way back whenever, he had wanted me in his wedding party. I didn't know what to think. Mark Quinn had even visited me in my Silesian village. After a tough-guy hug and after Mark had asked what century we were in, we had read quietly by the stove for several days. Why had I fully missed the notion, and opportunity, of him wanting me in his wedding? Lars Larson had also visited me in Prague at the end of those days. Lars, who with his Slovak boyfriend had been there even before the Curtain fell, had said as we had stared down at the dark river and ornate city, "Well, the end of the mystery." We had known that something was gone from those misty lanes around whose any corner one never knew what piece of handcrafted detail or what person of interesting ideas one might find. Gone was the misty feeling that had made one want to create some craft or some idea oneself. The feeling had simply disappeared from the air. But it hadn't, even today, faded from my insides.

Or maybe I had imagined the whole entire thing. Maybe there hadn't been anything there. But no, Lars had felt it. I took another tack on this Mark Quinn call. "Was Jana Stefackova at the Bologna thing?"

"Few Euros came over, other than those who walked from the World Bank, including Antonia, Jana's former housemate, if that counts."

"How's her face?"

"Her face? Well, it isn't quite Jessica Simpson. But otherwise normal."

"That's good. Who's Jessica Simpson? I know Lisa Simpson."

Mark didn't say anything. I called Catherine. I asked what she was up to. "Oh don't ask me that," she said. "I've been sleeping, basically sleeping and sleeping. I can't get up in the mornings now." At home I was helping her with new contact lists for another job search. The difference was that now I might've given myself the same task. I still knew I wanted to do great, and do good, and write epics, and keep the world from destroying itself. But I needed some serious rest first, somehow.

Jana Stefackova emailed that I should contact her acquaintance who was running charity programs over there. Catherine got a job offer in photography, if she agreed to do admin at the guy's house too. This press photographer gave her a camera to shoot an event, and I congratulated her with a hug, and then the photographer placed her photos onto the internet, and I praised her. And the caption read Catherine Rekstein. She was changing her driver's license too. I was slipping deeper and deeper.

On our way to Greenbelt service we stopped at the photographer's home to get some admin files, and Catherine walked to his door. The photographer opened up wearing no shirt and rubbing his chest for a while in conversation. He rubbed and talked. When we drove off, I said, "Sorry, CatCat, you'll find the right situation." Her little dreams were lodged inside me. They were part of me. They were sweet and sad. She looked over at me hopingly.

Civil Society Foundation Director Jiri Barta phone-interviewed me twice, and then I was telling Catherine that I had an opportunity in Prague. She nodded—the change would be good for us. We agreed I would go first to set things up. I told Terry the news privately upstairs. She was unfazed. She asked me to help find a replacement.

I revealed it at staff meeting. Tracie said, "You can't do that, you're the heart of this place." I smiled, nodded, shrugged, blinked. I coached Catherine what to bring over when she joined me. She listened. She said, "I'm so excited, Adventure Boy. I'll learn the language, don't worry." I hugged her. I hated her. She waited with me at the airplane gate. I squeezed her close again. We pecked. I said, "Don't cry, little CatCat."

She wiped her damp eyes. She handed me a thick, blank writing journal, and a little meditation book. I handed the clerk my boarding pass while the other passengers stepped up behind me. I turned back toward Catherine. Tears were pouring from her eyes. I said, "Baby, I'll see you so soon." She said, "I know. I can't help it. It's fine." I walked down the hall and I sat in my seat while the plane idled. I prepared to stand back up and leave the plane and go to her. My purpose in life was to prevent her from crying. God purposed it. It was clear enough, and cause enough. But the plane took off and I recalled that I was trying to leave her forever.

Aspen

"no move"

At my JFK gate, there were the Czechs. More were tangled here than I had seen all told in the eight years since. I was now standing silently among these people who had helped to blind me during a winter I considered enchanted, magic, special. My newly knotted emotions were unfair to them so I just tried to endure their pushiness and flashy new clothing and sweat-smell clothing and mullets and indifference to me. That's just who they were, in the end. I had thought, perhaps, they were something else, perhaps a holy people. They were no different though. The stunning, mean-faced girl was here too.

"The secret of meditation is relinquishing outward attachments and affirming divine freedom within." I had a long empty night to get through on this plane. The Czech guy next to me sat still and silent. I finally engaged with him and told him where I was going and why. I was glad to talk—I was an imperfect meditator. He responded, "Oh, that's interesting." But he was really still the passive guy who didn't want to bother.

Jiri Barta met me at the airport. My luggage did not. Jiri said, "You needn't come into the foundation this morning." As we drove, I shrugged off even a glance at the buildings and people and changes. My flat did have brand new furniture—Jiri said he hoped the place wasn't too small. Of course I only cared about the one thing and I immediately glanced out the lace curtains to the road below. It was three stories down and was thin like an alley and thus quiet, seemingly. Jiri Barta left.

I had no clothing, no luggage, nothing. I walked downstairs to the peopled streets. I could have called up Jana Stefackova. I could have gone to town and visited Jan Mraka or found climbers. Ivana and Yarda and the girls were still there too, of course. What could any of them really have done for me? They wouldn't understand where I was. I found an internet café and I wrote Colin a big long pouring out. I wrote Catherine that I was safe and preparing for her.

In the morning I walked around this quarter again, then returned to the internet café. Colin, to my surprise, had responded with a quick nothing, not a substantive word. Lenka was the one I called, little Lenka Rosolova from our brewery town who had gotten herself to America. I found her number right there on the internet. She was listed with some local corporation, where I now left a phone message. I walked back upstairs. "The secret to meditation is to sit very still, and gradually free yourself from the compulsion to move."

The foundation staff was all women except for me and Jiri. And among the dozen, unluckily, none was super attractive, super friendly, or really connectable. I deemed quickly that they were not going to be much of a source for filling my empty space.

We were paired in dim offices. My task was to design their new funding campaign. I still had no luggage. That evening I tried Lenka again. I had a landline at home this time around.

But Czech people seemed to all have these mobile phones, the sleek handy pocket things. Foundation staff had them—I had watched them speak and type into them on their way out for the weekend. Every tram and subway rider was punching away at them. I was riding to the main bus station. Then I walked amid the station fluorescence and the passing faces, everyone with somewhere to go. I watched their steady expressions. What was I doing over here? I looked at my watch. If I returned to the subway and rode to one end and then back, that would eat a piece of time. I wondered what Catherine was doing now, all alone. Maybe the Greenbelt people provided something for her a couple of times a week. I scraped along the station halls. In an hour, Lenka approached, carrying her rucksack. She was returning from a cottage trip. Here she stood, wearing a relaxed smile. She calmly looked me over.

We walked the city lanes. "You're kidding," I said. "You attended the world famous Great Books Program of St. John's College? Let me guess, you're the first girl from Jihlava to go there."

"First girl from behind the Iron Curtain." She led me to a bustling department store in the narrow center. One of the foundation's programs was "Smart Growth". Building this giant British store might have qualified even though it was amid the historic King's Route, where billboards now promoted everything from beer to insurance to breast implants. I didn't care. We walked the King's Route, still connecting little squares and old bridges and castle towers. People were handing out paper ads. I didn't take any but there were plenty to read on the ground, which was covered like snow. We sat down for dinner. I couldn't read her expression, there behind her smooth Slavic brow and round Slavic cheeks.

"Did you ever think of contacting me?"

"I called you and wrote you. I even invited you to my graduation," said Lenka Rosolova. "I never heard back from you. I wanted to thank you."

I was cursed with the memory of every silly stupid dusty detail here over the years but I had somehow forgotten Lenka's call until right now, just like I had missed Mark Quinn. I shook my head. Lenka added, "I heard you were in some church or something. Well, anyway, it doesn't matter. Meanwhile, a study has just identified us as the most secular country in the world. World's least faith here." Our entrees arrived. She said, "Another study shows that we are the most influenced by advertising. If you advertise to Czechs, they are the most likely to desire it and buy it."

I said, "I remember when they first put up a billboard in your town. It read, 'I am a billboard. I sell your products.' Everyone stared at it blankly. But I guess they learned. I just saw billboards that electronically switch ads, now for a new mall, now for a mobile phone, now for mortgages."

"I work for mobile phones. I'm Vice President of Marketing and Advertising."

"No."

"In our country of nine million, three million mobile phones were sold in year one. You can imagine what that looked like. Recently a small new company entered the market and I joined on."

I nodded and chewed. Lenka said, "Reks, your revolution did happen. You are just seeing things negatively." In a sentence she deleted my decade of thinking. She said, "The dream happened. This is it. It's a chance to think and earn. I don't know a better place to live. But then, I never minded life before the revolution."

I wanted to date her.

"So I am indeed using my classical education, thank you. Our company, in its first year, grew from fifty employees to eight hundred. Never has a company gotten market share so quickly, gotten its ads to be remembered so thoroughly. I won awards, Reks." Lenka had been living a single's life. She told me about some roommate situations, some relationship decisions, and how she was clear now about what she wanted from her ultimate partner. Lenka had been living based on being happy, as Ted Woods had tried to tell me. Lenka had been considering and choosing what would make her happy.

And I saw how differently I had been thinking. And I saw that I was in a big, big hole. I stared at my food. Lenka was watching me, unimpressed. God was here too, but distant. God was my best friend and was in my heart and thoughts and running dialogue. And for a long while I had been asking what would make God happy, what would make Catherine happy, what was serving, sacrificial, good for the world. They were not bad questions. But here I was.

She drove me home in her company car. "Smart Transport" was another foundation initiative. But it was nice to get this ride home across the city. I asked whether she had seen the study that showed Prague now having Europe's most cars per head. She said no. She shrugged about the idea of us meeting up again soon. I shook hands with Lenka Rosolova, the main female in *Both Sides of Winter*, a book that never was.

I did get an invite to Jiri Barta's flat. We sat with hot tea until his girlfriend came home with dinner. She jumped right into English—I was one of so many Americans over the decade, no doubt, as her boyfriend ran a western-funded foundation and she was a Prague girl working at the Arts Ministry. "A kiosk up the street makes good Chinese. I hope you don't mind that I haven't cooked."

Jiri added, "We're a modern couple."

I said, "If I hadn't come early tonight you could've served it as your own." We all smiled. The girlfriend passed the bowls around. She said, "I heard you've been in our country before. When were you here?"

"I came in 1990."

"Oh," she said, "the year of euphoria." Jiri took the serving bowl from me and smiled again. My mouth was flat. The girlfriend said, "We had an Australian teacher near that time and we thought he was so special we just wanted to touch him."

Jiri added, "That's really what it was, we didn't believe that here we were, actually able to touch a Westerner."

"Oh well," said the girlfriend.

"Oh well," I said.

She said, "But then I myself did a year of study in America."

Jiri added, "Lubbock, Texas. Do you know Lubbock, Texas?" He emphasized it with fun and irony. The girlfriend said, "Not a single bus. I couldn't get to the university. Just couldn't." Jiri added, "There weren't even sidewalks. No sidewalks." The girlfriend said, "So I walked on the road and the drivers honked angrily." And I was thinking, "How do I get out of this trap? How do I stop carrying their burden while they go along free?"

Jiri said, "It doesn't matter. Really." He smiled.

A barbed-wire fence separates Lenka from the rest of the world. When a playwright who has been in jail for writing against the regime is then carried into the castle and told he must be president, I fly in. American flags are flying. They are worn as pins on coats. Lenka is among the first of her kind to go west. She enrolls at St. Johns College and reads Aeschylus, Sophocles, Thucydides, Euripides, Aristophanes, Euclid, Plutarch, Ptolemy, Dante, Aquinas, Chaucer, Machiavelli, Luther, Pascal, Descartes, Milton, Spinoza, Newton, Kepler, Hume, Rousseau, Moliere, Kant, Hamilton, Hegel, Tocqueville, Kierkegaard, Marx, Melville, Nietzsche, the Bible, Freud, Einstein, Conrad, Darwin, and everything else. At the end of four years, no one in the world is better read than little Lenka Rosolova from her little town of medieval walls and communist coal stains.

She returns home and when her new corporate employer seeks to do a laundry detergent advertisement, Lenka must explain to these Westerners how the mind here is different: machines are tiny, the process takes hours, the soap is weaker, clothes are worn longer. So the company designs an ad stating that, with this detergent, consumers can wash their clothes at saner temperatures and do so as often as they want. "And look how white," says the blond wife on television. But the wisdom is Lenka's.

In the morning, I took my clothes down to the cyber laundromat. A decade ago there hadn't been a dryer in the entire land. Then an American entrepreneur, like so many comers and goers during my unnoticed absence, supplied ten beautiful Maytags. In an hour my clothes would be shiny clean and dry. Meanwhile, next to the humming machines, I checked emails.

I was surprised that Colin had still given nothing. Mary Dee had also never responded. Let's see, yes she had recently emailed Annie, "I feel like one of those flaky people who say they want to get together but just don't make the effort—I just looked at my Yann who was really sick and thought, better keep him home. You are very kind to offer the next weekend. But that doesn't sound so nice for your poor Darren on his birthday. Darren is good peeps and they are rare and it makes me happy to think of you. Reks! Gad! You know he never responded to my letter? Poor dude, I just had no idea he was so messed. Love you."

II

Prime Minister Vaclav Klaus, who had been chosen, instead of playwright Vaclav Havel, to lead during this previous decade, was now accused of manipulating the television news, censoring anything negative about himself, while exaggerating his own positive coverage. "The broadcasters have locked themselves in their office," reported my officemate. "They demand that his party stop controlling news!" Supporters were bucketing food up to them. A rally was urgently scheduled. We donned our coats and headed to the square.

We emerged from the subway right into the amassing evening crowd. And everyone felt it—we looked around with small smiles revealing so. It wasn't just me. The sea of heads was spread toward the top of the square, hands clapping in unison. An electric feeling was in the air, connecting us.

But who was going to overthrow anything now? Were they going to overthrow the three McDonalds around this square? Who would lead it, the new youth that had decided to deface the whole entire city with graffiti? This leader had been elected consistently, so he reminded everyone now, and he had enjoyed a decade of criticizing the ecological and humanist ideas of the too-placid Vaclav Havel, and no one had said a thing. I was soon back in Director Jiri's office thinking about Lenka and discussing the foundation's plan for surviving as U.S. funding ebbed.

Of course they could still call on their many American friends from over the decade, and some of these had written cards that were now collected on Jiri's wall. One was a thank-you for staff having attended the card-author's Slovakia wedding. "Thanks from Jan Surotchak."

"I know Jan Surotchak," I said.

Jiri nodded. Jiri knew a lot of people. He continued discussing my proposal writing. I said, "He was my friend." Finally Jiri confirmed that he was the same blond guy with a big chin and big smile and a history at a Boston think-tank.

When I was back at my desk, the phone rang. "Heyyy," said Jan Surotchak, calling from America. Despite his mature tone, the coincidence wasn't lost on him. He had worked at the sister foundation in Slovakia—I was hearing a familiar voice—and he had married a Bratislava gal named Lenka. They were coming back over next month. "Right now we're holed up in the lovely Lehigh Valley."

"Wow, that's where my wife's from," I said, despite myself.

"Okay," said Jan, "so we have a wife." It sounded so wrong.

"She'll be here next month too—I'm confirming her ticket this week."

Catherine called next. "I'm all packed, Snuggle Bunny. I'm a-coming, with my two suitcases only. I'm glad you finally got yours. Have you made any new friends, or dug up any of the old ones? How's work, and your director guy?"

"Baby," I said, "I'll pick you up at the airport, don't worry. You can teach English or something no problem. We'll do fine here. I haven't linked with old friends yet. I'll be visiting some international church this weekend. But it won't be the International Church of Christ that's for sure. Have you seen Elder Mike Fontenot on the subway or sidewalk?" She responded, "Yeah, right." Tomorrow I would go cancel her ticket.

First, I spent the morning drafting up the new proposal for Jiri. My head was swirling, today was the final day to cancel the ticket—did I have the courage? I stared into the enormous thought. With the remaining corner of my brain I was functioning, living, existing. I emailed the proposal over to Jiri's office. At lunch I took the tram down to the travel agency.

It stood on the corner of a little cobblestone square. I stared at its green wooden door. No, I wouldn't cancel her ticket—that would bring down upon her the full truth about my feelings. Yes it might finally free me up and improve my sleep. But maybe I'd feel other things instead, I didn't know.

Yet if I didn't cancel it, she'd be arriving here, and that would advance us a giant step in the wrong direction. Plus, I would have to deal with a typical middle-America girl here in this place, a girl going around saying she was my wife.

But again, if I did cancel it, how would I even let her know, how would I ever broach it? I had no move. Lunch hour was ending. I was still staring at the door. I took the tram back up to the foundation.

I took the tram right back down, and I stared at the green wooden door. I walked through it and sat down. The travel agent was a brown-haired thin guy who was surprisingly professional and pleasant, and I was relieved. "Refund this ticket please."

He smiled, then began typing into his computer, and I sat there silently. I stared at the world map on the wall behind him. His deleting, refunding, printing didn't take too long, and by the time he handed me the receipt, my mind had calmed a bit. I noticed the sunlight through the tall windows. I stood up and nodded. The agent said, "I'm here until five this evening."

I glared back at him. "You don't mean I can change my mind, change the cancellation?"

"Only until five this evening."

I went back to get Jiri's feedback on the proposal. I tried to focus on him. We were hosting a conference for foreign corporations. I asked, "Why not invite some local companies too?" Jiri asked, "Why?" I looked at my watch. I said, "Contributing is probably a longer education for them, but why not start it? They'll learn how they can gain positive exposure." Jiri said, "They'd probably like to be among such a crowd."

"Networking."

"Let's present it to the staff."

Everyone assembled and discussed which programs to emphasize, environment or children or the disabled or parks or transportation. I stood up and walked out and boarded the tram. It wound down through its five never-arriving stops.

I sat with the travel agent. We re-issued the ticket. He remained professional and pleasant. I boarded the tram and soon walked back into the foundation. The time was five o'clock. I wouldn't be disappointing Catherine at all. She was coming.

But she couldn't come. I couldn't have her here. I boarded the tram—maybe oh maybe he was still there. I raced to that corner. The green door was bolted. I ran around to the window. One of the women let me in and they knew my sad cause and they said, "He has left. Sorry. Or, is he dressing?"

They retrieved him from the back room. He was switching from his uniform to biking clothes—this guy biked to and from work. He said, "The computer is all shut down." He said it pleasantly and professionally.

He re-started the computer. I sat in my chair. Slowly, we canceled the ticket again. I would send her an email message tomorrow. I went back to the foundation and jumped right into my work. My officemate and others were still here. They didn't even know I was married. I didn't believe it myself.

After an hour, I logged onto the internet. I sat there dreading tomorrow's email. I stared at the blank screen. My officemate was staring at her screen. She had short blond hair. I remembered the term from the *International Tribune*, the paper where I had found Lenka's au-pair opportunity, beside which had been teeny print ads from Geneva, Brussels, Milan. The term was 'escort'. Now the internet was the place, no?

Yes, I found some advertisements, and then an address, not far from the office. When my officemate left, I picked up the phone. I put it down. I shook my head. This was crazy. My phone rang. "Heyyy," said Jan Surotchak. "Before you leave for the weekend, download Chat."

"What is that exactly?"

"That, for the few who still don't know, will allow you and me to type instantly to one another from our mutual offices, in case you have any burning questions about Slovak foundation history or the pleasures of Slovak wives, Christian I might add." I had always envisioned that some acquaintance from my path would unexpectedly become a rock-solid friend. And Jan's being a Christian—of course he wasn't truly—and his mentions of faith and prayer lifted my hopes a bit. Maybe my situation wasn't so impossible. He said, "Have a good weekend with all your foundation people."

When all the staff left, I remained seated and staring in the dim office. I looked at the screen and pulled up that ad again. Then I hurried out and rode the tram home and prayed to the God of Christ and then read my little meditation book about relinquishing attachments.

But I had that street address memorized. I decided just to eat and shower and get in bed and breathe through it. Around my mind went the Catherine turmoil and that street address. My mind slowed, but sleep still only flirted.

The next afternoon I buzzed the bell at that address. I considered walking away but soon a female voice in the little intercom told me a flat number. I walked up the shadowy stairs. I knocked. A blond woman answered, slightly older than expected, and more than slightly bitchy, as if she had just left her state-owned shop-assistant shift from another time and continued now to be disinterested in service.

I took none. I was safely out. It felt good, the clean spirit. I was probably better off tramming over to the foundation to draft that impossible email.

"Dear CatCat." I deleted it. I could blame my own situation, my misfiring mind and cardiac ache, which I now brought to work every morning except for the very rare day of real sleep. But I couldn't type it. I just sat there in the dead quiet.

And click, a message opened on the corner of my screen. Jan Surotchak had written, "What could you possibly be doing there on a Saturday?" I could sense his happy sarcasm. I wrote back, "Just stopped in. Wow, so we're talking together right now?"

He wrote, "You could say that. Or type it." I typed, "I'm so amazed. When I lived here last, well you know, because you were here afterward."

"Yep."

I glanced at my blank Catherine draft. I chose not to tell Jan about it. I did tell him I was visiting an American church tomorrow. He wrote a smiley face. He wrote, "We had another American at the Slovak foundation."

"How'd that go?"

"Unhappy."

"Really?"

"Well, she didn't look happy. Oh, and she didn't sound happy when she called me at three a.m. because she found a used condom under her bed."

"What?"

"I probably didn't sound happy on that call either. I never understood whether she was upset that the previous tenant left it, or that she never had an opportunity to soil one herself."

I wrote, "Oops, you can't say that." He typed an ashamed face. I did depart, achingly, for that church service the next afternoon. It began with some melodic singing and strumming. This stretched peacefully on. Between songs the lead musician said gently, "Worship however you need, however you choose."

I chose thinking about Catherine. The tall old room was uncrowded. Czechs and internationals were mixed sparsely among the pews, and there was a gal in the corner whose chosen form of worship was waving a silky flag back and forth to the music. The singer sang, "It's all about you, Lord. It's all about you." I stood, I sat. During every melancholy note I considered this woman, Catherine, who just wanted to be loved and who had thought this was in fact where God had lead her. She thought it was a marriage. She was devoted to poor pathetic me, who was trying to throw it away. And still they were singing warmly at this church of non-disciples. They were sitting, standing, singing, flagging, reaching, pacing, praying, swaying, and maybe someone else suffering with head down somewhere.

The singer had a beautiful voice indeed. "Over all the earth, you reign on high. Every mountain stream, every sunset sky. But my one request, Lord my only aim. Is that you reign in me again."

The pastor, eventually, came up for a sermon. He stood at the podium and didn't touch it as he spoke mild words. "If you have a problem, let it go.

Let God take care of it, whatever it is." He didn't open his Bible but he did quote, "'The sacrifices of God are a broken spirit, a broken and contrite heart.'" He was an American who had been here a few years. He had come with his wife.

When I arrived at work the next morning, I typed, "I can't handle this right now. I canceled your ticket. You don't know how sorry I am. I just haven't been thinking straight, for a while now." I sent it. It was gone. I was looking forward to Jan Surotchak's symbol lighting up. I was looking forward to his and Lenka Surotchak's visit. I suspected that Catherine would be calling me at the foundation today.

I was correct. Her voice was sharp, shrill, and cracking. "So, canceled it, just like that. That's what you had to do, huh?"

I responded, "I will try to come home soon on a work trip. We'll figure it out then."

"Figure out what? I'm all packed! I'm supposed to leave this week, Reks! I'm sorry for yelling. I know you hate that. I'm sorry."

I held the phone and my head. I had an ocean between us for safety. I again promised we would figure it out. I hung up with relief that I had avoided her arriving, and regret that I couldn't comfort her with hugs or feel her warm bare body against mine. "Heyyy," Jan lit up.

I still didn't mention what was going on. "Reks," said Jiri, popping his head into my office, "I believe we need to go over this month, sooner than expected, to visit the Czech-American community."

Oh, thank God. My salary was a small monthly handful of cash but now the foundation would be delivering me briefly home. I trammed to my flat to nap during lunch, but to no avail. At least I got horizontal and had the physical pain partly relieved for a stretch before tramming quickly back.

When I flew off with Jiri, he napped deeply beside me, shaking a few times in his sleep, just like Catherine. We were to cross over the whole of North America, en route to a Vancouver conference. I began a silent, focused prayer.

"God, you've been my best friend. You've been right here, I don't know exactly where, but with me surely. And there's no doubt about the fruit of the Spirit—love, joy, peace, patience, kindness, goodness, faithfulness, gentleness, self-control. I've been so different while living in you. I'm sorry for where we are, for what I don't understand. Father, take care of Catherine. Do you want me to take care of her? Is that really right? It doesn't feel right. But my life is not mine. Christ is my example. Be with me on this trip. Show me the way, as you've done for so long now."

III

The International Conference of Community Foundations was hosting its guests in a tall Vancouver Hilton. Jiri said, "Normally we would share one room but our two scholarships from the Michigan Consortium of Grantmakers allow this exception." We parted down separate halls. I said, "Enjoy." I had requested the quiet side, facing the water. I put my luggage on one bed and myself on the other.

I turned on some Expos baseball and reflected on the breakfast meeting many hours away. I counted some breaths and rolled over.

I didn't sleep this night. Three hundred diverse breakfasters convened and I didn't see in anyone's eyes what I felt in mine, the deep aching weakness. My chest was tight, my shoulders were stiff. Everyone could think more quickly than I, this I knew and saw. The workshops were a waste for me on this day, whereas the next day, when I again hadn't slept, I didn't even attend, but told Jiri false reports at the meals, between failed naps.

I worried that the lunch crowd could see my pain. My body was so tense and my chest so constricted that I was afraid to move. The Russian foundation members sat down at our table. How I wished, when I saw their two female staff, that I wasn't worthless, on the verge of breakdown or breaking in half. On the third day, I told Jiri, "I don't know whether you're experiencing any jet lag, but I haven't slept on this continent yet." His face didn't express much—he was serious about this conference and about our foundation's resources. I added, "I could possibly die before it ends."

He said, "You can't die from lack of sleep. Walk up to the store and buy some sleeping pills. Take the evening off, I'll see you at breakfast." That evening I tried Expos baseball again. When it was over I was alone with the night. My half pill hadn't worked, it just made my chest frighteningly tighter and my head cloudier. I lay down but could only think and ache. I got up and walked the silent halls.

Everyone was asleep but me—I saw no signs saying otherwise. I entered the empty fitness center and ran on the elliptical machine. At least I would keep a fit shell around my broken insides. I sat alone in the jacuzzi. My chest did not yet explode. I heard the hotel's first peeps, early risers entering for a workout before the big, final day. I went back to my room and showered and lay on the bed until it was time to dress for the workshops. I wouldn't attend them but nor would I tell the truth to Jiri this time. I would go to meals and otherwise avoid him.

After again failing at mid-day naps, I knew I'd be skipping the closing festivities too. My hollow eyes and scared body didn't fit with the other humans there. I glanced through the window at their happy drinking, their honoring the end of this year's week-long International Conference of Community Foundations. I was standing outside. My main regret at this moment, for whatever reason, was my not being able to schmooze the two Russian girls, the cute brunette and her director, the tall young blonde. They were on the inside, wearing heels. Back on my bed, I stared at the Expos game. The nighttime struggle awaited. I knew that my mouth was glum. I shook my head.

I missed the end of the game, I realized, because I had dozed off. I opened my eyes and stared afresh. This bit was all I needed to act human. I bounced up. But too late, the banquet was over. There was no point leaving my room. I could work on the Annie and Lenka portraits. Maybe I was ill but maybe too there was a story among these anecdotes. Maybe there was still a shot. First I hurried down to the gym.

It was very late on Friday night, but there in the jacuzzi sat the two Russian girls. They were smart and attractive and concerned and all mine now for this happy little dialogue in the water. I could now articulate, I could breathe calmly through my thoughts, I could smile. This brunette and blonde from a foundation deep in Russia, they asked me, "Were you at this conference?" We talked about emailing. They went off to the locker room for their banquet dresses. I ran on the elliptical—who knew how I would feel in the morning?

On our Chicago flight, I felt too pained to even reach and fasten my seatbelt. Jiri had us rolling right into meetings, where then the board of the Society of Czech Americans agreed to solicit their own membership for us. I didn't think they were anything special, these Midwestern ancestors of somebody. And they thought I was nothing special. In fact, they asked, "What are you even doing?" They didn't understand why I wasn't at least of Czech descent, with some connection to that little country They asked, "Why do you care?"

I cared only about surviving until sleeptime. First I would have to face Catherine. I called her from O'Hare, then she met me at my parents' house. We went to our room. There were cobwebs by the lamp. My lazy-boy recliner was gone—I'd left it at one of Ted's spec houses and then he'd emptied it into his wide industrial trash stream. I'd been too weak to retrieve my friend the chair. Catherine and I got under the big blanket. "Snuggling is a little weird," she said. "But I trust you."

In the morning, we drove off toward her father's new beach house. I lay on the sand with the usual tight silent pain. I considered how she always looked good in a bathing suit. The house was ours for the weekend—the house seemed to add to Catherine's value, to the reasons for staying committed. In a moment I realized the flaws in that thinking.

Her hair had grown long—she was insisting on wearing it with no bangs. We ate beach pizza and fries and gummy bears. Between bites we pecked on the lips. On the ride home, she said cutely, "Maybe you'd sleep better if we got an apartment in a really high New York building, away from any airports."

"There's no escape."

She said, "Or maybe if we lived in your lovely Europe. You said they have quiet villages right near cities. Maybe we could get jobs there."

I mustered the will to say, "I still don't know what's right for us. I want to figure it out." She stared forward as I drove. Her blue eyes began to leak onto her pinkening cheeks. "Great," she said, "you just go on figuring things out. Just go on." The cute voice was gone. She tumbled into uncontrollable tears. I pulled the car over. She asked, "Do you know what it's like for the person you love not to want to be with you? Do you know how that feels?"

Wow was I bad at this. I wished I could get Jan Surotchak's advice right now. Instead I hurried to make the peace, offering solutions such as twin beds that we could separate, after snuggling. "We'll just push them aside a bit—your shaking won't bother me. We'll still be together." I drove us onward. My voice took a different tack, "I don't know what God's thinking with this sleep plight. I've prayed a bunch. I've read *Job* a bunch. I've recognized my own powerlessness, thus allowing God to show his own work. But we were doing his work. Now I'm doing far less. Now I have nothing to give. Just anguish. I mean, night after night. I mean, traffic from three DC airports crosses right above our house, no joke."

She said, "I just don't hear them."

I said, "I just don't understand."

That night, she sat in the kitchen and I sat in the computer room and I punched in 'escort' to see what it might mean in America. Soon I was emailing some lady named Jessica J-Spot. I wasn't so interested, in fact it felt good to now just be logging off, done. Catherine walked in. "Let's see who you were writing."

She reached over me and switched it back on. Surprisingly, the "Dear Jessica" screen came right up. I switched it back off. Catherine switched it on. That screen would just not die. "Who's Jessica you're trying to meet with?"

"I'm asking you to not read that. I'm asking you to trust me and not read it."

"What?" Her voice was getting screechy again. "You're trying to meet with this woman and I'm supposed to trust you?"

"Yes, I'm asking you to trust me and not read that email." After several more volleys, we sat down for me to explain. "It's difficult to discuss. I had been considering something. I wasn't going to tell you, but here, fine. Jessica is a girl who works at the Slovak foundation. We spoke and she got pretty open about some hard times, even that she had thought about things like suicide." Catherine challenged, "Oh, so that's what your email was about?"

I told her that this was the embarrassing truth. I told her that I had thought about going down to that DC bridge where Eduardo and I used to walk. Catherine watched me silently. At JFK airport the next day, I found myself in the same cycle of pacing the terminal in isolation and guilt, then visiting the payphone to call and soothe her, then wishing her gone from my life. I looked into the long night ahead. As far as looking to Central Europe itself, I had no more illusions.

It was just a place, finally. It had nothing to give me except slightly reduced sprawl. I didn't expect to get anything from anyone, not even an idea, not even hope. We landed and the Sunday sun shone on the old city. I went home and successfully napped. I jumped up. I went out to the neighborhood with the doorbell to that rude escort lady, half hoping she wasn't home on this empty afternoon. While waiting in silence on the sidewalk, I stared at the daylight aglow on the tram tracks. I stared for a long quiet time.

The street door buzzed open. I walked up the four shadowy flights. Then I knocked. A younger girl answered. She was silent but not rude. She was alone in this flat. She wore a green negligee.

She sent me to wash up. I stood in the tub and held the warm flow on me. I could see down to the sunny street. When I eventually stepped into the little foyer, I had to recall the full meaning of where I was.

Where was the girl? I peeked into the bedroom. She was seated on the furthest corner of the bed. She had removed the negligee. She had brown hair to her shoulders, and she was leaned back on one arm. She was thin and tan. She said nothing. She lay back, and she pulled my hands across the bed and onto her. She was firm and soft and beginning to moan.

So I fucked her. During our quiet, sweaty afternoon, I shifted alongside her and held her leg. My other hand reached to her far breast. I walked out to the sunny street and crossed the tram tracks. I rode to the foundation office to prepare for the week.

Jan Surotchak flew in. He indeed knew Jiri Barta and the staff. We began some serious meetings and Lenka Surtochak attended too. I asked at lunch, "Continuing on to your Slovakia?"

Lenka said, "You should visit."

Blond-haired Jan said, "You should travel with me in the autumn. I'll be visiting some villages. And there's a cottage retreat."

I said, "Sounds great."

"Very great," said Lenka, "I'll get some free time from marriage." Jan nodded and smiled. His smile was wide and wise—he listened attentively then laughed after almost every sentence of ours. Tomorrow's meetings would be bigger, with more out-of-town strategizers and the entire board. Long discussions were scheduled, after which Jiri had reserved an evening pub. Some rest tonight was certainly needed. It was my prayer.

I prayed it meditatively before I lay down. Then I meditated on it while I lay there. I prayed again after an hour, and then deep in the wakeful night again. I noticed that the rare car passing on the thin lane below was actually audible. It was almost loud. I had thought it was just a trickle that died off at night. Now I heard it. I would enter the day in pain, that was now guaranteed. I would be worthless and pretending, I the only one so at these long meetings. I didn't care how imperfect their lives might have been, they didn't have this chest strain and brain weakness and tense tiredness, I could tell from their faces. They were rested people. It was that simple. I was not healthy. In the middle of the morning meeting I was gazing downward and remembering the Catherine problem. I shook my head very slowly.

I looked up and Jan and Lenka were watching me—I was sure they were following every beat of the meeting too. They had lives in both places, they were enjoying both sides. By the time I began anticipating my empty weekend, they were gone to Slovakia.

Obviously, I buzzed that door again. The brunette and I did the very same wonderful thing. But the following week, when I rose up in the stairwell, a blonde opened the door. She had the same youth but a different negligee and a distant lethargy.

We silently showered together. In every way, I held and caressed her tight pointy perfect body. Her teeth were slightly crooked and her few words were about disco-going not pertinent to me, but I again tried that alongside position. She was lying flat and I was lying on one shoulder. I came back the next day. This girl was very pretty, no better in the land. This was it.

At the foundation, Jiri Barta showed me Google so I could search for additional Czech-American groups and potential U.S. donors. I asked, "It knows about stuff in America?"

"It is American. But it searches the globe and more." He walked out of my office.

So it did. Today's Prague apparently had inexpensive girls in flats throughout its streets. I considered the mystery of what awaited behind all those doors.

At Prague Christian Fellowship, when the singing and strumming started, I began my Catherine sulk. I stood in one of the empty pews and I glanced at the arm raisers and flag wavers all in their separate spaces. It was a bad sleep day. My body ached like an old man's. I also wrote. I just sat down in the pew and revised those portraits and I again considered how I might thread them together. And the members sang and strummed.

At work I did the Google searching. I searched Lenka Rosolova, Benjamin Wallace, Stephanie Shrawder, Debbie Jaffee, Gilligan and Conehead too. I considered some past high schoolers. What had happened to people's lives?

In addition to marketing Oskar mobile phones, they were running businesses, managing investment accounts, selling pharmaceuticals, having children, living lives, smiling to the camera, publishing books. There was a certain high-schooler whom I couldn't find but I kept searching because I'd heard he might be writing out west somewhere.

"Tell me about your discos?" I asked the blonde when I next lay there and massaged her warm pointy breasts. She said, with crooked teeth and distant blue eyes, "It's on the main square."

"Maybe I'll see you there sometime."

"Who knows?" she shrugged.

I said, "Dancing queen." She nodded. I said, "Only seventeen." She stared off, flatly.

She said, "Here's my private number." I clasped it in my hand. Today was the rare good day, when I had gotten some morning sleep. I probably had some color in my face, as if healthy. "My name is Nika." She was my Lenka Rosolova, my Tess of the D'Urbervilles. I paid her.

But the next week, no one answered at the flat. And her mobile phone was out of credit, so it said. I searched online and finally found, among a thousand escort listings, the phone number listed with the address from that flat. I called from my office. A woman told me, "No one is answering at that flat because she's busy, she's occupied. But it might not be your Nika, she might be in another flat. Let me think. I'll let you know. Sometime."

My rush home for napping at lunch took twenty-two minutes on the tram, and the same back, just to collapse on my bed for a middle twenty of easing the anguish. That night, the cars vrooshed beneath my window. I stared at the ceiling. I flipped God off. I would have to survive yet another aching day.

My reprieve was smiley chats with Jan Surotchak. He was back at the Community Foundation of Lehigh Valley. He was sitting at his faraway desk and then would choose to just shoot out a message—about politics or our pasts or work issues such as green spaces and brown fields—and it would suddenly arrive to me.

Then he would call and we would discuss it in detail. At night, I might sit in an old pub or new bar. I could now just order the cheeseburger without thinking about global changes and revolutions and fairy tales. The warm breeze blew in the wide door open behind me. The bartender slid the burger and beer in front of me. I ate the burger, proud of my apathy. The bartender didn't care, he cared about tips. Tipping was fine with me, if he could say a few words, at least a hello. He disappeared somewhere while I sat waiting to pay.

Still waiting, I meandered to the front of the bar, then back to my seat. One more lap and then I looked at my bag. I picked it up and rushed out the door. My tram was there ahead—I sprinted through a dust-colored portico and across the cobblestone. I hugged my heavy bag close to my chest and I jumped onto the tram and felt a strain.

I lay in my bed that night and listened to the passing cars and prayed, "Lord, take this chest pain away. It's hurting me. It's scaring me. God my father, tonight I stole, and there's no excuse. I'm sorry. I will talk to Pastor John about it. I'll write a letter to Eduardo. I'll go back and tip the guy double, you know I will. I don't want to have a heart attack, Lord. I already wasn't sleeping and this certainly isn't helping." I laughed. I was staring with fear at the night ceiling. I even felt that maybe I hadn't appreciated my previous condition and blessings.

I prayed it all again in an hour. I was expected soon at the foundation, expected to achieve, to fundraise one million dollars this year. I prayed again for help and health. "Not this, not now. Wasn't I trying to serve you? Are you just humbling me? With thorns? I don't want to be Job anymore. Job is a parable, I'm in pain. Help me, Father."

Morning came and now I'd have to somehow get help. A car roared below the window. I looked over at my phone. I looked at the ceiling. I was short of breath. I flipped God off again. I was flipping off the ceiling—I held my middle finger at it—that's all it was, a ceiling. I was talking to the ceiling. I was alone in the room, alone in my ache. There was nothing else. I lifted myself a bit and then lay back down.

It was July 2001. I dragged myself to a doctor and she put me on a lab bike even though I said I was hurting and sleepless and scared. The stress test and EKGs were negative. That afternoon, the chest strain faded away, gone. I began searching around the Prague Fellowship for a quiet room. I gave them my office number.

The next day, Jan Surotchak and I chatted about the different one-star hotels on our upcoming road trip. I looked forward to having good talks with him in person. I figured I'd be secretly ill for most of them. I stayed late in the office to revise the big proposal. The phone rang.

The apartment madam said, "You want Nika?"

"I want."

"Go to the tall building at the east end. She's up on the twelfth." I had to tram across the whole city but it seemed fully worth it, and alas I was soon strutting down the long sidewalk that led to Nika's building. An old woman sat at the guard desk, a big listing before her. "Full name of tenant."

"Nika."

"Then you can't go up." She was obstructing my path. From a payphone I called the madam. She asked, "You sure you want her?"

"What? Yes I'm sure."

"Nika is in a different building." Was she testing me? I stayed silent. "Relax," she said. "It's just around the corner. Building Five-A."

After an eternity I arrived at Five-A. I rose up its bright stairs to the given floor. But I was just staring at a collection of closed doors. So I buzzed each one. None opened. I went back down and searched out another payphone—there were fewer these days. The madam said, "Not Five-A, Five-E." Who was this woman? I slogged down the row to the final building and then rose up its stairwell. I still hadn't been given an apartment number. I stood in silence on that floor. I could buzz each door again, or I could return to the payphone, or I could just quit this.

A door opened. I said with polite dismay, "You're not Nika."

"I'm Nikola. Will you choose to come in?"

She was more present than the fleeting Nika—she even bounced on her toes a bit there in the doorway. Her hair was actually a fairer blond. It was long and straight. I stepped in.

She closed the door and simply removed the shoulder straps of her black dress. Her top half was now naked. What a top half it was. She was a pleasant, pretty, slender girl. I got her into the position, and we stayed so for a long while.

She had smooth, fresh skin. My hand that hooked her leg also held the near breast while my far hand alternated between twining her inviting fingers and holding her other plump white breast.

At times she smiled, at times she moaned, at times I kneaded both those downy breasts. Talk about tall towers. I walked outside fully complete, elevated, satisfied. On the tram, I began thinking about when I would do it again.

Catherine called me. "Hi Snuggle Bunny, coming home ever?" I knew there was no middle, no halfway out—such tension was unlivable—so I kept it alive, gave her hope. She had mailed me a package of gummy bears and a note, "The beach misses you." Now I thanked her. We paused for long silences. Hanging up was a long, slow, delayed event, leaving her far away and alone, leaving me sitting at my desk, guilty, alone.

Jan Surotchak called. "Heyyy, I got great news from Lenka—she's going to join us at the end of our trip, for that celebrating at the cottage."

"Great. Celebrating what?"

Jan Surotchak laughed. "Maybe that was too strong a word. It's just friends down there who like to get together and have fun. They may not have the best restaurants or service—no they do not—but they still have a pretty good sense of community. I guess they call it celebrating."

Prague Fellowship's Isaac had a spare room facing a grassy court. He was a largish African with a weak handshake. "I am very grateful, Isaac." He responded, "Glory be to God. But isn't it far from your work?" I said, "I care only about the one thing."

Jiri Barta borrowed the foundation car to help move my bags. "It's far, no?" We were driving along the river, beyond the subway and near the final tram stop. I was embarrassed. I was living in remote, old Commie-cube projects.

Isaac's walls were thinner than I had realized. I listened for threatening sounds, clicking pipes. I was made of eggshells. I didn't nod off for a while. Then I slept in spurts. Then on my long commute, I practiced the breathing and the not looking for why—I was bending my mind away from seeking understanding. Finally Jan Surotchak flew in so we could take the long train to Bratislava. We sat across from one another in an empty cabin and I told him everything, my church struggle and the wedding morning and how I now needed out, and he listened.

I had now told someone the entire crisis. I no longer carried it by myself. Jan was nodding. I smiled, here on the train. Within the long click-clacking I felt safe. Jan told me how he had met Lenka at the Slovak foundation and how eventually one morning he realized he wanted her in his life always. "I never had any of that," I stated. "And I knew that it was supposed to be that way—I did know that once. But I lost touch with myself. Literally, I was not in touch with myself."

Jan nodded, I shook my head. There out our window the autumn sun glowed crisply. We were quiet. Eventually I said, "Poor Catherine."

The only plan we had here was to drive the Slovak foundation car relaxingly through the many sunny meadows, until that cottage celebration on the other end of Slovakia. In Rimskava Sobota we stayed in an old Commie hotel and Jan said, "I can do these periodically." I laughed and said, "These firm little beds are actually comfortable. Looks quiet here too."

"And," said Jan, "they have a fitness center." We threw our packs on the beds and dressed for the gym. Jan was unathletic but sinewy strong. We did the few weight machines. He pushed himself competitively, as if to prove something, but grinning always with his do-right chin. Back upstairs I prepared to shower but stopped to look in the mirror. I stuck out my belly. "Wow," I said, "there's something there. I mean, that's no flat stomach."

"No," said Jan. "There's definitely something there."

"Why am I shocked?"

"I'm a little surprised too," said Jan, "I don't know why." In the morning I opened my eyes right into that anguish of heart, brain, spine. I could not figure this out. I could not get right. Jan hadn't stirred for hours, there in his corner of the room. Eventually I caught his eye. But he didn't get up. We just tossed and laughed. I said, "What's there to see out there anyway?"

He said, "I'm more than happy to catch up on rest."

I said, "I'm just wondering whether they have room service." And Jan laughed big. I was worried about him having big expectations from me—I was powerless and worthless. Luckily he was still laughing about lying here until dinner.

And he napped right away. I mostly read the Krakauer and stared into the absolute corner of the walls. The next day, we passed castle ruins on the hill. Long deserted, their sprawling walls had once marked a frontier where invaders had finally been halted, here in these meadows. Jan and I squinted at it. "What does it mean?"

Jan answered, "Nothing if you're Henry Ford."

"What do you mean?"

"Ford said, 'History is bunk.'"

"Well," I said, "he was wrong. But I guess it worked for him." We bumped up to a two-star that night. "And lo'," said Jan, "a television. That might not inspire much room-leaving."

The guy knew how to chill and I was grateful. He could really sleep, except when walking naked to the shower and then back to his bed. I stayed curled in my sheets. He had us go from the gym straight to dinner so we could try some evening television back in the room. I asked, "Don't those multiple espressos hinder your rest?"

He shook his smiling head. "I sleep right through them. Wow, four channels. And lo', one is English." The channel was showing a documentary made by two tennis players who admitted they never fulfilled their potential—now they were taking some final swings at it, though with reduced expectations. They showed a clip in which one of the guys had beaten Pete Sampras as rookies, but Pete was the one who then skyrocketed, for whatever reason. For years then, our guy drove around between first-round losses. Now he was driving around between qualifying-round losses. The other guy held the camera.

They mixed in an interview with Andre Agassi, discussing his own journey. The interviewer asked, "Your classmates at the Academy, has there ever been such a bunch?" The screen showed a photograph. Andre said, "We were a talented group." I said, "That's Martin Blackman!"

He had been in my train story to Jan. Andre said, "There's Martin Blackman, Michael Chang, Dave Wheaton, Jim Courier, me." Jan Surotchak nodded. Everyone from the photo had become top-ten except for my Martin—Andre had listed him first—smiling there in the center, he once the country's number one youth, he now content leading his Greenbelt Bible Talk, expecting a child, and humbly but vocally worrying about Agassi's false sense of spiritual security.

Next our documenters were begging the organizers of the U.S. Open for a wildcard invitation into the doubles qualifier. They hadn't even qualified to qualify. "This is the lowest place we could be and still say we're on tour."

Their begging worked—they placed down the camera and rushed out to an obscure satellite court, to lose. Dismayed, one said he was done for good. The other, sweaty and tired in the fading light, said to the camera, "I'll probably keep at it, keep trying to qualify, trying to turn it around, trying in the hope to one day be a star."

Jan Surotchak wasn't trying to be a star. He was doing some good and was earning a living and so was his wife. Krakauer's thin-air climbers had been reaching for stars.

> ***Early on the foot path, there was loneliness as the sun set. I lay sinkingly as if my whole life lay behind me. Once on the mountain I knew—or trusted—that this would give way to total absorption with the task at hand. But at times I wondered if I had not come a long way only to find that what I really sought was something I had left behind.***

Jan and I were soon in the far corner of this country, ready to turn back. Jan said, "Well we sure did nothing in those rooms." We stopped at a nowhere station just as a long train squeaked to a stop. Along the many cars, one door alone opened. Lenka Surotchak calmly stepped down. I said, "Wow was that perfectly timed."

Jan said, "That's a life and wife over here." They reserved their own room that night, and the next day we traveled toward their cottage group. Jan said, "It'll just be good people, coming from towns all over."

I was thinking about single women being there. We searched for ice cream, today the last day that it would be served. Lenka said, "Colder weather tomorrow." I stayed seated in this Slovak square and I told them to go on alone, I would not get the ice cream. I had that sharp chest pain. I sat with my elbows on my knees. I didn't move, didn't talk, didn't pray. I just waited for it to pass. My heart sped and my breath shortened but I sat there without expression.

When Jan and Lenka returned, I faked conversation. They were all smiles. Soon we were driving. I sat motionless in the backseat. Happily, I felt myself dozing off. When I re-emerged, the stab was still there. So I had to tell them.

They pulled us off the highway at Banska Bystrica, to drive up the hill toward the Franklin D. Roosevelt Hospital emergency room. Old machinery and dedicated staff awaited. They began tests. They declared that, even though I passed the tests, I was to spend the night. I slipped into the required gown. Jan and Lenka and a doctor stood in the doorway. Jan wanted to make sure the doctor was doing enough—they'd be leaving for the cottage now. "Well," said the doctor, "I don't think it's his heart."

"What then?" challenged Jan. The doctor said, "It could be gas. It could be a muscle strain. Wasn't he carrying a sizeable rucksack?" Jan laughed. "Yeah, but look at those shoulders."

They left. I was to stay in this wide room of four beds and three old men who wanted my light turned off so they could sleep—there certainly wasn't anything else to do. The pain disappeared. I had to stay. I was stuck in this room, in my gown, in the dark. How did I get here? At the crack of dawn the nurse awoke us—this was why the grumbling old men retired early. The cottage celebration of good people was over. Jan and Lenka picked me up and we stopped in the nearest square—they looked for ice cream but only found coffee. We wore coats now though the sun still shone. I said, "I'm sorry. I just have to get out of this situation, somehow."

"Correct," said Jan.

It was my turn to speak again. I was sipping hot tea. I said, "I can't."

Lenka said in accent, "Reks, if you think you made a mistake then you just need to tell her."

Tears started down my face. "I can't."

"What choice do you have?" asked Jan. "Maybe now she'll do the math and help you."

Lenka said, "You must do it. Then some time will pass and you'll get out of these bad emotions."

"I understand." I took the long train alone back up to Prague. I didn't realize until the next afternoon, while searching Isaac's hard streets for a place to jog, that the clocks had changed. Winter hours had begun over here. I must have been late to work this morning.

The darkness fell on me hard. The foundation, still gloomy and unfriendly, was now further away. Autumn cold came quickly. Jogging on the hard lanes, with old shoes and unrested heart, hurt. And there in the dark, beneath the clouds above my building—not the next one but mine—came a low airplane, impossibly, because I was on the city's opposite corner from the airport.

But sure enough, at medium intervals here they came. My building was on the flight path. Isaac wouldn't hear it in a million years. Of course, I wouldn't miss one now.

I longed for Catherine, I cursed Catherine. I had finished the Krakauer so I curled up with *Man's Search for Meaning*. Sure I felt sorry for these Holocaust guys, but they did sleep.

> ***Though it was forbidden to take shoes up to the bunks, some people did use them secretly as pillows in spite of the fact that they were caked with mud. Otherwise, one's head had to rest on the crook of an almost dislocated arm, crowded and huddled against each other. And yet sleep came and brought relief from pain for a few hours.***

IV

> ***The most ghastly moment of camp life was when the three shrill blows of a whistle tore us pitilessly from our exhausted sleep and from the longings in our dreams. Then there were the usual moans and groans about the snapping of wires which replaced shoelaces. One morning I heard someone, whom I knew to be brave and dignified, cry like a child because he finally had to go to the snowy marching grounds in his bare feet, as his shoes were too shrunken for him to wear. In those ghastly minutes I found a little bit of comfort; a small piece of bread which I drew out of my pocket and munched with absorbed delight.***

Awaiting my first tram of the morning, I was afraid of quick movements, afraid of the long day, even just the ride itself. I feared reaching toward my pack for the book. In the evening, I sat in Jiri's dim office to draft our final proposal and to plan our New York event. Darkness had been at the windows for hours.

Chats with Jan were briefer now. To my paragraphs he responded with sentences. Slowly I realized he wasn't calling anymore. Sometimes I wrote our usual jokes but got nothing back at all in the little corner of my computer. My calls to the madam couldn't pin Nika down, and the madam said she'd never even heard of Nikola. I swore to her that I'd seen a Nikola and that I absolutely had to again. Oh my hands could still feel her.

I felt no guilt about fulfilling this, I felt only desire for my tram wait to not be long and for the driver to turn on the heated seats and for the deep emptiness to be filled by some miracle smile or hello or anything. Twenty-eight thousand feet was no place for morality.

Holiday kiosks had been erected already—I had bought a bulk bag of German gummies, bears and snakes and dinosaurs, and I slowly ate them now on the tram. Out the window, lovers kissed by the river. I did manage to read. I glanced up periodically. Each tram had a solitary driver. And when approaching another tram in the long labyrinth, each driver seemingly—I now discovered—blinked his left signal once, a hello to his momentary companion there in the dark front of a slowly passing tram.

How long it had been going on, who knew about it, why it happened, this wonder and sentiment dripped through me now in the heavy evening, unanswered. It happened with every single tram we passed. It happened on my next tram too. Now I knew, a final mystery of Prague, of people.

On the long ride to the foundation, I slipped a gummy bear up to my mouth. Sleepless, my whole body felt like an exposed wound. I jotted in the big, blank journal that Catherine had given me. It was official, I was writing this next story, a threading together of the characters and places—not just geographical—where my path had lead me this decade.

I arrived at work and checked my emails and thus survived the first hour. Jan Surotchak had faded fully away. His attentive friendship had been a safe wall to lean against, now gone. Annie was getting married—I checked her emails. Catherine wrote me, "Did you know that your Andy "Conehead" Erickson was just named head vintner for a top California label?" Yes, I had already googled him and found the press release about his dream come true. This googling still failed to find me that Eric Moe, the old high-schooler who might just be holed up writing somewhere, actually.

The stiffness in my chair, the darkness in the window, I could endure it as long as my officemate stayed. When she departed I tried to linger and draft out Jiri's funding strategy. But sitting here alone, I simply could not work.

I surfed. Nudies were not what I needed. I fled toward sports. Another World Series was approaching—this year the event had been postponed a bit. I was afraid to go out into the night. Its bustle had no connection to me. There was only tram riding, I just one lone face amid. If there were other solo riders, they held their mobile phones in hand, to not be alone. Maybe the drivers would have cared to know my thoughts, since they felt the need to break their own solitude with that one left blink in the night. Not once did they fail to signal each other when passing.

Finally I curled under the blankets in my cold little room, finally horizontal and done with the proposal writing and the pale short hellos and the painful jog. Then I woke in the middle of the night, my breathing refreshed and my heart finally rested. But it was likely two in the morning—I never dared to check—and was just a moment's respite. Sleep drifted from reach and I braced for every pipe and airplane.

On weekends, I didn't even have the piddling company of the foundation staff. Silent Saturday, and I crawled into the office and opened the internet and clicked and clicked. Sunday, and the singers moaned, "You're all I need. You're all I ever wanted. Nothing compares to the promise I have in you." The singing dissolved my periphery—my plight crystallized before me. I could look at it, here in my pew. "I sing for joy at the works of your hand. Forever I'll love you, forever I'll stand. Honor and glory and thanks to the Lamb." I saw the fraternity, the climbers, the forests, my DC biking and busing, all within this music. "We, the redeemed, shall be strong." I sighed, I sang, I stared, I felt Catherine's pain, I watched the flag wavers, I dreamed about sex with Nikola, I dreamed about health. This was the whole first hour of every service.

And I filled more pages of the journal. Here I went again, another decade-long project. Or maybe I was better at it these days. Pastor John now spoke while I jotted. He was all about grace—we were good in God, we were already there. I almost bought it. "Faith is having the courage to accept God's acceptance of you." Sunday night meant longer tram intervals. And I was approaching another night in that bed. When Isaac's light went off, I was alone. Yes, I missed my friend, God. But I was done talking to the ceiling. I was on the other side of believing. I looked back it.

Morning arrived and I rolled over and stared off for a quiet moment, letting thoughts come, entertaining none. I pulled myself up with the help of knowing I could go in and check the World Series score and stare hypnotically at the internet stats.

Wow, they were doing a lot of extra-inning comeback thrillers. Now I had to sit in this chair again for nine hours of anguished eyes, only to return home to the night. And home again, I stood in my doorway and stared at the bed, the place where it all occurred, or did not.

Finally I threw up my hands, careful not to strain anything. What the hell was I supposed to do with this? Friday was here again and I couldn't survive another empty weekend, couldn't cross that dark expanse. At lunch I took the tram down and stared at the green wooden door of the agency.

I stepped off the cobblestone curb. I sat down before my agent. This guy might have even thought I lived a normal life. I packed my bags—I left a sweater and my little meditation book for Isaac—and I boarded a plane.

In the air, I panicked. I stared into the seat in front of me. I was staring at the consequences. I was walking out on a job, a career. I didn't do this every day. The plane hummed above the ocean. I had taken a big step off the path, a big step toward having absolutely nothing happening. Andy Erickson had wine and a wife in Napa, Gilligan was a pharmaceutical mogul, Lenka was VP of Marketing, Annie was marrying the love-of-her-life, and that Eric Moe from my high school might have been successfully publishing somewhere as we speak. Colin was nowhere, turned out to be no one, not the friend to help me, save me. But who could've known?

Oh well, I guess I'd have to turn around and go back to Isaac's flat. I could re-board the plane in New York and fly right back, in time for Monday morning. I could meet Jiri Barta at the office and share a cup of coffee, chitchat about life, smile with energy, before bearing down for a patch of work.

But, my body had forgotten how to sleep. Not since white-haired Mike Fontenot's night of fierce scowls could I recall a normal pattern. At JFK, I grabbed my rucksack and cleared customs and switched terminals and walked the hall toward my DC gate.

And there it was out the window, that big old red-striped ex-Commie plane taking back off to Prague. Chance assured that I saw it speeding past the window, right here at huge JFK.

In the middle of my DC terminal stood smiling Catherine, a new reddish tint to her too-stringy hair, her feet pressed together cutely, her hands clapping nervously as I approached. We pecked. So I rolled in to America and caught the seventh game of the World Series. The Diamondbacks' scrappy Craig Counsel slapped in a late run and they were first-time champs. It was October 2001. I snuggled Catherine to sleep. The house was dark and silent when I picked up the phone to dial Jiri. As preparation, I reminded myself that my troubles were real.

"Oh, hello Reks."

"Jiri, I know you just saw me, but I'm calling from America. The reason, Jiri, is that I simply wasn't sleeping, wasn't functioning. I had to break out."

"Oh, okay. I guess you need to take care of your health." He went on to say all the right things, and he meant them. But life for some reason just didn't work this way, we both knew, and I heard so in his voice. I said, "Jiri, I'll get the New York invites out to the donors, and I'll review the brochure and maybe even print it here in good color. Then I can go meet the board early and be valuable in any way."

He said staidly, "No, no, you needn't see any of the board. Maybe you can get some of that other stuff done, if I get you our credit card number. But take care of yourself." I slipped back into my corner of the bed. Catherine would blow up soon. But I had survived another day.

She had been seeing a new counselor, and while the Greenbelt people had been neutral, this new Azora told me in no uncertain terms that I was just a guest at this morning appointment.

"I'm Catherine's cheerleader," said this small, spry, black woman. I was seated next to Catherine on the couch. "That's what Catherine needs," continued Azora. "And so that's me, her cheerleader—I'm reminding her how beautiful she is, inside and out." Catherine was crying and smiling. I nodded.

Azora said, "I remind her what's not healthy, but toxic. Catherine's in a toxic relationship." I nodded. I had awoken in the restless painful anguish today.

"Great," said Eduardo, "you're back from down there?" We were sitting at Bruce Lee's. In the past year, Eduardo's nudes had been displayed at DC's Artomatic and AC/DC Gallery and Adams-Morgan street festival, where he said he just observed the heated debate around him.

Now he revealed more about the ICC. "When I first told my discipler"—he made quote signs—"that no one seemed real, no one seemed happy, he, like, rebuked me or something. But I still believe we were doing the right thing out there, you and me, building something, building community. Why are you smiling?" When we parted, I took my JJ key and crept up to the third floor and emptied the petty cash. My heart was pounding. When I locked up the front and whisked around the corner, relief flowed through me.

Foundation staff flew in and our U.S. board escorted us up to the Rockefeller rural conference center for strategizing. We were surrounded by beautiful wealth and nature. We discussed how to advance the programs and funding. We walked to the old empty estate and put our faces up to its historic windows. Rockefeller history apparently had a brother jumping off a bridge to his death, because that was what he needed at the time, or because he couldn't get what he needed. We went back to the City and donned business attire and I had a night of VIPs and cocktails and faking.

Jan Surotchak was here and he was smiley but distant. Whatever he was, he had basically love-bombed me, building me up and then leaving me to fall. I knew I hadn't been easy to handle, but nor was calling oneself a Christian, a follower of that guy in that book. I handed Jiri the big proposal. The next day we met for lunch.

Jiri said, "I wanted to ask how you see your future at the foundation. Or actually, there is no future for you at the foundation." We sat through a slight pause. But he wasn't bad at this. He said, "It just wasn't the right fit." I nodded. He paid for lunch. I hadn't anticipated ever being fired in life. Jiri added, "You probably don't want to be over there anyway."

"No, I do want to be over there."

"Really? You really do? I'm surprised."

I walked out alone. Sunlight touched the tops of the buildings. I stopped on a corner where a great billboard read, "New York City. Twenty million people. One Mr. Right. You do the math." I arrived home in DC and removed my shoes only and got into bed. The covers felt heavy on me. I had nothing planned for the rest of the day, other than more jotting in that big journal. Maybe I could just do it here in bed. I looked for my bag. But I couldn't quite reach it. I was dripping.

I could reach my new read, *The Good Earth*, whose protagonist farmer was now entering his arranged marriage.

> ***He now had his woman, though not attractive—it seemed to him as he walked into the sharp sunshine of the dusty street that there was never a man filled with as good fortune as he. He thought of this at first with joy and then with fear. It did not do to be too fortunate. The air and the earth were filled with malignant spirits who could not endure the happiness of mortals. He turned abruptly into the candle-maker's shop and bought four sticks of incense, with which he went into the small temple of the gods.***

I rolled over. Oh guilt, whence do you come? The same farmer, not long afterward, strayed into dim-lit conversation with a madam.

He muttered, "I do not know that I want anything." And then his desire overcame him and he whispered, "The one with the little small face like a blossom of white and pink." At first it seemed to him that every man looked up and watched him, but when he took courage, he saw that none paid him any heed, except for one or two who called out, "Is it late enough then, to go to the women?" And there upon a bed covered with a flowered red quilt, sat a slender girl. If one had told him there were small hands like these he would not have believed it. All during that hot summer he loved this girl, yet never could he grasp her wholly, and this it was which kept him fevered and thirsty. He had never enough of her, and he went back to his house in the dawn, dazed and unsatisfied.

I tossed the book on the floor. I turned on sports radio. Some boxer was discussing his release from jail after a long sentence for rape. Apparently he still had a shot at some meaningless fight. "I made a mistake. Yeah, everyone out there, I advise you look yourselves in the mirror, face what's going on in you, face exactly where you're at. I strongly advise this."

I got out of bed and called Catherine at her sister's. "CatCat I'm not feeling great at the moment so I'm thinking it's better for my health if you stay there and I don't have anyone in the bed." She responded, "Do you mean you don't want me to stay with you there?" It was the sweetest, saddest voice in the world. Stabbed, I shook my head at this endless trap. I said, "Just for one night."

I packed up my car. Aspen awaited. I sped up the highway for thirty miles and then ramped left onto Interstate Seventy. As my windshield view arced westward into the dimming sunset, I pulled over. I stared across America.

I drowned in the vastness. I shook my head. I would never make it. NPR was playing on my radio but I would lose it once I headed into the night. I turned around and was back in time for Martin's Bible Talk. I smiled sincerely with everyone—it felt good to sit on the couch and hold the book and shoot the breeze. Catherine sat cross-legged on the floor, smiling behind her glasses. I didn't tell them I had left for Aspen or that I was an atheist. Martin read aloud:

Some men made an opening in the roof above Jesus and lowered a paralyzed man. When Jesus saw their faith, he said to the paralytic, "Son, your sins are forgiven." Some teachers of the law were sitting there thinking to themselves, "Why does this fellow blaspheme? Who can forgive sins but God alone?"

Martin looked up. I said, "So much irony." Martin smiled and continued on.

While Jesus was having dinner the teachers of the law asked his disciples, "Why does he eat with tax collectors and sinners?" On hearing this, Jesus said to them, "It is not the healthy who need a doctor, but the sick. I have not come to call the righteous, but sinners'"

Though Martin had a different discussion planned, I said again, "The irony."

"What do you mean?" asked Martin.

I opined, "By saying the guy's sins are forgiven, he's just provoking the leaders to react. But they don't get this. Then he tells them he isn't there to heal the righteous. But we know he doesn't consider them to be righteous. They miss that one too."

Catherine said, "Nice insight."

Sennait Blackman said, "That's really deep, Bro'. I didn't quite see it like that." I figured my ability to see into scripture was fading. Like Colin had enjoyed quoting, "'Hold to my teachings, then you'll see the truth.'" I spent the next day in bed. I couldn't even roll over. This was different than the usual stiff-hearted pain. Now I was paralyzed.

Finally, actual depression, I could confirm that it was something I'd never felt. The covers felt like lead on me. I could see some sunlight along the shades. I had missed the single years. I had no career. No one knew how bad I was hurting. Oh, and I had ruined this woman, Catherine. She needed some Azora as a cheerleader in her life. That I was really proud of.

I guess I got why people offed themselves, why they saw no way to change or continue. I rolled over. But why not go out with a bang, go out on a high? I mean, what really mattered anymore anyway? I picked the book up off the floor. Wang Lung's courtesan eventually moved right in, and his farmer wife just kept serving them all anyway. Eventually the wife fell so sick that the doctor said not even bed rest would solve it.

When the doctor was gone, Wang Lung went into the dark kitchen where Olan had lived her life for the most part, and where, now that she was not there, none would see him, and he turned his face to the blackened wall, and he wept.

I rolled back over. The depression streamed through my face and jaw. I remained beneath the heavy blanket and watched the daylight shadows shift. I switched the clock radio between NPR and sports. Then I sat up. I mean, why not? I got in the car and drove up toward the junior high. I drove down quiet suburban streets, searching. My fire burned. I nodded my head. Here came two teen girls jogging. But I needed just one. I needed gas. I pulled into a station and pumped quickly and pulled right back out. Screams stopped me. The nozzle was still in my tank. I braked hard.

I went back to bed. On NPR a female writer was saying she had no fear of her industry ever dying. "There're four things people will always need in life. Food, shelter, sex, and stories." I called Eduardo and we walked across the bridge. I said, "We met a lot of people."

He said, "I'm still meeting them. My message is a little different. Now it's, 'Wanna take off your clothes?'"

I added, "John Goodman always said, 'Wanna change the world, just open your mouth.'"

Eduardo laughed big toward the sky. He said, "So many people. So many characters. So much cluelessness." The bridge was actually in the epicenter of the two dozen hotels utilized by escorts here. But it wasn't the same as buzzing up to flats for seventeen-year old bodies costing fifty dollars. I had tapered off. Once again I had told Eduardo everything. I said now, "But I'm still looking for that white-haired Mike Fontenot on the subway, or on the sidewalk, or on the square." Eduardo said quickly, "Dream on. Bro', I gotta go shoot. Gotta go change the world." I shook his hand in that soulful snapful way that Jake the Inner-City Leader had taught us. At least I'd learned something. Eduardo hurried off, wearing a big grin.

I emptied the JJ petty cash again. I locked the front door and continued down the alley and climbed up on a dumpster and buried the key away, done, gone, decision made, for whatever reason.

I took a night subway down to the George Washington University Hospital, right beside the Campus Center and its bathroom stalls, and I underwent a sleep test. In a white comfortless room, the Ethiopian nurse--maybe she was Eritrean like Sennait Blackman--attached countless wires to me and explained, as far as I could understand, that I should stay in bed and urinate in this bottle and otherwise sleep normally. She left me there.

She left a red bulb shining right above my head--I didn't know what it was for but it certainly wasn't for soothing me to sleep. I stared upward and thought I would likely lay all night thinking. I tried to get more comfortable, gently leaning to one side, then eventually to the other. I noticed some muffled electronic sounds, somewhere.

I listened to the airplanes as they took off at all hours from DC National. I heard that muffled electronic blast again from above. Was it a voice? I slowly raised my wired head. There did seem to be a camera up in the red light. Was she watching me? The words came again. Was that English? She was saying, "No move." That's what she was telling me. "No move," she said again, from wherever she was. "No move."

I played pool with strong, blond Ted Woods. He was staffing asbestos and demolition jobs up and down the East Coast. He was engaged to marry again, with an old high-school gal whose path he had re-crossed. He had never started the foundation to find lost children. I asked about my reclining chair and he said he was too busy to track down little things like that in life. He had renovated and sold over a dozen Bethesda homes. In his own new estate he had put a big television in the bathroom. "Why not?"

I couldn't think of a reason. We took turns shooting and chatting and drinking. He had also bought a house in Vail. How had this guy, college-less, known at such an early age that breezy cloud shapes or sad guitar songs had no bearing? "What about the revolution?"

He asked, "What revolution?"

"You were going to march with me down into Harlem."

"And I would've. I guess you got distracted or something." He no longer asked about Debbie. He said, "But I'll never forget how we'd go out in Greensboro and you used to duck your head down to not see all the neon fast-food signs."

"I did that?" We both laughed small. Ted said, "Speaking of which, Reks, I heard some high-school news and I thought of you. It's not light."

"Go ahead."

"It's been out there a while but just reached me. Eric Moe jumped off that Adams-Morgan bridge."

"That's unbelievable."

"Apparently he came back from living in some Colorado ski-town and was staying at home here a while, not doing well. It's true."

"That is very very sad. And very hard to believe. I hadn't seen him in forever. But Ted, do you know I've been searching for him, trying to track him down?"

"It's one of the reasons I called you."

"I hadn't even seen him since high school—he was just a guy, one guy. Yet recently I'd begun thinking that he might have evolved into a real independent thinker, a creative thinker. I had a feeling. I heard something about him trying to write films."

Ted nodded. He said, "He didn't make it." This guy Eric had been at his parents' house up the street in Bethesda—I could've wandered up there, had I known. Ted and I quit pool and sat down for dinner. "Reks, I called for another reason too. Over this decade I've learned a lot about business. Why don't you hop back over to Russia or wherever you were and see if you can find me some good workers? The work ethic around here is so pitiful it makes me fucking depressed. Really, it's true. And it loses me about a million dollars a year."

I nodded calmly. If someone wanted to pay me during my current worthlessness, then yes, I could temporarily postpone my collapse. Out on the sidewalk we made plans to shoot pool again. I went home and packed a little bag for Catherine's sister's. We had their townhouse for the weekend.

While Catherine flipped through their magazines, I found an untouched Tolkien series on the shelf. I opened to the beginning—it didn't have the same intro as my version, which I had once even jotted into an odd notebook, probably saved from Ted and Betsy's Greensboro pyre. I had carried the meaningful quote, and notebook, around for a while.

> ***It's been fifteen years since I first came across LORD OF THE RINGS in the stacks at the Carnegie Library. I think of that time now—and the years after, when the trilogy continued to be hard to find and hard to explain to most friends—with an undeniable nostalgia. I've never thought it an accident that Tolkien's works waited more than ten years to explode into popularity almost overnight. The Sixties were no fouler a decade than the Fifties—they merely reaped the Fifties' foul harvest—but they were the years when millions of people grew aware that the industrial society had become paradoxically unlivable, incalculably immoral, and ultimately deadly. Progress lost its ancient holiness, and escape stopped being comically obscene. The impulse is being called reactionary now, but lovers of Middle-earth want to go there. I would, myself, like a shot.***

Give it up, dude. I didn't know who this whiner Peter Beagle was but hopefully he had found some way out, because apparently no millions of people ever lined up to join him in adjusting industrial society. Still, this had once been the publisher's introduction to the series, for whatever that was worth. I told Catherine I couldn't go to the beach house this week, I couldn't go anywhere, couldn't do anything. "I'm ill, I've been telling you."

She responded that it was okay. We sat around the couch instead. Bilbo was inching fearfully down the tunnel toward the dragon's lair.

> ***The rumble grew to the unmistakable gurgling noise of some vast animal snoring in its sleep down in the red glow before him.***

Catherine had her blow up. "It's because of my family—you're so superior." Her face was bitingly serious, her eyes shrunken.

I said, "Something just isn't working for me. Maybe I made a premature decision. Maybe I didn't decide at all, maybe I'm suddenly finding myself in this position. You don't have to take it entirely personally."

"Don't take it personally? I feel totally rejected by you. And it's because you can't handle shit!" She went upstairs. I would have to bring her back around or take that action that I could not. I was caught atop the cliff, needing to descend. But oh, that first turning step, over the edge, impossible.

> ***It was at this point in the tunnel that Bilbo stopped. Going on from there was the bravest thing he ever did. The tremendous things that happened afterwards were as nothing compared to it. He fought the real battle in the tunnel alone, before he ever saw the vast danger that lay in wait.***

I went upstairs and she was on the floor, bent forward, not in prayer, but crying devastation. I rubbed her stiff back and she may not have even noticed. I sat on the downstairs couch for another moment. Then I seized my bag and seized the chance to at least put a wedge between us, to get some space in there. I successfully drove off down the street.

There she came, running across the grass, barefoot and fit in her jeans outfit, determined and serious-faced, the poor thing. I stopped and went back in with her and made the peace.

I made it home at the end of the long weekend and I sat down at my old computer. My big journal was now full. I prepped my fingers like a pianist, an unknown and unfulfilled musician in the dim corner of his room.

My sentences did flow out a bit more deliberately and sharply, I hoped. My syntax-flawed first sculpture was history but the lessons could be applied to this new lump of clay, I hoped. I took a break in the TV room and flipped a few channels and stopped on "Jerry Maguire".

Wow, Tom Cruise's new bride approached unhappy him in the backyard and said she could see his struggle in this marriage and that it wasn't fair to him. And this wasn't fair to her. That was how she saw it. "I was just on some ride where I thought I was in love enough for both of us. It was me that did this. And at least I can do something about it now."

Jerry Maguire responded, "I'm not a guy who's going to run. I stick."

"I don't need you to stick."

"What do you want from me? My soul?"

"Why not? I deserve that much. If one of us doesn't say something now we might lose ten years being polite about it. I can't live that way."

Jerry nodded. I went back to my desk. I sat very still, just breathing, not moving. I walked back to the TV room and called Catherine and told her about the Jerry Maguire dialogue. She thought quietly and then said, "Okay, that makes some sense. But why are you telling me this exactly?"

I sighed, and I looked into my mind, and I said aloud, "We need a divorce."

It was really just a decision. Perhaps all this time I had just been making the decision. Perhaps I hadn't quite fully decided until now, because of the missing her, respecting her, snuggling her, the guilt or sex or God, whatever. On this day, I decided it would occur.

"Okay," she said. She didn't cry. "Okay," she repeated. I put down the phone and stared at the emotions ahead. I breathed. I went back to typing. I never saw the end of Jerry Maguire.

V

Ted flew me over to Prague. I was supposed to find him recruits. I got lucky—a Prague inn that I had heard of from foundation guests now provided me with a room facing a sunny soccer field and forest. It was dead quiet. It was the perfect little old simple Commie room, with the sad but solid wood walls.

After a couple days I took a bus across the meadows to the town. I walked up Economist Jan Mraka's stairwell and buzzed the bell. When he answered, I said with surprise, "You've gotten older." He said sharply, "You too." I told him about Ted's mission and he told me how to get in touch with Karel the Climber. I buzzed Ivana and Yarda's.

Here I stood, outside their tall red-plank fence, looking up at their back windows. I was pretty sure this wasn't a dream. Yarda opened the door.

Ivana was away at the grandmother's cottage and the girls were grown and had studied German—I told them in Czech how I was personally insulted. Yarda cooked me sausages on his courtyard grill. He said he rode his mountain bike for fun every afternoon. "Reks once had the only mountain bike in town, and now everyone has one." He rode off. He had made up a bed for me but I had glimpsed that old snide smirk—maybe I perceived things a bit better now—so I slept at the Mrakas, where Jitka said Yarda was cheating on Ivana.

The next afternoon, Ivana and Yarda buzzed the bell and we stood outside on the sidewalk and Ivana said, "Reks, you can stay with us, please, you are welcome." I shook my head, it was okay, everything was really okay. I tried to soothe her concerns. In the morning I returned to my Prague inn and went for a long slow jog around the sunny soccer field, and then I showered and lay on my bed, looking out the window for a long time.

Still a year later I could feel magical Nikola, I swear I could. I called pretty Nika and she picked up and I asked for the dancing queen. She agreed to meet at a café but then didn't recognize me, saying she had expected some Australian guy who had also spoken good Czech. She stared off vacantly. She was still attractive, very, but I didn't quite know how to behave with her. She said she didn't do that work anymore, that day was over. Neither did I, I told her. She said I could call again on my next visit.

Ted bought and modernized an old warehouse in Baltimore for our new headquarters. He bought twenty little rowhouses for the incoming workers, and I bought one for me, there amid the slum that was Baltimore. I didn't mind being in the business of brokering laborers, a renewable resource. My house overlooked my new garden and my trash-lined street. An interior room in the house had no windows. Maybe in this room I could sleep and heal a bit. I could walk to work just like I had walked to the Jihlava brewery from Ivana and Yarda's home on Tchaikovsky Street.

Well, it's time for me to sign off. No, I won't be killing myself. I'm going to battle on, wholeheartedly, with the goal of a few patches of happiness and then dying in a nice quiet bed on some distant day. I needn't battle on but I've decided to.

Down in DC I schedule a dinner with Grace. She treats me to perfectly subtle fine-dining, because she is Dr. Grace Goodell, Director of Change Economics, living alone, doing well and doing good, with her wrinkled unmade eyes and her wise ponytail and commanding voice and sincere listening.

She asks immediately about any new writing and I tell her that, indeed, I've begun a new project. She says, "Oh, that's so good." I also tell her that I'm no longer following Jesus nor teaching people not to fish. Grace says, "Faith isn't easy."

I tell her that there still lives, deep within me, a voice for some movement that would allow us to adjust our destructive habits and hearts. I say, "In Bologna there was a professor, not much taller than the podium, and not happy with our ignorance of history, but who said that Napoleon had acted himself out, had fully faced that voice inside him, and obeyed it, lived it. It's true that I can't really explain away Jesus and his special insight and Paul who sincerely loved him, and it's also true that they seem like guys who listened to that inner voice and gave their lives to it. But Hitler, I've read a lot about him, and it seems he did exactly that, just lived it all out. Turns out he was an agent of destruction, nothing more. Stalin, then, outdid him. I think my voice would have been for good, Grace, for some real good. And I was sure I was going to make it heard. I was sure this was my calling. It's becoming difficult to remember though. I got caught in a deep hole. Life grew so wrong for my mind and body that, well, I was considering killing myself."

She nods and says, "That sounds so interesting and difficult for you. So why didn't you?"

"Why didn't I? I didn't, because, well, it just seemed like a terrible waste of resources. I'm supposed to be strong and healthy and I can be so again. It seemed like a waste to throw that away and break it, physically break and destroy it. Now I can choose whatever principles I want, and I probably won't choose the whole list, but I've recently decided that I want to be honest, I'm not sure why. But I've decided it. I want to be an honest person. That's all. And I'll have written something real now. Maybe at least I can contribute that. It might have value, to have written something honest and real."

"That's not enough."

I say, "You're saying that's not enough?"

Grace says, "No, it must be noble. Art can't just have integrity. It must be noble. Because, you are correct, even Hitler acted out of integrity to himself."

"Yes," I nod. "But no, this is open and real. I'm giving them sincere real life, deep from the heart. This should have some value. True art operates on two levels, some good action and then some meaning below the surface if the patron cares to look."

Grace says, "Macbeth had them on the edge of their seat. But it's the story's nobility that makes it art."

I say, "My story is a sincere search. That's what I'm giving them."

"Not enough. Art needs to have a noble side. Painfully real problems might be a start, but Shakespeare always showed his star's high character." Kerouac she dismisses unsolicited, among several stabs at Hemingway, couched in more praise for Shakespeare's noble heroes. I say, "Dr. Goodell, you're telling me that my project doesn't even qualify as art."

She says, "Integrity must be joined by the fight for nobility. Without that fight, there's no point to integrity, no meaning. Art and life need nobility."

"Why?"

"Why?" she repeats back. "Because. Because of Hitler. Because there're Hitlers."

So it happens that Catherine buys a new little place and I bring her items there, including wedding gifts that I had hidden away but now face. I give them all to Catherine. Her sister is here and she points a sympathetic moan my way and I look into their eyes and nod.

But in several hours I find more items in my closet and I phone Catherine to arrange the next visit but she says she is unable to speak, she is out. I say, "Oh. What?" She says, "I'm out. I can't. I have to hang up."

I hang up. The revelation slams into my mind. Catherine is with someone. The sister's sympathetic moan had been for me.

In absolute panic and regret I speed back toward her apartment. Her door is locked, no answer. I huff and puff. My mind races for alternate possibilities. I check back again in half an hour. I sit on the freshly carpeted steps of her entrance hall. The air is chilled with fear and hopelessness. I walk across her complex to the twelve-theater cinema. I sit through segments of four movies and then I rush back over, praying to see her car. Yes it's parked over there, no that's not it, and the hour is getting really late.

I sit in the stairwell for another long patch. No one walks through the entrance. I drive home down the highway and turn on sports radio and I listen to the Orioles lose, and I listen to the post-game show, and I listen to the late-night sign off, "This is Scott Jackson, saying so long from Camden Yards. So long. So long." No, no, no, I exclaim, pounding my steering wheel. I come back at dawn. Everything is confirmed, by her continued absence.

That night, she walks into the entrance hall and up the stairs toward me. She says with a smile, "Hi, what are you doing here?"

"Where'd you sleep last night?"

"Oh, Reks, don't."

"How can you do this?" I implore her to stop it and I criticize her even though I know that this guy, whoever he is, is finally freeing me. He is my savior. Still, it hurts in my gut as deeply as possible. I say so to Eduardo on the phone at one in the morning, at three in the morning, and at five in the morning. Then back in her stairwell I say, "Thank heavens you're here tonight." But she just steps out and sits on the stairs with me and refuses to change anything.

"You are not being fair," she says, "I am just trying to save myself."

That's what she says. I can see the conflict and anguish on her face right in front of me. "Reks," she says, "you shouldn't be worrying about your life, you're funny and you're talented."

I say, "That's all you have to say about me, that I'm funny and talented?" She says, "Oh, Reks." I know I'm mistreating her here, and I know I do ache for her to be happy. But I still beg and twist. In truth all I need is a week more of calling Eduardo during the night and the pain will fade off.

Eduardo picks up every time. I tell it to Ted too, at our new warehouse office. Ted says, "You don't care about that." I nod in agreement. He adds, "Unless he's fucking her in the ass." That's what Ted says. Ted, who just wants to be known for calling it the way he sees it, takes me out for chicken wings.

I am considering buying a new lazy-boy recliner for my ghetto rowhouse. The Czech seasonal laborers are also living in the neighborhood and walking to work. Their streets are covered in trash too. But I'm thinking, maybe I'll let it be, maybe I'll just clean up my own block. On the weekend, I drive the climbers to a beach of their choosing.

They choose an isolated and protected national park, with wild grasses and the occasional wild horse and not a commercial wall or word. They walk in front of me, enjoying the sun and surf and breeze, Igor and Petr and Karel. It's I who arranged their visas. They are doing demolition for Ted. In fact, things are going a bit south with Ted—some of the things he had me promise the workers on that overseas trip aren't quite materializing here. Karel and I have discussed it over lunch—he is their unspoken leader. We've reassured each other that, no matter what, we have the friendship. But do we? Karel, who these days is meditative and

Buddhist and fully bald, appears to still be silently blaming me for the disconnect. On this protected beach today we don't address it. We all walk peacefully. The air is quiet. At least my Jihlava climbers have made it to America. This is something. It's pleasing. It's satisfying.

And so random.

The End

"And the days are dark, but the girls are fair. And the sparrows sing so sweetly on the Opera Square..."—meinke, warsaw, 1977

Made in the USA
Middletown, DE
13 May 2015